THE GLOBAL MANAGEMENT SERIES

Enterprise and its Business Environment

Norin Arshed, Julie McFarlane and Robert MacIntosh

(G) Goodfellow Publishers Ltd

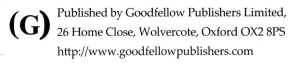

Published by Goodfellow Publishers Limited,
26 Home Close, Wolvercote, Oxford OX2 8PS
http://www.goodfellowpublishers.com

British Library Cataloguing in Publication Data: a catalogue record for this
title is available from the British Library.
Library of Congress Catalog Card Number: on file.

ISBN: 978-1-910158-79-1

 Design and typesetting by P.K. McBride, www.macbride.org.uk

Cover design by Cylinder

Printed by Marston Book Services, www.marston.co.uk

Contents

Biographies   vi

Preface   xi

1   **Business Organizations: The Internal Environment**   1
Julie McFarlane and Ross Curran

2   **Creativity, Innovation and Entrepreneurship**   21
Julie McFarlane

3   **The Legal Function: Starting a New Business – Getting the Structure Right**   41
Josephine Bisacre

4   **Employment Law**   59
Josh McLeod and Yvonne McLaren

5   **Research to Create Enterprise Value**   77
Geraldine McKay and Linda Phillips

6   **Marketing to Create Value**   95
Geraldine McKay

7   **The Human Resource Management Function**   117
Kehinde Olowookere and Katherine Sang

8   **Gender and Work-life Balance**   135
Steven Glasgow and Katherine Sang

9   **Porter's Five Forces and Generic Strategies**   151
Norin Arshed and Jaydeep Pancholi

10   **Operations Management**   169
Umit Bititci and Stavros Karamperidis

11   **Logistics and the Supply Chain**   195
Christine Rutherford and Christian König

12   **Corporate Social Responsibility and Corporate Governance**   215
Julie McFarlane and Keith Gori

Index   231

Dedications

I would like to thank all my colleagues who helped in writing this book.

NA

Your strength of will and your fortitude are where I got the strength to keep going even when, at times, it looked like I wanted to give up. You endured so much in this life, and it is seeing that strength of character that drives my own, so for that, I thank you. It's because of you I started, and for you that I finish. I just hope that wherever you are, you're proud of me. I miss you.

JMcF

To my beautiful wife Anne and our children Euan, Eilidh and Eva. Thank you for your patience and your company.

RMacI

Acknowledgments

We are grateful to all those who helped shape this project. Our authoring teams have been dedicated and patient as the interlocking parts of the manuscript came together over several rounds of editing. Our colleagues at Goodfellows helped mould the project and we remain indebted to Tim, Sally and Mac for their expertise and support. Kat Lloyd deserves special mention for her role in checking and polishing the manuscript in her first few weeks at Heriot-Watt. We are grateful to her for the speed and accuracy of her work. Finally to the many students in many countries who helped shape this text through their enthusiastic participation in classes and their constructive feedback, we owe you a huge debt of gratitude.

NA, JMcF & RMacI

Biographies

Norin Arshed is Programmes Director for the Leadership and Organizational Performance suite of MSc programmes in the Department of Business Management at Heriot-Watt University. She is an economist by background with professional experience in both the public and private sectors. Her work concentrates on enterprise policy, in particular, the role and contribution from those closely linked to the formulation process (ministers and civil servants), whilst also examining how enterprise policy is implemented (national, regional and local economic development agencies), and how entrepreneurs/SMEs experience and utilise such policy initiatives. Institutional theory is the theoretical lens used to highlight the dynamics of the enterprise policy process in her work.

Josephine Bisacre is an Associate Professor of Business Law and is the Director of Undergraduate Studies in the School of Management and Languages at Heriot-Watt University. She formerly worked as a solicitor in private practice in the field of corporate law. She is the author of various book chapters in the area of business law, the latest being in the third edition of Black, G (ed) (2015) *Business Law in Scotland* (2015) and the second edition of Johnson, D and Turner, C (2015) *European Business.*

Umit Bititci is the Professor of Business Performance at the Heriot-Watt University, School of Management and Languages, Edinburgh, UK. Until December 2013 he was the Director of Strathclyde Institute for Operations Management and the Professor of Technology and Enterprise Management at the University of Strathclyde. In the past he served as the Chairman of IFIP's Working Group on Advanced Production Management Systems and the Vice Chairman of the Institute of Operations Management. Currently he is a member of the Scottish Manufacturing Advisory Board. He has a blend of industrial and academic experience that spans across 35 years. He has dedicated his career to understanding what makes high-performing companies different. He has worked with an international portfolio of companies and public sector organizations. He has led several international research and development projects. He has published over 200 papers and regularly appears at international conferences and workshops as guest speaker.

Ross Curran is a PhD student at Heriot-Watt University, Edinburgh, where he is an active member of the Intercultural Research Centre. His primary research interests focus on improving volunteer management practises in the third sector, while he has published papers exploring PPT in the developed world, and authenticity consumption at tourist sites in Japan. His PhD thesis is concerned with fostering greater utilization of the heritage inherent in many third sector organizations.

Steven Glasgow is a PhD student in the School of Management and Languages at Heriot-Watt University. His research primarily focuses on how gender inequalities within the workplace are produced, maintained and disrupted. He has published a book review in *Feminism & Psychology* and is currently guest editing a special issue for the journal *Interdisciplinary Perspectives on Equality and Diversity* (IPED). Steven received his MA (Hons) in Business Management from Heriot-Watt University in 2014. His teaching commitments include Research Methods and Employee Relations.

Keith Gori is a doctoral student in SML at Heriot-Watt University. His doctoral research engages with Consumer Culture Theory and narratives of life on the British Home Front during World War Two. More widely his research interest lies in consumer and marketing history, the historical development of thought surrounding the social responsibilities of business, and in experiential marketing and consumption. He has presented both historical and contemporary research outputs at international marketing conferences and has published work in the *Journal of Marketing Management*. He teaches on global management and marketing courses in the Department of Business Management.

Stavros Karamperidis is an Assistant Professor in Shipping and International Logistics, in the School of Management and Languages at Heriot-Watt University. Stavros is also a Visiting Lecturer at Newcastle University and Associate of the Prime Maritime Transport Group (Newcastle University). Prior to joining Heriot-Watt, he has conducted research funded by research councils in various UK universities. His primary research interests are in maritime transport systems and logistics, indices development, container flows and transshipment. Before joining academia, Stavros worked in various companies ranging from SMEs to multinational companies. Stavros is a member of the Chartered Institute of Logistics and Transport.

Christian König is a PhD student in the School of Management and Languages at Heriot-Watt University, Edinburgh. He is an active member of the Logistics Research Centre and his primary research interests focus on the outsourcing strategies of focal firms and the continuous development of service providers. In his doctoral thesis, he investigates the role of systems integrators in the logistics industry using an exploratory approach.

Christian received an MSc. in Logistics and Supply Chain Management with distinction from Heriot-Watt University in Edinburgh in 2012.

Julie McFarlane is an Assistant Professor for the School of Management and Languages at Heriot-Watt University, teaching areas in business, marketing and enterprise. She recently completed a PhD in Entrepreneurial Business Models in the Creative industries at the University of Strathclyde's Hunter Centre for Entrepreneurship. Prior to her PhD Julie received a Master of Science award (with Distinction) in Innovation, Commercialization and Entrepreneurship from the University of Stirling as well as a Bachelor of Arts (with Honours) in Business Studies and Marketing, She has over 10 years' experience working closely with entrepreneurs. Julie also has an interest in dynamic business models, specifically the process of entrepreneurship in the music industry.

Geraldine McKay is an Associate Professor in Marketing and a Chartered Marketer with a special interest in the impact of branding across stakeholder groups. Following a career in marketing (financial services, publishing, industrial branding and enterprise development) she became a university lecturer, developing and leading a number of postgraduate, undergraduate and professional programmes. She moved to New Zealand where she managed an International project between a consortium of New Zealand universities and the Ministry of Higher Education in Oman. On returning to the UK she became Academic Head for the globally delivered Heriot-Watt Management Programmes. She is currently undertaking a PhD in Education investigating transnational education and the student experience.

Robert MacIntosh is Professor of Strategy and Head of the School of Management and Languages at Heriot-Watt University. He trained as an engineer and has worked at the Universities of Glasgow and Strathclyde. His research on the ways in which top teams develop strategy and on organizational change has been published in a wide range of outlets. He has a long-standing interest in research methods for business and management studies and has published on the relevance of management research using methods that include ethnography and action research. He has consulted extensively with public and private sector organizations and sits on the board of the charity Turning Point Scotland.

Yvonne McLaren is an Aberdeen University Law School Graduate currently based within The School of Management and Languages at Heriot-Watt University. In addition to her role as a director in Safeguard Technical Services Ltd., Yvonne has a variety of roles within the department, including

Course Leader in International Human Resource Management, Commercial Law and Marketing and Consumer Law. Pastoral duties include being the Third year co-ordinator and engaging with students in the role of Super Mentor. Yvonne has previously taught a variety of law subjects at Paisley University and Glasgow College of Commerce.

Joshua McLeod is a PhD student in the School of Management and Languages at Heriot-Watt University, where he teaches in Business Law and Global Management. His research focuses on the corporate governance practices of professional football clubs in Scotland. Further to this, his research interests include organizational change in the football industry, the feasibility of the supporter ownership model and football finance in a broader context.

Jaydeep Pancholi is a PhD student within the School of Management and Languages at Heriot-Watt University, Edinburgh. His PhD thesis is investigating business strategy within the context of conflict zones, reviewing stakeholder influences on strategic decision and conflict resolution. Prior to this Jaydeep had gained a BA (hons) in International Business and Marketing at the University of Strathclyde, Glasgow, including an exchange at Nanyang Technological University, Singapore, studying courses in management and culture. This was followed by working at a leading automotive manufacture in corporate fleet. Jaydeep's academic interests have been rooted from his extensive voluntary work in personal development and corporate sustainability while being a trainer for a global NGO.

Linda Phillips is the Academic Group Leader for Enterprise, Marketing and Services and Principal Lecturer at Staffordshire University. She is responsible for a team of marketing, tourism and events academic staff and has strategic responsibility for undergraduate Business, Marketing, Tourism and Events courses. Linda began her career working in industry with the BBC in London, the Australian government in Canberra, and for GEC in the Midlands, where latterly she worked as Senior Marketing Executive and Head of Marketing. Linda is a Chartered Marketer and since becoming a lecturer has taught, led and developed a range of courses at undergraduate level and also delivered postgraduate and professional level programmes.

Kehinde Olowookere is a PhD Student in the School of Management and Languages at Heriot-Watt University, Edinburgh. Her current research investigates the management and experiences of mental health conditions within the workplace, with particular focus on how difference is constructed within normative organizational contexts. She holds an MSc in International

Human Resource Management from Sheffield Hallam University (2013). More generally, her interests include the management of diversity in the workplace and identity construction at work.

Katherine Sang is an Associate Professor of Management in the School of Management and Languages, Heriot-Watt University. Her research examines the workplace as a site where gender and associated inequalities are (re)produced. In addition, her research examines posthumanism as a framework for understanding human/nonhuman relations in organizations. She teaches the sociology of work and research philosophy. Currently, Katherine is the Chair of the Feminist and Women's Studies Association UK & Ireland.

Preface

When Isaac Newton wrote to his contemporary Robert Hooke, he claimed to have seen a little further by standing on the shoulders of giants. In that same spirit we would acknowledge that this book builds on the contributions of many prior works by towering figures in the field of management and organization. In the last two decades, the fields of business and management, enterprise and entrepreneurship have developed rapidly, with the results that critics argue that business enterprise is merely a broad label under which a hodgepodge of loosely affiliated, sometimes contradictory research is housed. This book attempts to bring some structure to the field by organizing basic ideas and introducing them to those new to the study of business enterprises.

Often when we think of a business enterprise we default to those brand name, global businesses that are woven into the fabric of our everyday life. Google, Amazon, Apple and their contemporaries are amongst the most valuable businesses in the world, employing many thousands of people across developed and developing economies. Yet now, for the first time in history, more than half of the world's businesses are small in size. For example, in the UK alone 99% of the 5.2 million business registered are extremely small indeed. Small businesses have always played a vital role in the economy but the technological revolution of the last 20 to 30 years has meant that some small firms are 'born global', i.e. they operate in multiple markets and/or geographies from foundation. Business enterprises are creative, innovative and technology-savvy centres of excellence that challenge our traditional views. Many firms are larger than nation state economies. Some have better technological know-how than most governments. A few house art collections, employ security staff or know more about their customers than any political regime could imagine. As the global economy develops, firms large and small are at the heart of rapid and radical transformations in the way that we live our lives. The role of the business enterprise is to create value – value for the consumer, value for the market and value for those stakeholders who have a vested interest in the company. In a turbulent economy, businesses large and small must keep abreast of the external business environments where new competitors emerge, customer tastes change and new opportunities arise. Thus, to introduce new readers to the fascinating world of business enterprise, this book provides an insight into the inner workings of the firm.

This book touches upon the many challenges which organizations of all types need to consider today. This allows for a holistic approach to understanding businesses, their environment and, critically, the relationship between the two. Our aim is to examine globalization and its significance to organizations. We look at how organizations have been changed by evolving attitudes and cultures in the world economy. There are issues relating to the internal workings of the firm, external environments, legal issues, marketing (both planning and researching), human resource functions, strategies, business operations, logistics and finally, corporate governance and corporate social responsibility. Each represents an important area for business enterprises and chapter by chapter, we offer a comprehensive overview of these fundamental aspects of business. We explore the role of entrepreneurs, consumers and businesses, to understand how their roles affect the production and allocation of goods and services. Ultimately, such an overview can convey only a glimpse of the rapid changes facing business enterprises today. We hope however, to provide a solid base from which those new to the study of business can develop their own interests in relation to the most powerful economic and entrepreneurial forces shaping the world in which we live.

Norin Arshed, Julie McFarlane and Robert MacIntosh

1 Business Organizations: The Internal Environment

Julie McFarlane and Ross Curran

Anyone embarking upon a journey towards a genuine understanding of business must acquire an underpinning knowledge of the inner workings of the firm, how a firm sustains its operations, and the relationship between the firm and its external environment. This chapter gives a detailed definition of the internal business environment, and the main purpose of both business organizations and strategy are discussed. Furthermore, an understanding of the key concepts relating to business organizations and how such organizations continue to create value for the consumer in today's uncertain business environment will be developed.

The purpose of a business organization – its vision/mission

A **business organization** is an individual or group of individuals who collaborate in order to achieve certain commercial objectives; in essence, it is an economic system where goods and services are exchanged in return for profit. Business organizations come in a variety of forms, and each varies in type and size, from small family businesses to large multinational corporations. A business organization can be privately owned, not-for-profit, or state-owned. An example of a large corporate business is PepsiCo, while a small business such as an independently owned restaurant or shop is termed a private enterprise (Casadesus-Masanell and Ricart, 2010). These business organizations are usually formed to earn income for their owners, while the public or social enterprise is often founded to raise money and to utilise additional resources to provide or support public programmes. There are three common types of business organizations: public, private and voluntary, and there is often crossover between each type, as indicated by the arrows in Figure 1.1.

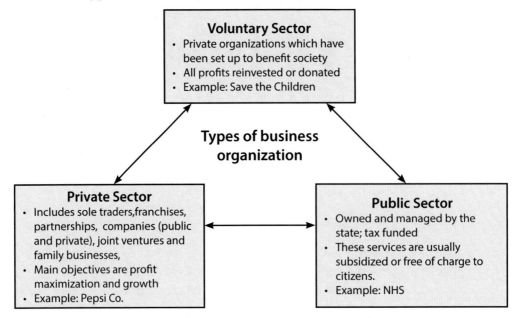

Figure 1.1: Types of organization

Defining business size can be surprisingly complex, as no single measure exists. Usually business size is determined by a combination of factors: the number of employees, the number of outlets or business units, total revenue, overall gross profit, capital investment and market value. However, the number of employees is the most common measure of the size of a business (Table 1.1).

Table 1.1: UK Business Statistics, 2014

Business type	Number of employees	Number of enterprises (000s)
Micro	0-9	5,010
Small	10-49	195
Medium	50-249	31
Large	250+	7

Source: Ward, M., and Rhodes, C., 2014. *Small Business and the UK Economy.* Standard Note: SN/EP/6078. (9 December 2014). Economic Policy and Statistics. House of Commons Library. P. 3.

Table 1.1 shows both the number of micro, and small and medium enterprises (SMEs) in the UK in 2014. There are a small number of multinational corporations (MNCs) (those with over 250 employees). In fact, in 2014 there were 4.9 million businesses in the UK, rising to 5.2 million businesses in 2015, and of those 99% were SMEs, accounting for 14.5 million in employment (Rhodes, 2013). This is significant in that many of these SMEs are micro in size with between 0-9 employees, and the number is growing with increased access to technologies. Thus, the contemporary business landscape in the UK comprises of a small number of dominant, influential organizations, contrasted by far more small and micro enterprises.

Exercise

Spend the next 5 minutes outlining what a business organization means to you.

How might you measure business success?

The strategic direction of an organization: Industries and markets

As well as establishing clear vision and aims for an organization, managers must also determine its direction. Strategy is therefore a fundamental part of the planning process, allowing firms to determine where they want to be in relation to where they currently are. There is no commonly agreed definition, and the term strategy means different things to different business organizations (Mintzberg *et al.*, 2005), not only in terms of what their strategy is, but also how they implement it. That said, most strategy scholars agree that the strategy of an organization should make clear the answers to key questions of identity, positioning and purpose. Regardless of size, type, or focus then, there should be a clear view of where the organization is, where it wants to be, and how it plans to get there.

According to McGoldrick (2002), these questions form a 'blueprint' upon which a firm will draw to achieve its objectives. Three levels of strategic decision-making are generally identified, (Table 1.2).

All three levels hold distinctive strategic concerns and draw on different sets of tools, techniques and approaches. Traditionally, corporate level strategy has set the direction for businesses, but we can see that there are occasions when corporate strategy emerges from, or is shaped by, functional level and business level decisions and actions (McIntosh and Maclean (2015). Thus, each level of strategy interacts in an iterative and dynamic manner with the others. For example, whilst marketing and advertising are seen as part of the functional role of the business strategy, corporate strategy cannot be set without a clear understanding of the consumer – this in essence is the purpose of marketing.

Table 1.2: Levels of strategic decision-making

Strategic Level	Description	Typical areas of decision
Corporate	Concerns the direction and composition of an organization, and the co-ordination of the businesses and activities that comprise large and diversified organizations.	• Mission of the organization • Unique attributes • Business portfolio management • Obtaining/retaining businesses • Priorities and portfolio
Business	Relates to the operation and direction of each of the individual businesses within a group of companies.	• Positioning to compete in strategically relevant markets • Product offerings • Internal management in support of chosen competitive approach
Functional	Concerns individual business functions and processes such as finance, marketing, manufacturing, technology and human resources.	• Translating higher-end strategies into operational terms. • Functions and processes organization

Source: Adapted from McGoldrick (2002)

Understanding strategy at all levels is essential. Strategy is concerned with creating value for the consumer and stakeholders of the business organization. Therefore business strategy is often heavily concerned with the wealth and well-being of the organization now and in the future. The strategic blueprint is also about articulating the values of the business, internally and externally, in assisting the implementation of ideas and ideals. Strategy also provides focus at all levels of a business, empowering those within to follow suit. Corporate strategy strengthens the brand while also providing motivation for employees towards achieving objectives. It strengthens the direction of the firm by empowering its employees, providing them with direction and achievable goals, while enriching management and the social contract within the organization. Tools such as **mission statements** can be used to provide general guidance on the internal strategic direction and values of the firm.

Mission statements can provide organizations with an opportunity to explain (both internally and externally) the company's goals, ethics, corporate culture, values and norms for decision-making. Usually, mission statements are one-sentence statements describing the reasons an organization exists, guiding subsequent decision-making about its priorities, actions, and responsibilities (MacIntosh and Maclean, 2015). The mission statement is also used internally, providing a clear idea of where the business is going and how it intends to get there. When these value statements are outlined to the public they are used to articulate the fundamental assumptions of the business.

■ The industries

Businesses operate in industry and service markets. According to Kotler (2007), an industry is a collection of sellers that provide goods and services, while the market is a collection of buyers who purchase these goods and services in exchange for money. The market communicates its needs, wants and desires to the industry and the industry provides information to the market about the goods and services available to fulfil those needs. This process is also called trade, commerce or exchange. Over 55 industrial sectors operate globally at any one time, consisting of various subsectors within which numerous organizations operate, as shown in Figure 1.2.

Accounting (23)	Defense (3)	Pension Funds (2)
Advertising (44)	Department Stores (3)	Pharmaceuticals (12)
Aerospace (5)	Education (82)	Privare Equity (8)
Agriculture (11)	Electronics (5)	Publishing (14)
Aircraft (1)	Energy (50)	Real Estate (35)
Airline (8)	Entertainment & Leisure (51)	Retail & Wholesale (75)
Apparel & Accessories (11)	Executive Search (6)	Securities & Commodity
Automotive (27)	Financial Services (120)	Exchanges (7)
Banking (71)	Food Beverage and Tobacco (32)	Service (15)
Biotechnology (15)	Grocery (9)	Soap & Detergent (2)
Broadcasting (6)	Health Care (93)	Software (36)
Brokerage (5)	Internet Publishing (28)	Sports (23)
Call Centers (1)	Investment Banking (25)	Technology (112)
Cargo Handling (1)	Legal (18)	Telecommunications (10)
Chemical (5)	Manufacturing (44)	Television (8)
Computer (25)	Motion Picture & Video (9)	Transportation (14)
Consulting (5)	Music (6)	Trucking (1)
Consumer Products (67)	Newspaper Publishers (8)	Venture Capital (29)
Cosmetics (8)	Online Auctions (9)	

Figure 1.2: 55 Harvard Business School industry classifications

Source: http://hbswk.hbs.edu/industries/

■ The market segment

The concept of market segmentation has evolved in tandem with increasingly sophisticated market information. Early segmentation in the 1950s was underpinned by demographic characteristics. However, in subsequent years as more market data became available an ability to target increasingly complex segments emerged (Wedel and Kamakura 2000). This segmentation process can be defined as "…identifying distinct groups of consumers whose purchasing behaviour differs from others in important ways" (Hill, 2011, p. 497).

Segmentation helps business organizations to identify groups of consumers with similar requirements in order to target and serve them effectively. This concept is at the heart of all marketing strategy and serves to form the basis by which organizations understand markets and develop strategies for serving segments better than their competition. Different bases of segmentation are presented in Figure 1.3 below; overlap between segmentation bases is common, and contextually dependent.

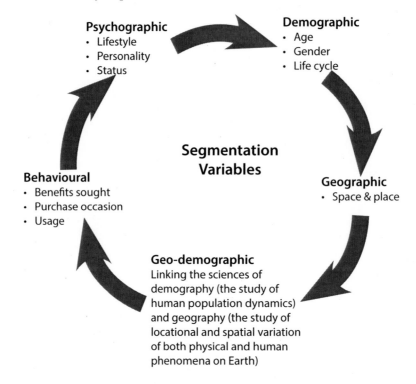

Psychographic
- Lifestyle
- Personality
- Status

Demographic
- Age
- Gender
- Life cycle

Segmentation Variables

Behavioural
- Benefits sought
- Purchase occasion
- Usage

Geographic
- Space & place

Geo-demographic
Linking the sciences of demography (the study of human population dynamics) and geography (the study of locational and spatial variation of both physical and human phenomena on Earth)

Figure 1.3: Segmentation variables

Organizations should be able to identify the segmented variables and create a profile of their target consumers in order to fulfil the segment's needs. For example, consumers with lower household incomes shopping in supermarkets such as Tesco may choose to purchase 'own-label' products. Tesco (one of the UK's largest supermarket chains), works closely with Dunnhumby, a market intelligence agency who use segmentation and profiling to assist the retailer in understanding their consumers in a detailed way. Essentially, by record-ing purchases through providing consumers with loyalty cards (which allow consumers to earn discounts through purchases made), the retailer creates a database of consumer information allowing them to target promotions at certain consumers. The former Tesco Chief Executive who oversaw the introduction of loyalty cards (termed the Tesco Clubcard) believed that it didn't really buy loyalty but did buy consumer insight. Such loyalty card schemes allow organizations to determine if a consumer is male or female, has pets, has children, or is on a diet. The list of variables is long, and the level of understanding accrued is believed not only to lead to more satisfied consumers, but also to reduce costs and increased profits.

> **Tip:** The segmentation concept is explored more extensively in Chapter 6.

Exercise

How might a manufacturer of toothpaste look to segment their market?

Using Figure 1.3 as a guide, select a brand of your choice and outline target segments of the market and how their product(s) fulfils those needs.

How businesses create value

Knowing who you're competing against is simply good business sense. Defining who your competitors are is a hugely important task for any business organization. While the key for small and large businesses is to analyse the market, it is much more important they understand how their business or idea is different.

By looking again at Tesco, the UK's largest retailer, we can give example answers to the above questions. They provide food products, clothing, homewares, electrical equipment and financial services. According to Dunnhumby, Tesco have the consumer at the core of what they do and aim to provide superior customer service. They are located across the UK and have an international presence whilst their growth and competitive position is achieved through a differentiation strategy. Asda (another popular UK supermarket chain), on the other hand, have a similar portfolio but compete more aggressively on price.

Ultimately, businesses compete in a number of ways, from price competition to differentiation strategies; however, the underlying principle is to add value for the consumer. This value-added focus helps organizations articulate what makes their idea different, and gives them insights into why the consumer will choose them over a competitor. Four key elements are identified:

1 A well-defined business opportunity;

2 A benefit or value that is measurable;

3 A favourable price/benefit ratio, and;

4 A short payback period.

Figure 1.4 illustrates some examples of each.

Exemplar case: RightNow Software

RightNow is a software designer that specialises in back-room customer service support.

1 A well-defined business opportunity

Internet sites provide notoriously bad customer service, mainly due to inferior systems failing to get the customer query – 26% of customers never get a response. In addition the number of calls to retailers due to online issues is costly and time-consuming. Right-Now provides a solution to this.

2 A benefit or value that is measurable

RightNow reduces costs for the busines of dealing with customer queries' it increases customer satisfaciton and retention due to the ability to gather data on purchasing habits. For example, the tangible evidence for Ben & Jerry's would be that onine problems reduced by 90%. Another example is of a firm where RightNow was able to reduce incoming calls and save them $250,000

3 A favourable price/benefit ratio

RightNow provides a service comparable to others on the market, only they compete on price rather than on differentiation. They offer a similar service for a much lower price.

4 A short payback period

RightNow charge $29,000 for a 2-year licence of the software and a further $10,000 for any additional modules. The company receives payback in a matter of months, or in some cases more quickly.

Figure 1.4: RightNow Software Exemplar Case

The example above reveals that this company does two things that markedly differentiates them from their competitors: they quantify the savings they provide to the consumer at both time-saved and money-saved levels. Thus, business organizations must not only evaluate their overall strategic direction but also do the same for each product or service to make sure that it adds value and does not become a waste of resources.

Ultimately, any business seeks to add value by offering one of three things:

☐ Tangible benefit.

☐ Time savings.

☐ Money savings.

Exercise

Take 5 minutes to think about Apple's competition, and how they compete.

Think about who they are. What do they do? Why do they do it? Where do they do it? And how do they do it?

How business organizations operate: The role of management and the corporate culture

How a business operates is just as important as who it is or what it does, and is perhaps even the most important part of understanding business organizations of any size. Internally, the organization is concerned with the immediate context of management and the elements of the organization. Externally, the organization operates within micro and macro environments in which past, present and future events also have an impact. These two distinct environments also interact with one another. Worthington and Britton (2009) discuss the business organization not as an entity but as a transformative system, consisting of **inputs** and **outputs**, impacted by both their internal processes and their external environment.

The **inputs** can be anything from the initial resources utilized in the organization's set-up, which usually include human, financial, material and technological resources. The **outputs** are usually the goods and/or services that are provided by the business, organization or firm, which in most cases are then consumed in return for profit. The transformative nature of this process means that profits are usually reinvested into the business organization and used for the acquisition of further resources to enhance the business.

It should be noted that this is not a linear process whereby the inputs are transformed into outputs for consumption; rather, the process is cyclical and is dependent on the external environment and the feedback loop linked to the organization's consumers, as Figure 1.5 shows.

Additionally, external environmental factors such as political, economic, social, technological, environmental and legal situations, will all have an impact on the nature of the available inputs and the success of the overall business process. Many retailers have suppliers and manufacturers globally located, from Europe to South East Asia. Operating in these countries, while bringing cost reductions through labour and manufacturing savings, creates issues due to complexities arising from operating in different environments. For example, in some countries international trade tariffs are set by local governments, and more often than not these are subject to change, generating issues with production and, in some cases, shipping. Another example is the recent economic recession in the UK, limiting SMEs' funding and start-up investment. Therefore, both the external environment and the feedback loop from consumers have a major impact on the inputs and outputs that businesses use, and how each business operates.

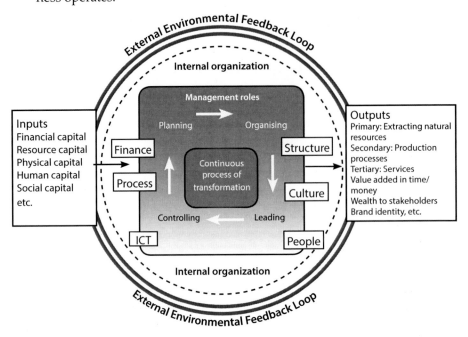

Figure 1.5: Inputs and Outputs – The Internal and External Feedback Loop

Source: Boddy, (2009, p. 6)

Alternatively, the business organization can be viewed as a **techno-system** and/or a **socio-system.** The former refers to a business organization with technology at its core. Systems, processes and routines are prominent in the techno-systemic organization. Its supply chains are efficient and it focuses on quality management, innovation, consumer relationship management, network relationships, knowledge exchange and integration. The techno-system is results driven and has efficiency at its core. Meanwhile, the socio-systemic entity focuses on leadership, learning, empowerment, a community of practice, corporate governance, and flexibility to ensure internal efficiency. The social culture of the organization is vital in this latter system. While these two contrasting formulations of the business organization exist in today's business environment, neither will work in isolation. While efficiency is key to the business processes, so too is the management of people; an organization therefore has to be a combination of both techno and socio-systems (Ruppel *et al.,* 2012).

> **Tip**: Remember, organizations necessitate management of both technological systems and people. They require vastly differing yet complimentary approaches.

The **Sociotechnical systems (STS)** view combines both the techno and socio systems approaches described above, recognising the interaction between people and technology in organizational development. This view was first developed by Trist and Bamforth (1951), whose study observed that despite the introduction of technology to improve organizational efficiency, productivity had become ever more reliant on the social context of the organization. Thus, it is actually the interaction of both social and technical factors that creates the conditions for efficient and effective optimal organizational performance. While Trist and Bamforth's (1951) analysis introduced the terms "socio" and "technical", sociotechnical theory is about joint optimization, i.e. a combination of socio-system and techno-system that works well.

Sociotechnical theory advocates adaptability not only through the technical processes but also in the internal leadership of the organization; this is a key part of the organization's overall strategy. Figure 1.6 shows how a combination of both approaches can create strategic direction for a business. In order to reduce cost the business can look both at optimising the supply chain or distribution channels and also at improving its work practices. Or, a business may look internally to its employees for ideas as well as to their consumers, as Toyota in Japan does in order to develop its brand. There are numerous examples in the literature of situations where internal environments that are conducive to the exchange of ideas facilitate the development of new products or processes (Litchfield *et al.*, 2015).

As previously highlighted, the main role of the business organization is to add value to its resources in order to survive, thrive and grow. One key area is the management of these value-adding activities and another relates to the value adding process itself. Managers within the business organization facilitate the directing of resources in order to transform them into a product/service that they can provide to consumers. A number of different types of managers and leaders help to set the direction of the firm, ranging from general management to the functional line, staff and project managers, each of whom manage staff, managers and/or business processes.

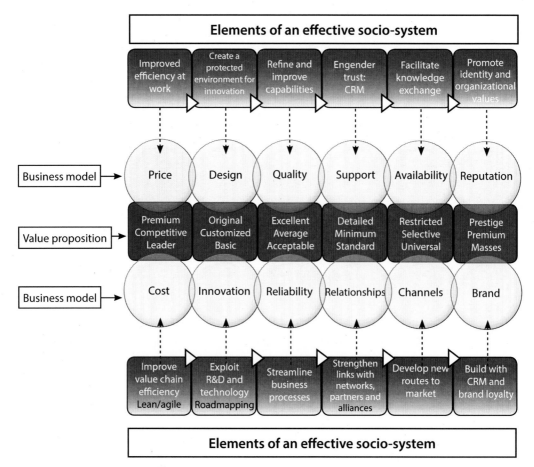

Figure 1.6: Delivering strategy

Source: Adapted from Finkelstein, et al. (2007)

The role of the manager in influencing others and motivating them continues to be debated, but was rather succinctly, although arguably simplistically, described by Rosemary Stewart (1967) as 'someone who gets things done with the aid of people and other resources'. In her study, Stewart sought to understand not only who these managers were, but also what they did. After asking 160 senior and middle managers at Oxford University to keep a diary of their activities for four weeks, the study showed that the ways they worked were diverse (in size and scope), fragmented (in terms of role) and interrupted (by internal and external factors in the environment), and this diversity has not significantly changed in the decades since. The study found a great variety in types of managers, and hypothesized five distinguishing profiles based on how managers spent their time, as distinct from their official level or function. These are now summarized.

- ☐ **Emissaries:** managers who spend most of their time outside of the organization, meeting consumers, suppliers or contractors.

- ☐ **Writers:** managers who spend their time reading and writing, and working on processes.

- ☐ **Discussers:** managers who spent most time with other colleagues.

- ☐ **Troubleshooters:** managers with the most fragmented roles in any of the departments, with many brief contacts.

- ☐ **Committee members:** managers who spend much of their time in meetings and who have a wide range of internal contacts.

This indicative list of five types offers a brief representation of what many managers spend their time doing. Henry Mintzberg (1973) took this idea further by observing how (five) chief executives spent their time, and used this data to create a frequently-quoted model of management roles. Like Stewart, he noted that managers' work was varied and fragmented and listed ten roles falling into three categories – informational, interpersonal and decisional.

- ☐ Within the **informational** category, Mintzberg described a *monitor role*, which involves seeking out and screening information to understand the organization and its context. The *disseminator role* then shares the information by forwarding reports or briefing staff, while the *spokesperson* transmits information outside the organization.

- ☐ Within the **interpersonal** roles, the *figurehead* is a symbol representing the unit in ceremonial or legal duties, while the *leader* defines the manager's relationship with others and facilitates motivation, communication and the development of employee skills and confidence. The *liaison role* focuses on contacts with people outside the immediate unit.

- ☐ Within **decisional** roles, *entrepreneurial* managers are those who demonstrate creativity and initiate change. *Disturbance-handlers* deal with problems and unexpected change, while *resource-allocators* efficiently allocate all resources, from human to financial, to meet organizational objectives.

Tip: Not all managers will fit under each of the titles or categories listed by either Stewart (1967) or Mintzberg (1973); often managers could be classified under a number of these categories and fulfil a number of these roles. While some believe that those who achieve promotion are those who network (i.e., 'it's not what you know but who you know'), in fact the most effective managers are said to spend more time on the management of people as opposed to processes (MacIntosh & Maclean, 2015). In essence, it is this combined sociotechnical system that allows organizations to ensure the efficient transfer of inputs to outputs.

Regardless of their role and status, all managers must plan, organise, control and lead. They must **plan** the overall direction of work, whether at the strategic/corporate level or at the functional level. They must **allocate** resources to every area of the business from procurement to logistics, and of course marketing. They must allocate not only financial resources but also human resources in the form of time and effort, and decide on where each will be most effectively and efficiently spent. The manager must be the networker, politician and leader in that they must ensure they **inspire** the team. They must convey the vision or mission of the business while also generating commitment towards achieving those objectives, at all levels. Finally, managers must **control** the direction of the business. They must monitor its progress, plan for the future, make adjustments and be ready to implement contingencies. Subsequently, regardless of the organization's size, each process always applies, with each done iteratively.

Ultimately, effective managers can be visionaries or pragmatists but must ensure that their organization's internal processes are efficient and that they achieve its overall strategic goals. Thus, managers should ensure that the processes are effective while possessing the ability to identify challenges and provide solutions. Through this critical thinking they must understand and recognise the importance of context and have the vision to imagine and explore alternative paths and, of course, to identify limits. Those with true management capabilities are few and far between so not all managers truly exhibit them. The most successful managers will place the values of the organization at the heart of any strategy and ensure that their people and processes are at the heart of any decision.

Exercise

Below is a table of various leadership and managerial capabilities, associated behaviours and the significance of each approach. Take 5 minutes to select a well-known leader who fits one of these roles (as opposed to all).

Capabilities	Associated Behaviours	Significance
Positive	Visioning. Articulating. Inspiring. Deciding. Resolving. Selling.	Positive projection of future inspires confidence, belief and commitment.
Negative	Waiting. Listening. Contemplating. Testing. Feeling. Absorbing.	Enables engagement with complex issues and maintenance of focus when uncertainty is rife, preventing dispersal into unfocused activity.
Conceptual	Analysing. Auditing. Appraising. Strategizing. Researching. Theorising.	Well-grounded and realisable strategies follow from the application of abstract reasoning and the evaluation of evidence.

Creative	Experimenting. Interacting. Harmonizing. Patterning. Imagining.	Enterprise and innovation follow from creative engagement with market and other business imperatives.
Relational	Communication. Empathizing. Building. Solidarity. Reaching out. Giving. Demonstrating competence.	Trust, confidence and reputational gain are the products of relational excellence. Each is vital to the effective management of networks and alliances.

Source: Adapted from Finkelstein et al (2007)

Aligning the business model with the value proposition

Throughout this chapter we have discussed the concept of the business organization reallocating its resources in order to create a value proposition for the consumer. This section revisits the concept of value and explores best alignment practice between the business model and the value proposition. Value is a subjective concept, as what may be of value to one person may not be to another.

Zeithaml (1988) defined consumer value as having four elements:

1 Value is low price

2 Value is whatever I want in a product

3 Value is the quality I get for the price I pay

4 Value is what I get for what I give

These elements influence a consumer's mind-set when deciding whether or not a product or service is worth buying. The types of value consumers place on certain products can be even more subjective and the ways in which a business organization meets those needs involves complex processes.

The **Business Model Canvas** is a strategic lean-startup template for developing new ideas or documenting existing business models. It is a visual representation chart that describes an organization's or a product's value proposition, infrastructure, consumers, and finances (Osterwalder, 2010), and can be summarized as follows:

Infrastructure

☐ **Key activities**: An example would be creating an efficient supply chain to reduce costs.

☐ **Key resources:** These could be human, financial, physical, technological and intellectual.

☐ **Partner network:** These are the complementary business alliances or strategic alliances.

Offering

☐ **Value proposition**: The portfolio of products and services a business offers to meet its consumers' needs.

☐ **Distinguishing**: Separates a company's value proposition them from their competition.

☐ **Quantifiable**: Should offer savings in time or money for the consumer as well as through newness, performance, customization, efficiency, design quality, brand status/reputation/legitimacy, price, accessibility, and convenience/usability.

☐ As well as price and efficiency, overall consumer experience and outcomes are vital.

Customers

☐ **Consumer segments**: Some businesses serve multiple consumer segments with different needs and characteristics.

☐ **Channels**: The route(s) by which the company delivers its value proposition to its targeted market.

☐ **Consumer relationships:** It is vital to identify consumers and build relationships with them.

Finances

☐ **Cost structure**: This describes the monetary inputs under different business models.

☐ **Revenue streams**: This refers to the income stream from all operating activities in the delivery of the value proposition.

> **Tip**: The value proposition itself is related to price, product or service, quality, support, availability, and reputation, while the business model is focused on cost minimization, innovation, reliability, relationship management, channels of distribution and brand value.

In order to suitably align the business model with the value proposition, the internal processes of the organization must work together to create value. Michael Porter (1985) identified six stages in the analysis of a business organization's value proposition. The 'value chain' model he created is a means of analysing an organization's strategically relevant activities in order to understand its cost behaviour. Porter (1985) breaks the value chain (VC) model into primary and support activities. The model suggests that regardless of an organization's size, its primary activities can be conceptualized into five generic stages:

1   Inbound logistics,

2   Operations,

3   Outbound logistics,

4   Marketing and sales, and

5   Service.

These primary stages are, in turn, supported by the organization's infrastructure:

1   Human resource management (HRM),

2   Technology development,

3   Purchasing, and

4   Procurement.

The value chain should not be seen in isolation but instead as part of the wider context which includes the interactions between each stage, not just within the processes. The relationship between sales and marketing, for instance, can be used to determine what stock is carried and how much inventory should be held. This only happens when all an organization's functional areas work together towards ensuring that the value proposition is at the forefront of all activities.

Tip: Remember, the value chain should not be viewed in isolation,. It is part of the wider business context and involves interactions between stages, not just within processes. The work of Porter is further discussed in Chapter 9.

Thus far this chapter has focused on the inner workings of the business organization. The main theme has been the importance of the value proposition to organizations of all shapes and sizes, and the question of how organizations of all sizes align their business models with their value propositions. We have discussed the concept of the corporate strategy that sets the blueprint for action, and the functional strategies at the business unit level.

All these factors must be working together to create or add value in new ways. For example, while price and cost have a direct impact the value proposition, adding new features and the quality of innovations can also have an impact on the price and the cost of production. Therefore, businesses of all shapes and sizes must add value in new ways, while ensuring that the value proposition remains aligned with the business model is also essential.

Exercise

What value are people who buy from the following brands looking for from the product?

■ Prada Jeans

■ Next Jeans

■ Tesco Jeans

Conclusions

The majority of business organizations, both large and small, begin with an idea of who they are and where they want to be. Getting there is a different undertaking for different organizations. At the strategic level, the organization decides on its direction, and based on that, all processes, functions and resources are directed towards the achievement of its set goals. The business itself involves a transformative process of inputs and outputs that are heavily impacted by the external environment and industry as well as by the market they are serving. The management of such a system requires a dual focus on the management of both processes and people, aligned to create value for the consumer. The role of management in this process is key, as the manager has to be a leader, a networker and the politician responsible for the planning, implementation and control of decisions that add or create value. Managers undertake the process of managing, the task of managing and shaping the business contexts.

The role of management in business organizations has therefore extended beyond operational responsibilities to strategic roles. The functional departments and primary activities within the organization that contribute to developing its products or services are supported by the organization's infrastructure in aiming to reduce costs and add value, as illustrated in the afore-mentioned exemplar paper (Osterwalder, 2004). Smaller enterprises may have differing strategies, stages, operations and styles of management of people but all organizations must seek to add value and align those value adding activities with their business models, if necessary in less formalized ways.

Exemplar paper

Osterwalder, A. (2004). The business model ontology: A proposition in a design science approach.

Osterwalder (2004) investigates ways in which contemporary businesses express the processes and logic behind operations and provides the first global, business oriented model ontology. Osterwalder presents the four pillars of his business model as: customer interface, infrastructure, finance, and the product. These elements are said to be useful in guiding strategy formation, which shapes the product element through answering questions of 'what' the business is, while the interface element focuses on answering the question of 'who' the consumers are. Finally, the infrastructure element describes 'how' the business works. Ultimately, the model serves as a holistic resource for strategy planners and managers.

Who to read

While the range of the topics covered in this chapter are intended as merely an introductory overview, Henry Mintzberg's substantive contributions offer valuable insight. Mintzberg's (1989) work offers analysis at managerial, firm, sectorial and societal levels. Mintzberg holds that management pertains to people perfecting systems rather than systems controlling people. Michael Porter (2013) has also made seminal contributions to management research, particularly the field of competitive strategy. A compilation of several of his papers is available as *'On Competition'*.

References

Boddy, D. (2009). *Management*. 5th Edition. US: Financial Times/Prentice Hall.

Casadesus-Masanell, R., & Ricart, J. E. (2010). From strategy to business models and onto tactics. *Long range planning*, **43**(2), 195-215.

Finkelstein, S., Harvey, C., and Lawton, T. (2007). Breakout strategy: meeting the challenge of double digit growth. McGraw Hill. Available at: http://www.comp. nus.edu.sg/~wongls/icaas-web/events/Thomas-Lawton-apr07-ppt.pdf.

Hill, C. (2011). *Global Business Today* (7th edition). New York: McGraw Hill.

Litchfield, R. C., Gilson, L. L., and Gilson, P. W. (2015) Defining creative ideas toward a more nuanced approach. *Group & Organization Management*, **9**(40), pp. 238-265.

MacIntosh, R., & Maclean, D. (2015). *Strategic Management: Strategists at Work*. Palgrave Macmillan.

McGoldrick, P. (2002). *Retail Marketing*. 1st Edition. New York: McGraw Hill.

Mintzberg, H. (1973). *The Nature of Managerial Work*. New York: Harper and Row.

Mintzberg, H. (1989). *Mintzberg on Management: Inside our Strange World of Organizations*. New York: Free Press.

Mintzberg, H., Ahlstrand, B. W., Ahlstrand, B. and Lampel, J. (2005) *Strategy Safari: A Guided Tour Through The Wilds of Strategic Management.* New York: Free Press.

Osterwalder, A. (2010). *The Business Model Ontology: A Proposition in a Design Science Approach.* New Jersey: Wiley

Porter, M. E.(1985) *The Competitive Advantage: Creating and Sustaining Superior Performance.* NY: Free Press.

Porter, M. (2013) *On Competition,* Boston: Harvard Business Review Press.

Ruppel, C., Tworoger, L., & Tworoger, T. (2012). Telework: Identifying a personal dimension to work-related socio-technical theory. *Advances in Business Research,* **3**(1), pp. 12-24.

Stewart, R. (1967) *Managers and their Jobs,* Macmillan

Trist, E. L. and K. W. Bamforth (1951). Some social and psychological consequences of the longwall method of coal getting. *Human Relations,* **4**(3)

Ward, M., & Rhodes, C. (2014). Small Business and the UK Economy. Standard Note: SN/EP/6078. (9 December 2014). Economic Policy and Statistics. House of Commons Library.

Wedel, M. & Kamakura, W. (2000). *Market Segmentation: Conceptual and Methodological Foundations.* 2nd Edition. Springer Science and Business Media.

Worthington, I. and Britton, C. (2009) *The Business Environment,* Prentice Hall

Zeithaml, V. A. (1988), Consumer perceptions of price, quality, and value: *Journal of Marketing,* **52**(3).

2 Creativity, Innovation and Entrepreneurship

Julie McFarlane

Since the 1990s, creativity and innovation have become more prominent within the fields of business and management, since it is increasingly the case that new markets, or even market growth, may best be attained via creative and innovative solutions. Studies of entrepreneurs, entrepreneurship and growth have catalysed identification and promotion of innovative knowledge industries, rendering their economic importance increasingly significant. For the first time in history, more than half of the world's businesses are now small-scale, creative and innovative, reflecting recent economic transitions around the world. Thus, to appreciate the role of creativity and innovation, it is necessary to understand the nature of entrepreneurship and, specifically, the creativity required to identify and exploit opportunities.

Creativity defined: Past, present and future

Traditionally, being creative was to "unleash, harness, and empower potential from whatever source" (Landry, 2005, p. 53). Indeed, for many "the artist is a channel for a superior power, creativity a gift from the gods, and the imagination a divine spark" (Throsby, 2001, p. 94). Creativity was thought of as "spiritual experiences in the service of whatever muse held the artist in her thrall" (Ibid, p. 95). According to Hisrich, Peters and Shepherd (2012, p. 8), the "ability to innovate and create can be observed throughout history; although the fundamental tools may have changed the ability has been present in every civilization". Examples include classical Athens, with its complex exchange arrangements; the 'guild craft cities' (Hall, 1998), of Renaissance Florence in the fourteenth century, seventeenth century Vienna, and eighteenth century Paris, both with their strong atelier traditions. Each of these cities was a birthplace for renewal in disciplines including art, technology, science and literature. The city of Edinburgh, for example, experienced an intense period of multidisciplinary breakthroughs in philosophy (David Hume), economics (Adam Smith) and architecture (Patrick Geddes).

For creative thinkers like Edward de Bono (2008), without these places and people, there would have been no progress. For de Bono, it is those people who turned creative thought to turn into creative action; the alternative is that ideas remain just ideas. The concept of creativity as a commercial concept emerged in the late 1940s and the economist Joseph Schumpeter popularized the term *creative destruction* to describe the process of one business model, technology or industry disrupting and replacing another. For many, interest in creativity was grounded in the changes in the world economy after both world wars, while for others in industry it was more about the reformation of wealth (Schumpeter, 1976) or the collapse of industrial and manufacturing dominance in the Western world. With the growing commercialization and commoditization of film, music and media, creativity as a core concept became "both a major force of production and formative mode of social organization and control" (Kellner, 2007, p. 56). The response was the first critical theory of the cultural industries, distinguishing between traditional creative arts and industrially produced forms of mass culture. Two distinct views of creativity emerged; the 'born' versus the 'made' (Figure 2.1).

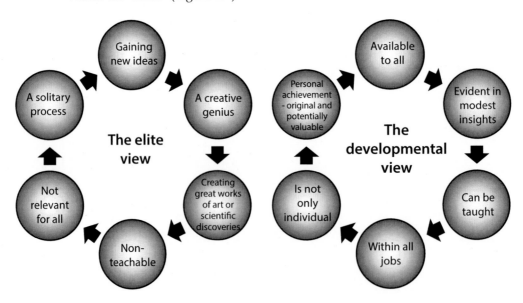

Figure 2.1: Feldman's (1979) elitist and developmental view of creativity.
Source: Adapted from Feldman (1979, p.660-663)

The elitist view sees the creative process as an individual spiritual experience; an innate ability that cannot be harnessed. Here, creativity is ground-breaking, from great works of art to architecture and design. In the developmental view, creativity is a process, not an event, and something that can be harnessed and supported. In essence, creativity is in us all, not a select few, and is a problem-solving process. It can be learned, practiced and applied by anyone. Some research suggests there are a number of tools individuals can use to enhance creativity, while others have suggested that those entering the creative process must have the relevant skills and be strongly motivated.

Thus creativity has been slowly democratized, and popularized. We are now witnessing the convergence of new kinds of artistic and technological creativity, where individuals, businesses and even rich, affluent, cultural cities sell their beauty, philosophies, music and arts to the rest of the world (Hall, 1998). Yet we mustn't forget the skill and talent in innovation is people. Thus it is human creativity that will fill in the gaps left by the past and help to change the future.

Exercise

Take 5 minutes and think about what creativity means to you.

Note down your own definition.

How creative thought can turn into innovation

"May we be wakened by the Spirit of Creativity in this coming century" (Fox, 2002, p.1).

While the concept of creativity has been hotly debated in recent years, the discussion on how creative thought can turn into creative action and innovation also needs to be acknowledged. Fox (2002) suggests we are now in an era where creativity has the ability to change the way we do things. A clear understanding of what it means to innovate is required (Goffin and Mitchell, 2005). To innovate, according to the New Oxford Dictionary (2004, p. 942), is to: 'Make changes in something established, especially by introducing new methods, ideas, or products'. Joseph Schumpeter (1950) was among the first to categorise innovation as the creation of something 'new' that creates and adds value for those to whom it was intended. Something 'new' can also mean the updating of something which exists to take advantage of a specific segment or market.

Many of our greatest innovations come from natural sources, and without them our lives would be more difficult (Figure 2.2).

Nature's creation?	or	Human creation
Venoms and poisons	or	Anaesthetics
The leaf	or	Solar Panel (energy from light)
Brain	or	Computer/electronic circuitry
DNA	or	Computer program
Ear drum	or	Microphone
Eye	or	Camera (lens, focus, iris, film)
Eye lid	or	Windshield wiper
Tears	or	Wiper fluid
Incisor teeth	or	Knife
Heart	or	Pump
Spinal chord/nervous system	or	Communication/telephone cables
Song birds	or	Music

Figure 2.2: Nature's creations turned into human innovation

Ultimately, innovation falls into two categories; functional and design-driven. The former is focused on the functional elements of the products, for example: does it work? Does it meet customer needs? The Apple iPhone operating system is part of the functional characteristics of the product, while the way it is designed for ease of use is a remnant of the design element. In design-driven innovations the key focus is on the symbolic nature of the product. What does it mean to the consumer? How do they feel when they use the product? Ultimately the innovation must add value in terms of price, quality, and functionality, but it also has to fulfil a number of intangible requirements, for example how it makes a consumer 'feel'.

Another seminal theorist in the field, Clayton Christensen (1997), identifies two types of innovations: *disruptive* innovations and *sustaining* innovations. The former introduces a new value proposition; here, new markets are created, or alternatively, such innovations reshape existing markets. The effect is to dis-equilibrate and to alter the existing market structure, then wait until the process eventually settles down for the next wave of innovation.

Entrepreneurs innovate not just by figuring out how to use inventions, but also by introducing new means of production, new products, and new forms of organization (Figure 2.3). These innovations, he argued, take just as much skill and daring as the process of invention.

Type	A new process	A new market	A new supply chain	A new business/ industry	A new product
	New method of production	Opening a new market	A new source of supply	A new type of organization	A new product or improvement
Examples of Innovation	Manufacturing & assembly lines	Analogue to digital	International air travel	The Internet	The mobile phone

Figure 2.3: Schumpeter's five types of innovation

One example of a **disruptive** innovation is the impact of Apple's iTunes on the music industry. When Apple observed the impact of MP3 technology they designed the first generation iPod and, following the success of Napster, they created the first legal online music service, iTunes, in April 2003 (Vaccaro and Cohn, 2004). Apple did not just create an innovation in terms of the way music was played – they also had an impact on the way music was listened to. Subsequently, this meant changes in how it was produced, manufactured and distributed, with an inevitable impact on overall profits.

In contrast, **sustaining** innovations are incremental improvements to existing products, processes or markets. However, consumers never see many of these sustaining innovations. They include, for example, process improvement in organizations to make supply chains more efficient, such as with Spanish retailer Zara, whose in-house supply chain makes them more efficient in response to changing consumer demands or trends. Some other examples include making the organization more streamlined, diversifying operations and divestment activities. By taking a resource-based view of the organization and focusing on utilising its core competencies, the search for new techniques to improve business processes has subsequently grown, both internally and externally.

While we usually think of innovations as things that shake the foundations of how we live, often innovation refers to customization and specialization through harnessing creativity and knowledge (Hisrich *et al.*, 2005). Innovation can be radical or incremental, but it is multi-dimensional and should be thought of as a process rather than an activity.

Exercise

Can you think of any other disruptive or sustaining innovations?

Note them down and then think about why you define them in this way.

Opportunity identification: Individual and organizational creativity in innovation

Creating an organization built to innovate requires more than simply defining innovation; an understanding of how innovation is achieved is also needed. Researchers have focused on individual creativity, however, further research (Goffin and Mitchell, 2005) has revealed that innovation is often about working as part of a team to build what Porter calls 'competitive advantage' (1990); often innovation management is about the people you employ. For organizations to become innovators they must begin with an environment that fosters innovation and allows creativity to flourish. Innovation strategy should be set out in a clear 'vision', and set of objectives that seek to change and implement innovative approaches should be identified. Innovative organizations require a set of core competences; these are usually located within the organization as resources or externally as part of technical collaboration or knowledge-sharing initiatives. However, while competences and capacities can be acquired externally, the values which create an organizational culture that encourages innovation need to be embedded within. With a clear focus on communication, *kaizen* (continuous improvement and monitoring management) must also allow for diversity and creativity.

Innovation is complex and though it can occur accidentally, it works most effectively when resources, structure, planning and strategy are aligned to encourage both innovation and the diffusion or adoption of innovative ideas. Akio Morita of Sony once stated that: "Ordinary people cannot innovate all of the time" (Goffin and Mitchell, 2005, p. 265). The majority of innovations are harnessed through an organization's supportive structure and culture. Innovative organizations today require an integrated set of components which can create and reinforce innovation continuously and allow it to flourish. Creativity by itself is insufficient in coming up with ideas and reaping the benefits. Today, creativity is defined as a personal problem-solving process of a non-routine kind, which can be learned, practiced and successfully applied by anyone.

Exercise

Take 5 minutes and think about whether innovation is a 'team game'.

Many of the greatest opportunities for innovation began as ways to solve a problem. According to Lumpkin and Lichtenstein (2005) there are five stages to creative problem solving (Figure 2.4).

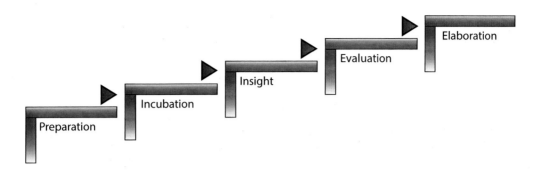

Figure 2.4: Stages in creative problem solving

Source: Adapted from: Lumpkin and Lichtenstein(2005, p. 458)

These stages are malleable, forming a toolkit for organizations' innovation development processes. Ideas can be prepared in brainstorming sessions, then internalized and refined before market tests. Once disseminated to customers or the test market, insights gained are evaluated internally before changes are made prior to commercialization. However, this is a simplified version of the creative process and in reality it is much more complex and often ad-hoc in organizations, due to changing business environments. Some evidence suggests creativity is a problem-solving activity, some still argue for the 'hero' – the individual with the drive to make an idea reality. But the secret to success is far more about having "the nerve, energy, passion, commitment and skill to build a business, than it is about a great idea" (Barrow *et al.*, 2005, p. 16).

Not all creative thought is actioned and not all ideas are creative. Nor do all creative ideas align with a lucrative commercial opportunity. Scholars agree that somewhere early in the creative process an individual encounters an opportunity (Dimov, 2011). Opportunities may be derived through new technologies, market inefficiencies, or through political, regulatory or demographic change (Shane and Venkataraman, 2000). Schumpeter (1934) identified such changes as catalysts which can either generate or close off entrepreneurial opportunities (Eckhardt and Shane, 2003).

How and why particular opportunities are discovered is determined by a complex mix of factors. While it is most often conceptualized as an outcome, opportunity can also be seen as an unfolding process. As Dimov (2011, p. 133) explains, opportunities are "situated expressions of prospective entrepreneurs' motivation, knowledge, and cognitive and learning abilities". Previous research has shown that individuals differ in their ability to identify entrepreneurial opportunities, to perceive particular market changes, or to know how to create specific products or services. One reason for this is that information is imperfectly distributed, so that "no two people share all of the same information at the same time" (Shane and Venkataraman, 2000, p. 221). World-renowned 18th Century economist Adam Smith (1967) distinguished between a craftsman, motivated by intrinsic rewards such as autonomy and driven by a need for independence, and an opportunist, focused on the functional activities associated with management and motivated by the prospect of growth. Timmons and Spinelli (2015, 2007) distinguished between lifestyle and high-growth entrepreneurs. The former focused on running a business to sustain a comfortable lifestyle, while the latter seeks to expand his/her business.

Many researchers have argued that the main objectives for most entrepreneurs are profit and growth; others that personal motives take precedence (Cyert and March, 1963). Beyond this, experience and education and the support of family, friends and others can all help to determine an individual's propensity to enter the creative process (Lumpkin and Dess, 1996). Bhave (1994, p. 230) suggests a trigger when "the prospective individuals [experience], or [are] introduced to, needs that [can]not be fulfilled by others". Seeing an opportunity, the entrepreneur takes the necessary action to capitalise upon it. This implies a match between the market, on one hand, and the knowledge, skills and competencies of the entrepreneur on the other. But, opportunities do not come pre-packaged (Venkataraman, 1997), and the opportunity recognition process is not straightforward. The literature usually recommends that entrepreneurs should systematically search for opportunities, yet some suggest this is impossible since opportunity, by definition, is always unknown until it is discovered or created. Aspiring entrepreneurs must therefore be alert.

Exercise

Using one business organization, describe the alignment between an innovation introduced by that organization and the opportunity created. Note down your thoughts.

Entrepreneurial opportunities are not exclusively serendipitous; most research suggests that prior knowledge, work experience, education, personal experience, networks and other factors may all play a part, either alone or in combination. Research suggests that many would-be entrepreneurs forego alertness and instead utilise contacts in their chosen industry to help them spot gaps that others may have missed (Burns, 2001).

Aspiring entrepreneurs often fail to identify a variety of opportunities, or identify the wrong ones. Moreover, as Singh (2001, p. 11) explains, entrepreneurs may spot the right opportunity but then fail to act optimally. Good planning involving idea preparation, incubation of key skills and resources, insights from market research, evaluation of consumer feedback and elaboration of idea development is needed. Additionally, domain-relevant skills, intrinsic (internal) motivation or drive to create, and the process of creation are all prominent (Venkataraman and Sarasvathy, 2000).

Exercise

Below is a list of different opportunity types. Identify a current enterprise that engages with each one of these opportunity types.

1   New products/services

2   Solutions to existing problems

3   New customer markets

4   New industries

5   Experience industries

6   New operating/manufacturing process

7   New supply chain

Who are these creative entrepreneurs?

Who is an entrepreneur? A universally accepted definition has yet to emerge. The entrepreneur was identified in the 13th Century; however the first proper noun for an entrepreneur emerged from the 17th Century French verb *entreprendre* (to undertake). The entrepreneur is therefore someone who undertakes to make things happen (Kirby, 2010, p. 3). They exercise high levels of initiative and willingness to take risks, although arguably this could cover a wide range of occupations. Schumpeter (1934) "gave us the modern definition of an entrepreneur as an individual who shakes the foundations of the existing economic order by introducing new products and services, and or exploiting new ways of doing things" (Bygrave, 2003, p. 1). For him, the entrepreneur is an extraordinary individual with the ability to bring about change through new technological processes or products, "altering convention through innovative activity, bringing about extraordinary events" (Deakins and Freel, 2006, p. 5). For Baumol (1990, p. 4), only Schumpeter has "succeeded in infusing the entrepreneur with life". Yet others see the entrepreneur as a risk taker, an individual with foresight, and a facility for organization, a born leader, a capitalist, an innovator and someone who is alert to opportunities. Economic theorists hold various views, from Adam Smith (1776) to Israel Kirzner (1973) on the entrepreneur as a risk taker or a capitalist, (Figure 2.5).

Economic theories of entrepreneurship

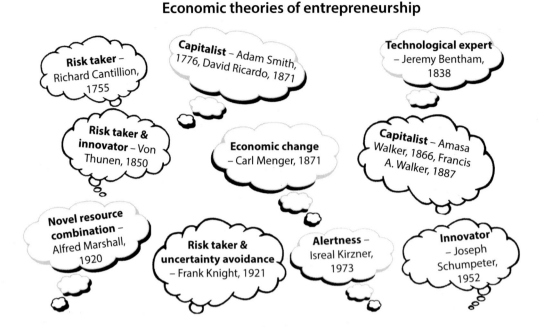

Figure 2.5: Economic theories of entrepreneurship

> **Tip:** The term *Creative Destruction* was used to describe how the activities of individuals or businesses can alter existing economic structures and reconfigure them in order to make way for new wealth. Today the term is used in various contexts, from product development to new disruptive technology and marketing strategies, with the best example being the introduction of the smartphone, which completely restructured the mobile phone industry, among many other things. In recent years it has been suggested that very few new ventures will have the potential to initiate the "Schumpeterian 'gale' of creative-destruction", (Burns 2001, p 316). It is therefore imperative to understand that not only is the ability to create and conceptualise needed; the ability to understand all the forces at work in the environment is also required.

Perhaps reflecting the diversity of definitions, we can be sure that entrepreneurs are all different, and have had different experiences (Kirby, 2010, p. 117). Thus, perhaps no individual displays the full range of entrepreneurial attitudes displayed above.

Exercise

Select an entrepreneur. Take 5 minutes and discuss which of the definitions from Figure 2.5 seems to most accurately describe to them.

What is entrepreneurship? Key theories and concepts

Entrepreneurship is an economic phenomenon involving "a nexus of two phenomena: the presence of lucrative opportunities and the presence of enterprising individuals" (Shane and Venkataraman, 2000, p. 218). Both prioritise the creation of wealth rather than its transfer. The economics literature is now acknowledging their central role in "economic development, prosperity, and evolutionary change" (Shane, 2000, p. 448).

Leading entrepreneurship and management theorist William. B. Gartner (1985, p. 697) previously presented a useful conceptual framework for describing the phenomenon of entrepreneurship, setting out the four major elements in the venture creation process, (Figure 2.6).

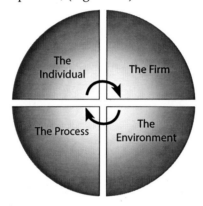

Figure 2.6: Gartner's conceptual framework. Adapted from Gartner (1985)

According to Gartner, the venture creation process is complex because: "entrepreneurs and their firms vary widely; the actions they take or do not take and the environments they operate in and respond to are equally diverse – and all these elements form complex and unique combinations in the creation of each new venture" (Gartner, 1985, p. 697). Entrepreneurship can therefore only be comprehensively described by including all these key elements.

Researchers have attempted to describe how entrepreneurs search for information influenced through cognition style (Shane, 2000). Other researchers have focused on gaining greater understanding of entrepreneurs' behaviour and typologies (nascent, novice, serial and portfolio entrepreneurs) (Gartner, Carter and Reynolds, 2010). Gartner, Starr and Bhat (1999) identified three role identities (Figure 2.7).

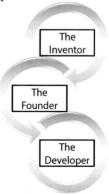

Figure 2.7: The three role identities

The early stages of the entrepreneurial process activities are typically linked to the *inventor* identity. For example, seeking out new ideas, developing products and/or scanning the environment for market-disruptive opportunities (Wilson and Stokes, 2005). In later stages, activities are more likely to be related to the *founder* identity as they assemble the tangible and intangible resources necessary to create a firm. As the venture becomes more formalized, the entrepreneur takes on the role of *developer* – a transition many entrepreneurs struggle to come to terms with.

Exercise

Using the three identity types, select an entrepreneur and describe each trait relating to the entrepreneur and detail his or her journey through each stage.

Some researchers have explored the resources entrepreneurs acquire and where these come from, both in terms of finance and labour. Those writing within the entrepreneurial network literature argue that personal and professional networks not only provide access to finance, information, advice and support, but also that they can enhance an entrepreneur's legitimacy, reputation and status (Baum and Oliver, 1991). Entrepreneurship has "evolved beyond the classic start-up to include companies of all types and in all stages" (Timmons and Spinelli, 2015, 2007, p. 79). As Hindle (2010) suggests, much is already known about the six inextricably linked, generic questions at the heart of entrepreneurship research: *who, why, what, how, when* and *where*. Yet, current theory is underdeveloped and, more critically, it is unsupported by systematic evidence. Moroz and Hindle (2012) argue that the problem is made worse because of the complexity of human action and the variety of circumstances, which make theorising difficult. We are left with "multidisciplinary theories that investigate entrepreneurship in narrowly themed contexts" (Moroz and Hindle, 2012, p. 789).

The process of enterprise

Researchers argue that entrepreneurship constitutes a set of activities best studied as processes. According to expert Per Davidsson (2008, p. 4), the entrepreneurial process is "the creation of economic activity that is new to the market," by an individual who "perceives an opportunity, in turn creating a medium to pursue it, while bringing together available resources and undertaking all necessary functions, and activities, to achieve realization" (Bygrave, 2003, p. 7). This involves all functions, actions and activities associated with the identification and discovery of opportunities and creating organizations to exploit them.

Bhave (1994) views the entrepreneurial process as being both "internally and externally stimulated". The latter characteristic is more goal-oriented; in this case, the entrepreneurial process:

> …starts with a decision or desire to launch a new venture, the potential entrepreneur(s) begins actively searching for opportunities, typically selecting several alternate ideas that are considered and evaluated ('opportunity filtration') before one is chosen. The selected idea is then elaborated and adapted, until a relatively complete business idea that is judged viable has been developed by the entrepreneur, who then decides to exploit 'it' (Davidsson, 2008, p.8).

The internally stimulated process is the opposite, though according to some studies it is just as common. In it:

> …the individual has no prior intention to go into business, yet experienced or were introduced to needs that could not be fulfilled. Finding a solution, the individual becomes aware of others with the same problem, and in turn enters the entrepreneurial process (Davidsson, 2008, p. 8).

Again, the process is discussed from a variety of perspectives and has produced a range of views. Moroz and Hindle (2012) reviewed the entrepreneurial process models presented in peer reviewed journals and scholarly books over the last 40 years. Selecting 32 of these models, the authors looked for commonalities and concluded that the models fell into four distinct groups: static frameworks (11), stage models (12), process dynamic models (8) and quantification sequences (1) (Moroz and Hindle, 2012, p. 811) (Figure 2.8).

Static Frameworks (11)	Gartner's (1985) framework is static as it does not consider the dynamic nature of each of the stages. Each is studied in isolation as in Shane's (2003) model of recognition, discover and exploitation.
Stage Models (12)	Bhave's (1884) *internally* and *externally* stimulated processes are said to encompass a stage model that signifies key events or milestones in the venture creation process.
Process Dynamic Models (8)	Sarasvathy's (2001) model of effectuation is a process dynamic model that focuses on the inputs and outputs of the process. Each feeds the next and each can be used in isolation or as a group. The process itself takes into account the context of the venture itself.
Quantification Sequences (1)	Carter, Gartner & Reynolds (1996) was the only quantification of the activities of entrepreneurs from those that were: up and running; still trying; or who had given up. However, even this was in stages.

Figure 2.8: 4 Process model classifications. Adapted from Moroz & Hindle (2012)

Despite their apparent focus on process, the majority of the models were identified as static frameworks, and were typically found in studies addressing the overall process of venture creation. Gartner's process model was also classed as static because it discusses venture creation "without examining the sequence of activities, consists of a limited set of variables connected by speculative causal links (e.g., Gartner, 1985); process oriented but do not capture sequence of dynamics" (Moroz and Hindle, 2012, p. 811). Moroz and Hindle (2012, p. 800) also found that stage models were commonly used to understand the developmental steps in an organization's evolution, as marked by key events or milestones in the venture creation process. In other words, start with an idea and create a business around it.

Entrepreneurship is generally considered nonlinear in nature. Sarasvathy's (2001) model of effectuation offers an alternative view by focusing on the dynamic nature of inputs and outputs of the process. Entrepreneurs must be clear about who they are, what they know and whom they know, and they must use this information to decide between a range of possible outcomes. In this view, the individual is responsible for initiating the process.

In Sarasvathy's (2001) process model, the individual gets the idea for a new venture either through a deliberate search or by a chance encounter. Sarasvathy (2008) further argues that the individual begins the entrepreneurial process in one of two ways: causation or effectuation. The causation process is goal-oriented. It begins with a multitude of possible alternatives, from which the potential entrepreneur chooses the most suitable idea for their skills and resources (Bygrave, 2003). In the effectuation process, the set of means is taken as a given; rather than planning around an uncertain future, the entrepreneur works with "who they are, what they know, and whom they know" (Sarasvathy, 2001). The individual looks to expand their horizons, from a variety of "localized possibilities to increasingly complex and enduring opportunities fabricated in a contingent fashion over time" (Sarasvathy, 2003, p. 208).

The difference between causation and effectuation can be illustrated using a simple cooking analogy. If you follow causational logic, you will decide on the menu, determine and purchase the required ingredients, and then prepare them. If you follow effectuation logic, you will take whatever ingredients are available to you and work with them as best you can (Davidsson, 2008). The specific strategies adopted are characterized as action rather than outcome. Sarasvathy's central argument places causation and effectuation at opposite ends of a continuum, with five principles (Figure 2.9) positioned in a spectrum between the two: *the bird-in-hand principle, the affordable loss principle, the crazy quilt principle, the lemonade principle and the pilot-in-the-plane principle*. At each step of the entrepreneurial process, entrepreneurs use and adapt the principles as and when they are required. Sometimes more than one principle will be used. In many cases all will be used (Sarasvathy, 2008).

The bird-in-hand principle

The creation of something using existing means (as opposed to discovering new ways and means to achieve goals): the entrepreneur therefore asks in the scenario: 'what do I have?' rather than asking: 'what do I need?' For Sarasvathy, the effectual entrepreneur begins with who they are, what they know and whom they know.

The affordable-loss principle

The entrepreneur then decides, based on their current financial status and psychological willingness to invest, how much they are willing to sacrifice to undertake the process (rather than investing based on expected returns) (*ibid*).

The crazy-quilt principle

Refers to instances where a venture develops from an isolated phenomenon to become part of a socially embedded process as the entrepreneur co-develops his or her business with others.

The lemonade principle

Given that today's business environment is increasingly global, the wise entrepreneur acknowledges and appropriates contingencies by leveraging surprises rather than trying to avoid or adapt to them. In essence: when life throws you lemons, make lemonade.

The pilot-in-the-plane principle

Urges entrepreneurs to focus on activities within their control: for example, business now exploiting the technological advances that have brought such turblence to the industry to their own advantage.

Figure 2.9: The five principles of effectuation. Adapted from Sarasvathy (2001, p. 247)

Although the various process models outlined above fundamentally differ, they all imply that prospective entrepreneurs seek ideas which will allow them to leverage their own unique interests and skills, rather than venturing into completely unknown territory. The most common model describes the entrepreneur who discovers and exploits existing opportunities, rather than the effectual entrepreneur who fabricates them "from the mundane realities of life" (Sarasvathy, 2008, p. xiii). But as scholars compare the processes, it has become apparent that the empirical evidence to support either view is scarce. However, since the success of a new venture depends on "opportunity recognition, acquisition of essential resources (financial and human), and the capacity to respond quickly and effectively to rapid change in highly dynamic environments," process should be the central focus (Baron, 2008, p. 332).

Exercise

Which process model seems to you to offer the most helpful explanation of entrepreneurship? Why?

Conclusions

This chapter has provided an overview of the presence of creativity and innovation. We have discussed who entrepreneurial individuals are, and what they do in light of the current theory. We have developed an understanding of current theories of the firm. Finally, the chapter has looked at the study of process, and explained that the process itself is not linear but is, rather, dynamic, and that inclusion and understanding of not only who the entrepreneur is, but what they do, why they do it, where they do it, when they do it and of course how, are of greater importance than purely focusing on who they are.

Exemplar paper

Shane, S. and Venkataraman, S., (2000). The promise of entrepreneurship as a field of research. *Academy of Management Review*, 25(1), pp. 217-226.

The authors provide a detailed definition of the field of entrepreneurship, and give an explanation of why it is important. They also provide us with an understanding of how opportunities are created and why some and not others are exploited, as well as considering the different modes of exploitation. Finally the authors attempt to create a framework that best describes entrepreneurship as a research agenda. Ultimately, they organise previously fragmented research and create a logical framework by which to understand the field of entrepreneurship.

Who to read

William B. Gartner is a world-renowned Professor of Entrepreneurial Leadership and over the last 25 years has written a number of articles on entrepreneurship theory and new venture creation. Gartner's (1985) views on entrepreneurship have been hugely influential in terms of education and research, however with his own ties to industry Gartner is able to bridge the gap between theory and practice in a seamless manner. He was one of the first to conduct a nationwide study of nascent entrepreneurs and create a framework that highlights how entrepreneurs identify opportunities, acquire resources in order to solve problems, and take action to successfully launch new ventures.

References

Baron, R. (2008) The role of affect in the entrepreneurial process. *Academy of Management Review,* **33**(2), 328-340.

Barrow, C., Burke, G., Molian, D. and Brown, R. (2005) *Enterprise Development: The Challenges of Starting, Growing and Selling Businesses.* UK: Thomson, pp. 1-51.

Baumol, W. (1990) Entrepreneurship: productive, unproductive, and destructive. *Journal of Political Economy,* **98**(5), 893-921.

Bhave, M. (1994) A process model of entrepreneurial venture creation. *Journal of Business Venturing,* **9**(3), 223-242.

Burns, P. (2001) *Entrepreneurship and Small Business,* Palgrave MacMillan.

Bygrave, W.D. (2003) The entrepreneurial process. In: W. Bygrave & A. Zacharakis, eds. *The Portable MBA in Entrepreneurship.* 3rd ed. New York: John Wiley and Sons Publishing, pp. 1-26.

Christensen, C. M. (1997) *The Innovator's Dilemma When New Technologies Cause Great Firms to Fail.* Cambridge, MA: Harvard Business School Press.

Cyert, Richard M. and March, James G. (1963), *A Behavioral Theory of the Firm,* Englewood Cliffs, NJ: Prentice-Hall.

Davidsson, P. (2008) *The Entrepreneurship Research Challenge.* Cheltenham, UK: Edward Elgar Publishing.

Deakins, R. and Freel, M. (2006) *Entrepreneurship and Small Firms,* 4th Edition, UK: McGraw Hill.

De Bono, E. (2008) *Six Frames For Thinking about Information.* London: Vermilion.

Dimov, D. (2011) Entrepreneurial opportunities. In: S. Carter & D. Jones-Evans, eds. *Enterprise and Small Business: Principles, Practice and Policy.* 3rd ed. Oxford: Financial Times/Prentice Hall, pp. 129-150

Eckhardt, J. & Shane, S. (2003) Opportunities and entrepreneurship. *Journal of Management,* **29**(3), pp. 333-349.

Feldman, D. (1979) Toward a nonelitist conception of giftedness. *Phi Delta Kappan,* **60**(9), 660-663.

Fox, M. (2002) *Creativity: Where the Divine and the Human Meet,* 1st Edition. New York: Tarcher/Putnam

Gartner, W.B. (1985) A conceptual framework for describing the phenomenon of new venture creation. *The Academy of Management Review,* B(4), pp. 696-706.

Gartner, W.B., Carter, N. & Reynolds, P. (2010) Entrepreneurial behavior: firm organizing processes. In: Z. J. Acs & D. B. Audretsch, eds. *Handbook of Entrepreneurship Research: An Interdisciplinary Survey and Introduction.* New York: Springer, pp. 99-128.

Gartner, W.B., Starr, J.A. & Bhat, S, (1999) Predicting New Venture Survival: An Analysis of "Anatomy of a Startup", Cases from Inc. Magazine. *Journal of Business Venturing*, **14**(2), pp. 215-232.

Goffin, K., & Mitchell, R. (2005) *Innovation Management*, Palgrave Macmillan.

Hall, P. (1998) *Cities and Civilization: Culture, Innovation, and Urban Order*. London: Weidenfeld & Nicolson.

Hindle, K. (2010). Skillful dreaming: testing a general model of entrepreneurial process with a specific narrative of venture creation. In: W.B. Gartner, ed. *ENTER: Entrepreneurial Narrative Theory Ethnomethodology and Reflexivity*. South Carolina: Clemson University Digital Press, pp. 97-135.

Hisrich, R.D., Peters, M.P. and Shepherd, D.A. (2012, 2005) *Entrepreneurship*, 9th Edition, USA: McGraw Hill Irwin, pp. 6.

Kellner, D. (2007). The Frankfurt School. In: T. Edwards, ed. *Cultural Theory: Classical and Contemporary Positions*. London: Sage Publications, pp. 49-68.

Kirby, D.A. (2010) *Entrepreneurship*, UK: McGraw Hill, pp. 1-206.

Landry, C. (2005). Lineages of the creative city. In: S. Franke & E. Verhhagen, eds. *Creativity and the City: How the Creative Economy is Changing the City*. Rotterdam: NAI Publishing, pp. 42-55.

Lumpkin, G. & Dess, G. (1996). Clarifying the entrepreneurial orientation construct and linking it to performance, *Academy of Management Review*, **21** (1), 135 - 172.

Lumpkin, G. T., & Lichtenstein, B. B. (2005). The role of organizational learning in the opportunity-recognition process. *Entrepreneurship Theory and Practice*, **29**(4), 451-472.

Moroz, P. & Hindle, K. (2012). Entrepreneurship as a process: toward harmonizing multiple perspectives. *Entrepreneurship Theory and Practice*, **36**(4), 781-818.

Sarasvathy, S. (2001). Causation and effectuation: towards a theoretical shift from economic inevitability to entrepreneurial contingency. *Academy of Management Review*, **26**(2), 243-288.

Sarasvathy, S. (2003). Entrepreneurship as a science of the artificial. *Journal of Economic Psychology*, **24**(2), 203-220.

Sarasvathy, S. (2008). *Effectuation: Elements of Entrepreneurial Expertise*. Cheltenham, UK: Edward Elgar Publishing.

Schumpeter, J.A. (1934). *The Theory of Economic Development*. Cambridge, Mass: Harvard University Press.

Schumpeter, J. A. (1950). *Capitalism, Socialism, and Democracy*. 3d Ed. New York, Harper [1962].

Schumpeter, J.A. (1976) *Capitalism, Socialism and Democracy*. 5th Edition. London:

George Allen & Unwin, Original 1942.

Shane, S., (2000). Prior knowledge and the discovery of entrepreneurial opportunities. *Organization Science,* **11**(4), 448-466.

Shane, S. & Venkataraman, S., (2000). The promise of entrepreneurship as a field of research. *Academy of Management Review,* **25**(1), 217-226.

Singh, R. (2001). A comment on developing the field of entrepreneurship through the study of opportunity recognition and exploitation. *Academy of Management Review,* **26**(1), 10-12.

Timmons, J., Spinelli, S. & Adams, R. (2015) *New Venture Creation: Entrepreneurship for the 21st Century.* 10th Edition. McGrawHill. Ch 3 & 4.

The New Oxford Dictionary (2001*), Oxford University Press, UK, 2nd Edition.,*

Throsby, D., 2001. Economics and culture. Cambridge: Cambridge University Press.

Vaccaro, V. & Cohn, D. (2004). The evolution of business models and marketing strategies in the music industry. *International Journal on Media Management,* **6**(1-2), . 46-58.

Venkataraman, S., (1997). The distinctive domain of entrepreneurship research: an editor's perspective. In: *Advances in Entrepreneurship, Firm Emergence and Growth.* Greenwich, CT: JAI Press, pp. 119–138.

Venkataraman, S. & Sarasvathy, S., (2000). Strategy and entrepreneurship: outlines of an untold story. In: M. Hitt, R. Freeman & J. Harrison, eds. *The Handbook of Strategic Management.* Oxford: Blackwell Publishing, pp. 650-658.

Wilson, N. & Stokes, D. (2005). Managing creativity and the challenge for cultural entrepreneurs. *Journal of Small Business and Enterprise Development,* **12**(3), 366-378.

3 The Legal Function: Starting a New Business – Getting the Structure Right

Josephine Bisacre

When we look at business, we generally focus on large global businesses, such as Apple, Shell or Rolls Royce. While there are around 5.2 million businesses in the UK, in fact 99% of them are extremely small (HM Government, 2014). Despite the rate of business failure being high in the early years, overall numbers of businesses are slowly growing. Most new businesses start small, with a view to expansion. This narrows the choice of business medium, as some forms may not suit a particular business at its current stage of development. The focus of this chapter is on the legal structures for doing business. It adopts terminology from the UK's legal system, but similar structures apply in other countries. The objective is to show when a particular legal structure might be appropriate and to highlight key differences between legal structures for enterprises. We also examine the concept of legal personality, which allows a business to be considered as a separate entity from its members, and allows the members of some organizations to have limited liability for business obligations. Most countries have some business forms where the proprietors carry unlimited liability and others where they can avail themselves of limited liability.

Businesses are either *unincorporated* or *incorporated*. This refers to whether or not a business has been formed by an act of law as a body corporate. Examples of incorporated businesses are British Airways plc, incorporated in the UK, and PetroChina Company Limited, incorporated in China. Unincorporated businesses are used by many tradespeople such as plumbers, and also by some professionals such as doctors and solicitors, though both of these groups also often use the incorporated business forms.

In the UK, incorporated businesses have to be registered at Companies House. Its website is https://www.gov.uk/government/organizations/companies-house

> ## Tip
>
> The primary source of most of the law in this chapter is from the UK Acts of Parliament, also called statutes. These are a formal source of law, and are public information that we are all presumed to know. Therefore you do not need to reference them beyond giving their name and year. The main statutes referred to here are:
>
> Partnership Act 1890
>
> Limited Partnerships Act 1907
>
> Limited Liability Partnerships Act 2000
>
> Companies Act 2006
>
> Insolvency Act 1986
>
> You can look them up for free using www.legislation.gov.uk, and there are also subscription databases such as Westlaw. In this chapter there are some references to sections of statutes. Statutes are divided into smaller parts called sections, for example section 1 of the Companies Act 2006.
>
> While devolution of law-making means that parts of the law differ between different parts of the United Kingdom, the statutes discussed in this chapter generally apply to the whole of the UK, with relatively few differences.
>
> Some of the law comes also from cases decided in the courts.

Running your business solo – the sole trader

This is the first of the unincorporated forms of business and the simplest option. There are around 3.3 million sole traders in the UK, or around 62% of all businesses (Federation of Small Businesses, 2014). When deciding to set up as a sole trader, it is important to review one's talents and experience, and do extensive market research. This can be a business form that works well in conjunction with an innovative product, where there is a desire to launch early and at small scale. In the UK there are few formalities, apart from contacting the UK tax authority within 3 months of the start-up date.

Sole traders are not employed, though they often call themselves self-employed. Instead, they are running a business on their own account, and may have employees themselves. However, while they might like to keep their business assets separate from their private assets, in law there is no such separation. This means that should the business fail, personal assets may have to be sold to pay business debts. If all the debts cannot be paid the sole trader may become personally bankrupt and have to sell the family home and other assets.

However this form of business suits many people. Sole traders should obtain insurance against liability to their customers and the public. There is less paperwork involved in being a sole trader than any other legal form: all that is needed is to pay National Insurance contributions, and submit an annual tax return. Any business whose turnover is over a certain limit (£82,000 at the time of writing) needs to register for Value Added Tax (VAT), though businesses may choose to do this even where turnover is below this threshold. The same turnover thresholds and obligation to register for VAT apply to all the business forms discussed in this chapter.

This is a very popular form, particularly when starting a small business. Examples include plumbers and beauticians, as well as accountants and solicitors.

3

Exercise

What are the attractions of operating your business as a sole trader, and what are the potential pitfalls?

Running a business in partnership

For some, the way to succeed is to work with other like-minded people to spark ideas off each other. There are about 460,000 partnerships in the UK, which amounts to around 9% of all businesses (Federation of Small Businesses, 2014).

There are three forms of partnership in the UK: the partnership under the Partnership Act 1890 (PA 1890), the limited partnership under the Limited Partnerships Act 1907 (LPA 1907), and the relatively new limited liability partnership under the Limited Liability Partnerships Act 2000 (LLPA 2000).

■ The partnership

This business form is regulated by the Partnership Act 1890 (PA 1890). The partnership is defined in that statute as "the relation which subsists between two or more persons carrying on business in common with a view of profit." The people who form a partnership must be in 'business' in a general sense, though the term includes professionals. They must aim to make a profit, even if they do not actually make one. There is no upper limit on numbers of partners nowadays. It is not possible to be a 'sole partner'.

This form of partnership is created by contract, and a written agreement is unnecessary, though it would be useful in case of dispute. This agreement is a private one between the partners. Partnership is therefore not one of the business forms where the entity is formed by incorporation. The PA 1890 contains many rules, for example on how partners share profits and losses, which only apply if the partners have not created their own rules. This provides useful flexibility for partnerships.

In Scotland, though not in England, a partnership is a *legal person*. This key concept will be discussed later. A legal person is treated by the law as being separate from the people who make it up, and it can sue them and be sued by them. However, despite the fact that a partnership in Scotland is a legal person, its personality is incomplete. The statute goes on to say that individual partners may face a claim as a result of an action brought against the firm, and if they, or more than one of them, have to pay, they would have a right of relief against the firm and the other partners. Partners in Scotland are *jointly and severally liable* for debts and obligations of the firm that are incurred while they are partners. The same applies where there have been claims against the firm for wrongful acts by the partnership.

Example

A partnership has failed to pay a debt under contract or has committed a *delict* (the term for a civil wrong in Scotland – in England called *tort*) against a third party. For example the firm has done a bad job installing central heating for a customer (breach of contract), or a brick from a roof under repair falls on the head of a passer-by causing injury (delict).

If the partnership is sued, the joint and several liability of the partners works like this:

Step 1: the other party demands payment of the price or damages from the partnership and the partnership fails to pay.

If nothing happens

Step 2: The other party can now demand that **any one or more or all partners** pay what is owed. Those who do pay have a right of relief against the partnership and their fellow partners.

With joint and several liability, the partners are often sued in the same action with the partnership. This potential for facing unlimited personal liability while the partnership is trading can be a problem for partners. Partners must be chosen carefully to ensure they are adequately funded and sufficiently competent.

There are other things to be mindful of in relation to partnership structures. While in many cases partners will agree before they make contracts, in fact all partners have considerable authority to act autonomously as agents for the partnership, even where they have not been authorized. This is *implied authority*. Under the PA 1890, even if they have not been authorized expressly, every partner has the power to do acts "for carrying on in the usual way business of the kind carried on by the firm." This applies unless the other party knows the partner had no authority or does not know or believe the person to be a partner. Because of this, a partner, who might even have been forbidden to do an act, can bind a partnership in a contract that the other partners would not have wished to make. It might be that the firm would have a right of action against that partner for exceeding their authority, but it is probably bound to carry out that contract, like it or not.

3

Two cases illustrate how this works. In *Mercantile Credit Co Ltd v Garrod* (1962), the partners in a garage partnership had an internal agreement that they would not sell cars. One of the partners sold a car to a finance company. The court held that because a third party with no information about the internal agreement would naturally assume that partners in a garage partnership would be able to sell cars, the partnership was held liable to the finance company. By contrast, in the case of *Paterson Brothers v Gladstone* (1891), a partner in a firm of builders was not allowed by the partnership to borrow money for the partnership, but nevertheless borrowed in the firm's name at 40% interest from a money-lender, a debt which was not repaid. The partnership was sued. The court held that the implied authority of a partner did not apply here, as the transaction was so unusual that it should have set alarm-bells ringing for the money-lenders. They should have sought confirmation from the partnership. So, in this case, the money-lenders lost out.

Partners owe each other positive duties of loyalty and good faith, called *fiduciary duties*. Under the statute they must account to their fellow partners for everything that relates to the partnership ; also they must account for any private profit that may come their way through any connection to the partnership; and they have a duty not to compete with the firm.

Setting up in partnership is not difficult: once the partners have made their agreement, the tax authorities must be informed that a partnership has been formed. Annual accounts and tax returns must be prepared for the tax authority. Income tax is payable on each partner's share of the profits. The form of partnership is often used by doctors in general practice in the UK, and also by solicitors, though many are now making use of the limited liability partnership.

Exercise

You are thinking of going into partnership with the two students sitting next to you in class. You all bring different things to the partnership: Student A is wealthier than the others, B has relevant skills and experience but no money, and C has useful business contacts, though he/she is often reckless and unbusinesslike. Discuss with your fellow students what legal problems might arise if the three of you do go into partnership.

■ The limited partnership

This is a variant on the partnership described above. It is regulated by the Limited Partnerships Act 1907 (LPA 1907) and also PA 1890. It has the following characteristics:

☐ It is a legal person in Scotland (though not in England), like a partnership.

☐ Some partners may have limited liability for partnership obligations, provided that at least one partner bears unlimited liability, as in a general partnership.

☐ Limited partners invest in the business, but are barred from taking part in management. If they do take part in management, they become jointly and severally liable like any general partner.

☐ Limited partnerships are formed by agreement, like partnerships, but must be publicly registered at Companies House.

This form of partnership has not proved popular, because businesses generally want all their members to have limited liability if possible. However, it is used for some agricultural tenancies in Scotland and both the Scottish and English variants are used as a vehicle for certain financial products and in tax planning. By March 2014 there were around 27,300 limited partnerships on the register in the UK (Companies House, 2014).

■ Limited liability partnership (LLP)

This is one of the incorporated business forms. The reason that it was created was because the big firms of auditors were facing potentially enormous negligence claims if they missed something when auditing the accounts of large companies. While these claims can be insured against, all insurance has a financial limit. These large accountancy firms were at that time run as partnerships under PA 1890, in which every partner faced unlimited liability. One of the Channel Islands, Jersey, offered a form of limited liability partnership in which every partner could have limited liability, and the big auditing firms, who have a lot of clout, threatened to use the Jersey limited liability partnership. The UK Parliament therefore passed the Limited Liability Partnerships Act 2000 (LLPA 2000).

The LLP is a cross between a partnership and a limited company. Parts of the Companies Act 2006 (CA 2006) and the Insolvency Act 1986 (IA 1986) apply alongside the LLPA 2000. The PA 1890 does not apply.

The following box shows the main characteristics of an LLP and how it differs from a partnership and a company.

LLPs and limited companies

Under the LLPA 2000 the entity is a full legal person throughout the UK and all partners have limited liability.

All partners (called 'members') can take part in management as in a partnership and unlike the limited partnership.

It is formed by incorporation by filing an application to be registered as a LLP at Companies House, and is granted a certificate of incorporation, like a company and unlike a partnership.

It faces similar publicity requirements to a company: it must publish its accounts and make an annual return to Companies House.

Like a company (and unlike a partnership or a sole trader) it can grant a security to a lender for borrowed money in the form of a floating charge, which can be granted over most types of assets. Borrowing may therefore be cheaper than for a partnership.

The LLP must have at least two 'designated members' who are its managers.

Like a partnership, the LLP is available where two or more persons carry on lawful business together with a view to profit, but it is mainly used by professionals, such as accountants and solicitors.

LLPs are taxed similarly to partnerships, in that members normally pay income tax.

Some provisions of company law apply, such as those on fraudulent trading and wrongful trading, which are discussed later.

At the end of June 2015, there were around fifty-six thousand LLPs on the register in the UK (Companies House, 2015).

This relatively new business form has been widely adopted by accountants and solicitors throughout the UK. For example, the UK member firms of Price Waterhouse Coopers (PWC), (one of the 'big four' global accountancy firms), use this business form.

Finally, all three forms of partnership may be used to carry out joint ventures. These are agreements between businesses to pool resources to do something together, at home or abroad. Some countries only permit foreign investors to operate in their countries along with a domestic partner, through joint ventures, to ensure that domestic businesses benefit and are not harmed by foreign competition.

Key concept: Limited liability

Limited liability refers to the liability of *participants in the business*, rather than the business itself. If a business has legal personality, it is liable for its own obligations to the full extent of its assets. Partners in an LLP or members of a limited liability company are liable to the extent of their agreed contribution, but no further. Those who made their financial contribution in full when they joined the business cannot be forced to contribute more. Those who have not yet paid their whole contribution remain liable for the balance. The reason why limited liability is attractive to those involved in business is that from the outset they know exactly what they stand to lose if the business becomes insolvent.

For example, if I agree to buy 100 shares in a company, costing £1 each, I as a member (shareholder) have met my liability to the company in full once I have paid £100 to that company.

■ **Remember:** it is not the *business* that has limited liability, but the *members*.

Using the corporate form to run a business: What is a company?

Some people go straight to the company form when they set up a business, while others go through a stage of first being a sole trader or partnership. The main attraction of the corporate form is the availability of limited liability for the members.

Unlike partnerships which are formed by agreement, companies, like LLPs, are formed by the legal process of *incorporation*, which is done by filing incorporation papers at Companies House. All companies, like LLPs, are legal persons, and they acquire this status when they receive their certificate of incorporation.

NB: The main statute that regulates companies in the UK is the **Companies Act 2006** (CA 2006).

Unlike partnerships, companies have *members* and *directors* who are not necessarily the same. The directors are in charge of strategic management and monitoring how the company operates. A member of a company does not have an automatic right to take part in management, unlike a partner in a general partnership. If the company issues shares, these members are called shareholders.

Unlike sole traders and partners in all forms of partnership who pay income tax, companies pay corporation tax on their profits.

Every company belongs in two categories: it is either (1) *unlimited* or *limited* and also either (2) *public or private.*

■ Unlimited companies

In an unlimited company, every member agrees to be liable to an unlimited extent for the company's debts if it should fail. Unlike a partnership under the PA 1890, this liability does not kick in while the company is still trading. Since most people prefer to use the limited company, the unlimited company is little used, and there were only 5,084 of them on the register as at March 2014 (Companies House, 2014).

3

Unlimited companies have one special feature: because all the members carry unlimited liability, unlimited companies are exempted from the requirement to publish their accounts. This might be attractive to a business that values keeping its affairs secret from its rivals, provided that risks of liability and business failure can be tempered by a good regime of risk management and by insurance.

Current examples of unlimited companies in the UK are C. Hoare & Co, a private bank, and Credit Suisse International, the UK arm of Credit Suisse.

■ Limited companies

There are two forms of limited company: *companies limited by shares* or *limited by guarantee.* In a *company limited by shares*, the members are called shareholders'. These members contract to buy shares at an agreed price. Their names are entered in the register of members and they become the legal owners of the shares, which they can sell if they want. This is a very popular business form: at January 2015, there were over 3 million such companies on the register in the UK, of which 1.5 million were actively trading, representing 29% of all businesses (HM Government, 2014).

In a *company limited by guarantee*, the members agree that should the company go into insolvent liquidation they would pay a sum of money, which is usually fairly nominal, for example £100 each. The company limited by guarantee is a useful form for non-trading organizations. It is used by some professional bodies, charities such as Cancer Research UK and sports and other clubs, which want limited liability for their office-bearers and members. As of March 2014 there were just under 100,000 companies limited by guarantee on the register in the UK (Companies House, 2014).

Every company is also either *private* or *public.*

■ Private companies

The vast majority of companies are private companies – around 99%. They range in size from one-person companies with no employees to very large and important companies employing thousands such as Dyson Limited, famous for manufacture of bagless vacuum cleaners, with around 3,000 employees world-wide.

The main characteristics of private companies are:

☐ They can be run as unlimited companies, companies limited by shares and companies limited by guarantee, though most opt for the company limited by shares.

☐ A private limited company has the word 'limited' or 'Ltd' after its name.

☐ People who choose this business form need to remember is that under CA 2006 it is not possible to offer shares in a private company limited by shares by advertising them to the public - only a public company can use the Stock Exchange or other public markets to raise money by issuing shares. A private company would have to contact prospective purchasers directly.

☐ No minimum issued share capital is needed, provided they issue at least one share at, usually, £1. In some other European Union member states there is a sizeable minimum issued share capital requirement.

☐ There is a less demanding regime than for public companies. Small private companies normally do not have to have their accounts audited. Small and medium-sized enterprises (SMEs) are allowed to file simplified accounts at Companies House and from 2013 the smallest companies (micro-entities) can file even simpler accounts. Full accounts still need to be filed with the tax authority, however. An annual return also has to be filed at Companies House by all companies.

☐ While the members of public companies must transact their business at meetings (though audio and videoconferencing are permitted), the members of private companies can dispense with meetings and use written resolutions. A private company might choose to hold an annual general meeting, but this is optional.

☐ While both public and private companies can be formed with just one member, a private company can be formed with just one director (manager) whereas a public company needs at least two. There is no need for a company secretary, unlike a public company.

■ Public companies

Whereas there are over three million private companies in the UK, there are only around 6,500 public companies (Companies House, 2015). These include most of the famous names in UK corporate life such as the armaments company BAE Systems plc, the clothing and food retailer Marks & Spencer plc, the oil company BP plc, the pharmaceutical company GlaxoSmithKline plc and the Scottish oil engineering company the Wood Group plc. Often a company will start out as private and once it has grown and acquired a good trading record, it may re-register as a public company.

The main characteristics of public companies

They can only be formed as **companies limited by shares** and not as either of the other forms discussed for private companies.

The name states the business form: it ends in 'public limited company' or 'plc'.

There are capital restrictions: before the public company can trade or borrow money, it must issue a minimum amount of share capital, which is £50,000 ('authorized minimum'). It must receive one quarter of this sum (£12,500) from its members, and, if the shares are sold for more than their par value, (e.g. £1.50 if the shares are one pound shares, where there is a 50p premium per share), the whole of that premium.

Example: ABC plc has just been formed as a public company and issues 50,000 one pound shares, which are to be sold for £1.50 each. This means that before ABC plc can trade or borrow, it must receive £12,500 (one quarter of the nominal value) from its members plus £25,000 in premiums. Those premiums are paid into a separate share premium account.

One very important reason for choosing a public company is to raise money by issuing shares to the public – a private company cannot do this. There are various public markets in the UK, most notably the London Stock Exchange. When a company seeks a listing for new shares, it issues a prospectus to the public, to inform investors about the company and about the investment, and how it will be used. If a public company has its shares listed, the shareholders can easily resell them, which is not always easy in unlisted companies. However, a listing is expensive for the company, and it has to make much more disclosure about its affairs than non-listed companies, to provide investors with the information they need. There are no accounting privileges for public companies: they must file a full set of audited accounts at Companies House as well as annual returns.

Unlike private companies, public companies must hold annual general meetings (AGMs). This is a chance for the shareholders to hear how the year has gone and about the directors' plans for the future. Shareholders also have a chance to ask questions and, may put items on the agenda for discussion and vote. At the AGM, there is some business which

3

regularly appears on the agenda: consideration and approval by the shareholders of the annual accounts, the declaration of a dividend on the shares by the shareholders, (if a dividend is to be paid), appointment of the auditor, and appointment of directors.

A public company is not allowed to use written resolutions, which means that if there is business for shareholders to transact, extraordinary general meetings (EGMs) must be convened.

A public limited company is allowed to have a single member, (however unlikely that is in reality) but unlike a private company, it must have two or more directors, and a company secretary. The secretary's job is to organise general meetings and board meetings, and to advise the board of directors on the law and practice of meetings. The secretary may also act as share registrar.

- **Remember**: a public company may, **but does not have to** have its shares listed on the Stock Exchange.

Exercise

Consider why it might be considered more attractive to use the corporate form to run your business than to run it as a partnership under PA 1890.

Key concept: Legal personality

We have already looked at various business forms that have legal personality. We now need to focus on this concept a bit more. Legal personality is really a fiction by which businesses may be granted many of the attributes of natural persons (human beings). They are regarded as being legally separate from their members. Here are some attributes of the legal personality of a registered company:

- It is liable for its own obligations (contracts and delicts).

- It owns its own property.

- It can commit some (though not all) crimes.

- Courts have recognised that a legal person can have some (but not all) human rights contained in the European Convention on Human Rights and Fundamental Freedoms, e.g. freedom of expression, right to a fair trial and the right to peaceful enjoyment of one's possessions (Council of Europe, 1950) .

- It can contract with other parties including its own members.

- It has a quality called *perpetual succession, which* means that its legal personality survives the death of a member or the departure of a member from the corporate body – this is important as in listed public companies the membership is changing constantly. Note that a partnership under the PA 1890 does not have this quality.

The company as a legal person

Legal personality makes it easier for business people to keep their personal and business assets separate (Davies, 2010), which is a problem for the sole trader described earlier. The leading case on legal personality is *Salomon v Salomon & Co Ltd* (1897). The facts were that Salomon had run a boot-making business as a sole trader, before incorporating his business as a company, in which he, his wife and sons all held shares. All went well until there was a downturn in the market for boots and the company went into insolvent liquidation. Salomon had acquired a secured loan, which made him the first-ranking creditor. Salomon contended that as the first-ranking creditor, he should be paid first, which meant that other creditors would get nothing. The liquidator and the other creditors did not agree and the lower courts held that incorporation was not meant to be used for family companies, that what Salomon did was fraudulent, and therefore he should pay the company rather than it paying him. However, the House of Lords (at that time the final court of civil appeal in the UK) took the opposite view: the legislation did not prevent Salomon using the corporate form for a family business, and what he did was not fraud. Therefore the court held that the company was a separate legal person from Salomon: Salomon could be the first-ranking creditor of the company, with the effect that other creditors got nothing. Lord Halsbury stated:

> ...it seems to be impossible to dispute that once the company is legally incorporated it must be treated like any other independent person with its rights and liabilities appropriate to itself, and that the motives of those who took part in the promotion of the company are absolutely irrelevant in discussing what those rights and liabilities are.

Legal personality is a very important concept, as the legal separation between the members and the organization makes limited liability possible. It also allows businesses to separate their activities, for example by forming subsidiary companies which might each be responsible for an aspect of the business, or might be used by a multinational company to operate globally through local subsidiaries in each country. It is a useful concept in tax planning.

When people elect to run their businesses through a company, they sometimes forget a crucial point: if they were originally sole traders and owned assets, at that time they owned those assets personally. If the business is now run as a company, the company now owns those assets, not them. This important message was ignored by Macaura in the case of *Macaura v Northern Assurance Co Ltd* (1925). Macaura had owned a timber estate, but later the business was incorporated. However, the insurance of the timber was left in the Macaura's name. Fire destroyed the timber and an insurance claim was made. However, the insurance company refused to pay out, contending that Macaura had no insurable interest directly in the property, which was owned by the company: the court agreed.

In a very small company, there is often one member who is also the sole director, and who carries out multiple roles, with no other employees. That person may have no formal contract of employment. Nevertheless, if the evidence is there, that sole member/director may be considered to be an employee, even though he may never have considered himself employed. That was what happened in *Lee v Lee's Air Farming Ltd* (1961). The business of this company was aerial crop-spraying. It was a one-person company in which Lee owned nearly all the shares, and also did the spraying. Lee was killed while working. His widow claimed compensation, and the issue turned on whether Lee was an employee. The court held that he could be an employee, as a person could act in more than one capacity (as director and as employee) with the result that the company could have contracted through the agency of Lee as director for Lee to be an employee of the company, and Mrs Lee could therefore claim compensation. Chapter 4 of this book looks at the issue of the contract of employment in more detail.

Problems with legal personality – and solutions

While legal personality has undoubtedly been a great asset to business, it has its dark side too. The concept has the potential to be used as a way of escaping liability for one's contractual obligations, to carry out tax evasion, to hide money and property during a divorce, and for money-laundering and fraud. The law therefore has to step in and set some limits to what is allowable. Both Parliament and the courts have done this. This is done very sparingly, to keep the concept itself intact, as business hates uncertainty.

What follows are a few examples of the exceptions recognised by Parliament and the courts:

■ Statutory liability – fraudulent trading and wrongful trading

If a company suffers financial difficulties and cannot pay its bills, it might be tempting for the directors to carry on business as usual in the hope that trade will pick up. This is very dangerous. If they continue to accept advance payments for goods and services when the company is insolvent, and the company goes into insolvent liquidation, the customers will not get their goods or services and will probably not recover their deposits. This is fraud if done intentionally. Under **section 213 of the Insolvency Act 1986**, any person (not only the directors) who allows a company to trade with intent to defraud creditors may be taken to court by the liquidator if the company fails, seeking a contribution towards paying the creditors (fraudulent trading). Section 214, which prohibits wrongful trading, is similar, though it does not need proof of fraud, so is easier to prove. Under section 214, directors may be taken to court by a liquidator in an insolvent liquidation, on the grounds that they continued to trade after they knew or ought to have concluded that the company had no reasonable prospect of avoiding going into insolvent liquidation. Again, the liquidator would be seeking a contribution from the directors to help to pay the creditors. There is a statutory defence to liability under this section, and this section only affects directors. The two provisions apply to LLPs as well.

■ Evasion of contractual obligations – the courts

The courts have intervened on rare occasions as well. The leading case at common law is *Gilford Motor Co Ltd v Horne* (1933). Horne was an employee of the Gilford Motor Co Ltd and had access to confidential customer lists. His contract of employment prohibited him from using those customer lists if he left his job. Horne left his employment and in order to get round the prohibition, he got his wife to set up a company in which he took care not to be a member or a director. The company then made use of the customer lists of the Gilford Motor Co Ltd, on the basis that the new company was a different legal person from Horne as an individual, and not subject to the prohibition. The court was unimpressed and took the view that Horne was seeking to evade his contractual obligations, and that the company was a sham: both Horne and the company were held to be subject to the prohibition. This decision puts a stop to what would be a popular way to avoid liability for contractual obligations.

■ Cheating a spouse out of their share of assets on divorce – common law

In recent years the UK Supreme Court has made clear that the veil of incorporation must only be pierced as a last resort, and other legal solutions should be preferred if available. One recent leading matrimonial case is *Prest v Petrodel Resources Ltd* (2013). According to Cheng-Han (2015), in this judgment the Supreme Court made a welcome effort to take a principled approach to veil-piercing. Mrs Prest, the wife of a wealthy oil trader, had been awarded her divorce settlement, but she was having trouble getting her husband to pay it. In the end she went to court to argue that she should be paid out of the proceeds of residential properties owned by companies in which Mr Prest held shares. Note that Mr Prest was not the owner of the properties: the companies owned them. The Supreme Court took a restrictive line: courts should find other ways of dealing with such problems rather than piercing the veil of incorporation if possible. Only cases similar to the *Gilford Motor Co Ltd v Horne,* where sham companies are used to get out of one's obligations or where a company was being used to frustrate the operation of law or do something illegal, would be recognised. In the *Prest* case, the Supreme Court found words in the relevant matrimonial statute that would allow it to say that as Mr Prest was the shareholder of the companies, he was 'entitled' to them, on the basis that the companies held the properties for Mr Prest's benefit. Mrs Prest therefore had a right to have her divorce settlement satisfied out of their assets.

Conclusion

When starting up in business, the choice of business medium is one of the important decisions to be made. The level of risk and how it can be managed needs to be considered carefully in making this choice. This may dictate that limited liability is needed. However, limited liability brings with it much more accountability and paperwork. How profits will be taxed may be a deciding factor as to whether or not the sole trader or one of the partnership formats would be preferred to forming a company. It is important to remember that very often a business may pass through various phases of development, and the legal structure may need to change over time as the business grows. While legal personality and limited liability are undoubtedly important to business, in allowing for a higher level of risk-taking, the chapter ends by looking at some of the legal limits which aim to prevent the concept being unduly exploited.

Further reading

Bisacre, J., and McFadzean, C., (2011) *Company Law*. Dundee: Dundee University Press, pp. 17-40 and 45-48.

Black, G. (2015) *Business Law in Scotland*. 3rd edition Edinburgh: W Green, pp. 72-113, 519-547, 548-641 and 638-663.

Companies House, Home page, https://www.gov.uk/government/organizations/companies-house [Accessed 5 October 2015]

Davidson, F. and Macgregor, L. (2014) *Commercial Law in Scotland*. 3rd edition, Edinburgh: W Green, pp. 339-365.

Davies, P. (2010) *Introduction to Company Law*. 2nd edition, Oxford: Oxford University Press, pp. 1-30 and 31-52.

Department of Business Innovation and Skills. A Guide to Legal Forms for Business https://www.gov.uk/government/uploads/system/uploads/attachment_data/file/31676/11-1399-guide-legal-forms-for-business.pdf [Accessed 4 August 2015].

Grier, N. *Company Law* 4th edition, Edinburgh: W Green, 2014.

Grier, N. (2014) Case Comment, Piercing the corporate veil: Prest v Petrodel Resources Ltd *Edinburgh Law Review*, **18**(2), pp. 275-279.

HM Government (2015). Choose a Legal Structure for your Business https://www.gov.uk/business-legal-structures/overview [Accessed 4 August 2015].

London Stock Exchange. www.londonstockexchange.com/home/homepage.htm [accessed 4 August 2015]

National Archives (2015) UK Legislation http://www.legislation.gov.uk [Accessed 4 August 2015]

Nyombi, C. (2014) Lifting the veil of incorporation under common law and statute *International Journal of Law & Management*, **56**(1), pp. 66-81.

Table of cases

Gilford Motor Co Ltd v Horne [1933] Ch. 935

Lee v Lee's Air Farming Ltd [1961] A.C.12

Macaura v Northern Assurance Co Ltd [1925] A.C. 619, HL

Mercantile Credit Co Ltd v Garrod [1962] 3 All E.R.1103

Paterson Brothers v Gladstone (1891) 18 R. 403

Prest v Petrodel Resources Ltd [2013] UKSC 34

Salomon v Salomon & Co Ltd [1897] A.C. 22, HL

References

Cheng-Han, T. (2015). Veil-piercing: a fresh start. *Journal of Business Law* **1**, 20-36.

Companies House (2015) Statistical Release: Incorporated Companies in the United Kingdom - June 2015, https://www.gov.uk/government/statistics/incorporated-companies-in-the-united-kingdom-june-2015 [Accessed 4 August 2015]

Companies House (2014) Statistical release: Companies Register Activities 2013-2014 https://www.gov.uk/government/uploads/system/uploads/attachment_data/file/380779/CompaniesRegisterActivities2013-2014.pdf [Accessed 4 August 2015]

Council of Europe (1950) Convention for the Protection of Human Rights and Fundamental Freedoms http://www.echr.coe.int/Documents/Convention_ENG.pdf [Accessed 4 August 2015]

Davies, P., (2010) *Introduction to Company Law.* 2nd edition. Oxford: Oxford University Press.

Federation of Small Businesses (2014) Small Business Statistics http://www.fsb.org.uk/stats [Accessed 4 August 2015]

HM Government (2014). Business Population Estimates for the UK and the Regions. https://www.gov.uk/government/uploads/system/uploads/attachment_data/file/377934/bpe_2014_statistical_release.pdf [Accessed 4 August 2015].

4 Employment Law

Josh McLeod and Yvonne McLaren

Employment laws are put in place to protect employees from any mistreatment from their employers, and are a vital part of a country's efforts to protect its citizens. Some countries are regarded as having very restrictive employment laws whilst others are regarded as more relaxed. According to the Organization for Economic Co-operation and Development (OECD), who analyse and compare employment protections in various countries, the UK, Canada and the USA have the most lenient laws whereas France, Spain and Turkey have the strictest. This chapter will focus on UK employment law, where workers' rights can be traced back to the 1300s and significant changes are still occurring today. By examining the UK's history of employment law, the contract of employment, corresponding rights and duties of both the employer and employee and the circumstances in which the contract of employment might come to an end, students will gain a valuable insight into a unique area of UK business law.

The history of employment law

Until the 1950s, the relationship between employer and employee involved little regulation from UK government. This meant that the terms of any employment contracts were either determined by the customs and practices of the particular trade in which the employee engaged, or by the employer. Employers have historically enjoyed a stronger bargaining position than the employee, with the relationship often characterized as 'master and servant'.

The 1970s to 1990s saw increased legislative interventions by UK government which moved further towards a system of employment protections emanating from a desire to afford the employee a better bargaining position within organizations. Examples of this increased protection include the **Equal Pay Act 1970**; the **Health and Safety at Work Act 1974**; the **Sex Discrimination Act 1975**; the **Race Relations Act 1976**; the **Employment Protection (Consolidation) Act 1978** (now contained in the **Employment Rights Act 1996**).

The Employment Rights Act 1996

This is a statutory law. A statutory law is a written law, where right and wrong is expressly stated. The ERA 1996 is one of the most pertinent statutes underpinning employment law. You can access all of the statutes for this Act at: www.legislation.gov.uk

---

In thinking about employment law it is helpful to have a basic understanding of the legal principles of **contract law.** Here, we will review the **Scots law of delict** (in England this is known as **tort law**) and of course, other countries will have their own equivalents.

Contract law

Contracts are agreements voluntarily entered into by two or more parties, each of whom intend to create a legal obligation between them. Contract law refers to the body of law that governs these agreements and is concerned with aspects such as the nature of contracts, contractual obligations and termination.

Delict

A delict is a legal wrong. Where a person has suffered wrongful loss at the hands of another, they are entitled to reparation for this loss.

It is important to note that reference to these areas of law is reflected in **Common Law** decisions and principles (case law). However, more recent developments will have significant reference to statutory law such as the ERA 1996.

The Common Law

The part of the law that is derived from judicial precedent rather that statute. This means that instead of having the law set out in writing like the ERA 1996, decisions are made in consideration of similar cases that have happened in the past.

The institutions involved in employment law

Various institutions of employment law exist that seek to resolve employment disputes before they take escalate. In the UK these include the Advisory Conciliation and Arbitration Service (ACAS), the Central Arbitration Committee (CAC), and the Equality and Human Rights Commission. After a dispute takes place, it must be resolved via the domestic courts. In Scotland this includes the Sheriff Court and the Court of Session. In England, the County Court and the High Court will perform a similar function. Most disputes, however, will begin their journey via the employment tribunal with appeals then being referred to the Employment Appeal Tribunal where appropriate. These tribunals were created specifically to enforce employment rights which have been created via statute.

■ Employment tribunals

These independent judicial bodies were established via the **Industrial Training Act 1964**. The modern day employment tribunals started their lifespan as industrial tribunals with a name change from the 1ˢᵗ August 1998 via the **Employment Rights (Dispute Resolution) Act 1998**.

Employment tribunals are specialist tribunals generally comprised of one legally qualified chairperson (the employment judge), an individual nominated by an employer association and another person appointed by the Trades-Union Congress (TUC). The tribunals are constituted under the **Employment Tribunals (Constitution and Rules of Procedure) (Scotland) Regulations 2013**, while the jurisdictions and powers of employment tribunals are set out in the **Employment Tribunals Act 1996**.

A significant advantage of these specialist tribunals relates to the relative speed and informality of the process; there are no complicated procedural rules and an unrepresented party may be given assistance from the employment judge or lay members where matters are complicated. Further advantages might reflect the physical environment which will be less formal than a court. For example, no-one is likely to wear a wig or gown. This certainly supports the modern day alternative dispute resolution techniques which consider time, cost and control essential for parties in any dispute.

Within the Employment Tribunals, almost all hearings are open to the public, and evidence will be given under oath or affirmation. Decisions are based on the majority and a claim must generally be brought within three months of the effective date of termination of the contract of employment. Note that a person must have been employed for a minimum of two years in order to pursue a case via the Employment Tribunals.

■ The Employment Appeals Tribunal (EAT)

The EAT is a wholly appellate tribunal, which means that no cases will begin their journey here. Primarily, its role was established to hear appeals from employment tribunals on questions of law only. Appeals on questions of fact are only allowed in exceptional circumstances, on the grounds that a tribunal decision was so substantially defective that no reasonable tribunal could have arrived at that decision in ordinary circumstances. It may also hear appeals from decisions of the Certification Officer and The Central Arbitration Committee.

An individual may represent themselves at an EAT hearing or may be represented by any other person of their choosing (who may or may not be a lawyer). The main hearing of an appeal is held in public before the judge, who sits alone, unless the judge has directed that the appeal will also be heard by lay members. The hearing itself usually consists of legal arguments from each side, with the appellant making submissions first. Judgment may be given orally at the end of the hearing or may be reserved to be handed down at a later date. The Court of Session will hear appeals from the EAT, but permission must be given by the EAT.

The employment contract

Only individuals employed under a 'contract of employment', otherwise known as a 'contract *of* service', have the legal status of being an employee.

Other workers who are employed to provide services for an employer, but do not have a contract of employment, are defined as independent contractors. This is known as a 'contract *for* services'. It is not uncommon for companies to have a mixture of employees and independent contractors working within their organization. However, there a number of implications for workers who do not work under a contract of employment. Perhaps the most significant distinction is that statutes, such as the ERA 1996, confer employment protection rights only upon employees, which includes protection against unfair dismissal, entitlement to compensation in case of redundancy and a right to a minimum notice period of termination. In addition, employers may be liable for delicts committed by employees during the course of employment, but this is not the case for independent contractors. There are also a variety of terms that are implied into a contract of employment such as the duty of faithful and loyal service. In some instances, this duty means that an employee cannot carry out the same work for an employer's competitor. An independent contractor, however, has no duty of faithful and loyal service.

Contract of employment

A contract of employment is an agreement between employer and employee that acts as the basis for the employment relationship. It will set out the employment rights, responsibilities and duties. Although most employment contracts do not need to be in writing to be legally valid, this is desirable in case of a dispute.

■ Classifying employees and workers

☐ **Employee** – A person is generally considered an 'employee' if: they have an employment contract to do work or services; their reward for work is financial, and there is a promise of future work. Employment duties must be personally carried out by the employee; they do not have a right to send someone else to perform the work for them.

If an individual is classified as an employee then they may be entitled to employment rights including: the national minimum-wage, protection against unlawful deductions from wages, the statutory minimum level of paid holiday leave, the statutory minimum length of rest breaks, the right not to have to work more than 48 hours per working week and protection against unlawful discrimination. Employees may also be entitled to statutory maternity/paternity pay, maternity/paternity leave, redundancy pay and the right to request flexible working hours. Some of these rights require a minimum length of continuous employment before an employee qualifies for them. The employment contract may state how long this qualification period is.

☐ **Agency worker** – this category of worker will have specific rights from the first day at work including minimum wage, holiday pay and details of job vacancies with the hirer. However, they are not usually entitled to minimum notice periods if their employment is being terminated, the right to request flexible working, time off for emergencies and statutory redundancy pay. Importantly for agency workers, if they are employed continuously for 12 weeks in the same organization, they will be entitled to the same terms and conditions are a regular employee under a contract of service.

☐ **Workers (independent contractors)** – a person is likely to be a worker if they only occasionally do work for a specific business, the business is not obligated to offer them future work and they do not have to accept the work. This kind of worker, who is an independent contractor, may have a contract that includes terms such as 'casual', 'freelance', 'zero hours', 'as required' or similar. Workers will be required to agree to such terms and conditions to get the work – either verbally or in writing. They are still under the supervision of the company's management, but they may have to provide their own materials, tools and equipment to carry out the work.

4

Worker or employee?

The case of **Torith Ltd v Flynn (EAT 0017/02)** effectively illustrates the circumstances in which an individual may be classed as a worker. The case, which was heard by the EAT, involved a self-employed joiner who worked exclusively for a firm of building contractors. Despite working exclusively for the company, the joiner was still considered to be a worker because he paid his own taxes and supplied his own tools. Therefore, statutory employment protection was not available.

Exercise

Consider the differences in rights that employees and casual workers possess. Do you think it is fair that the employee has stronger protections?

The employment tests

As you have learned, a significant issue in the area of employment law relates to whether an individual is in a position of 'employment', or merely providing a 'service'. As discussed in the previous section, there are a number of implications for individuals who are not considered employees. Because workers are not afforded the same employment protections, employers may attempt to avoid giving workers a contract of employment in order to maintain a flexible position where they do not have to give redundancy payments or notices of termination. For this reason, various tests have been constructed by the courts to determine whether an individual should be considered an employee. These are now discussed in turn.

■ Control test

The control test has been applied in some form or another since the 19th century, and still retains a certain force today. The test involves examining whether the employer controlled, or had the right to control, not only what the worker did, but also the manner in which he did it (*Yewens v Noakes*, 1880). However, as the pace of technological change increased, the control test was criticised for its rigidity. It became obviously unrealistic to conceive that employers have the knowledge to control high skilled workers such as surgeons, airline pilots and research chemists.

■ Integration test

An alternative to the control test was formulated in *Stevenson, Jordan and Harrison Ltd v Macdonald and Evans* (1952) by Lord Denning, who viewed the decisive question as whether the person under consideration was *fully integrated* into the employer's organization. Thus, under a contract for services, an individual's work is only an accessory of the organization, whereas, a contract of employment requires full integration of an individual into the workplace.

■ Economic reality test

The economic reality test essentially asks whether the worker is in business on his or her own account, as an entrepreneur, or working for someone else who ultimately takes the risk of profit or loss. Casual or irregular workers and others who may have a high degree of autonomy in their working arrangements may still be employees under this test providing that they are economically dependent on one principal employer (*Market Investigations Ltd v Minister of Social Security*, 1969).

■ Mutuality of obligation test

The mutuality of obligation test refers to the obligation of an employer to provide work and remunerate for it, together with the obligation of the employee to personally do the work. If such obligations are implied in the employment contract, then employment status will be established. In the leading case of *Kelly v Trusthouse Forte plc* (1983), the applicants, who were wine waiters, were employed by a hotel chain as so-called 'regular casuals'. This meant that they were employed periodically to work on a particular catering job. The EAT decided that there was no contract of employment, and that the applicants had entered into a relationship with the company with the expectation that they would be provided with casual work whenever it was available. Thus, there was no obligation for the company to provide work and no obligation on the workers to carry out work, which made them independent contractors. Generally, when the courts are establishing whether an individual has the status of employee, the mutuality of obligation test will be the foundation of the decision. However, consideration may also be given to more than one test in the same case.

Exercise

Imagine you are a judge that must decide a case that has been brought to an employment tribunal. What do you think is the fairest test for establishing whether an individual is an employee?

Contracts

Within any contractual agreement, all parties have corresponding rights and obligations. Contracts within Scots law are administered by two sources: statutory law and the common law. In terms of hierarchy, statute law is the first port-of-call, since it will often provide express intentions and conditions that the employment contract will be required to include. Any right that is not expressly given may have to be determined via common law sources and we can thereafter determine that such terms may be implied into the contract between employer and employee.

■ Express terms

Section 230(2) of the ERA restates the common law position that a contract of employment may be made expressly or implied. In Scotland, employment contracts do not have to be in written form or witnessed by a third party, and therefore, it is completely legitimate to have a contract which is verbal in nature.

Section 1 of the ERA 1996 determines that employees must be issued with a written statement which will contain the terms and particulars of their contract of employment. This statement must be issued within two months of the start of their employment contract and if one is not provided the employee may take the employer to the Employment Tribunal, as part of an unfair dismissal claim for failure to issue such a statement.

Some of the main terms and conditions of employment within the written statement should contain the following: the employer's and employee's names; the date of commencement of employment; wages/salary details; location and working hour details; (or information about overseas conditions); holiday entitlement; sick pay entitlement and pensionable service requirements; notice requirements; job title and brief description of the job. As far as possible, the document should include as much relevant information as possible, although today with the reliance on technology it may well be appropriate to refer to relevant employer websites wherein a complete schedule of information may be accessed.

Section 38 of the **Employment Act 2002** provides that failure to issue the written statement of particulars may result in an employee being able to claim up to 4 weeks' wages as damages.

■ Implied terms

At common law, there may be several terms that are implied into a contract of employment, and these may be applicable to both the employee and the employer. Implied terms are, effectively, obligations on both the parties to refrain from acting in a way which might destroy or seriously damage the trust and confidence on which the employment relationship is ultimately based.

For the **employee** some of the implied duties may include the following:

☐ *The duty to provide personal service* – The main aspect of this duty is that the employer expects the employee to carry out performance of the task personally with no substitution, unless permitted. This has been validated via the Court of Appeal in *Ready Mixed Concrete (South East) Ltd v Minister of Pensions* (1968) where it was held that the contract could be defined as one **for** services due to the driver being unable to appoint a substitute.

☐ *The duty of faithful and loyal service* – This duty prohibits the employee from doing anything that would harm the employer's business, such as carrying out work for the employer's competitor. In *Forster & Sons Ltd v Suggett* (1918) the court held that the pursuers were entitled to enforce the contractual restraint in order to protect business secrets, where an employee had learned confidential production methods during the course of his or her service.

☐ *The duty to obey lawful and reasonable orders* – In *Ottoman Bank v Chakarian* (1930) the Privy Council held that the bank's order to Chakarian was unreasonable, after they had ordered the plaintiff to relocate to Turkey. Chakarian was Armenian and had already been sentenced to death by the Turkish authorities. Clearly, this order did not constitute as a 'reasonable' order.

☐ *The duty to use reasonable care and skill in the discharge of their duties* – An employee must attempt to perform his or her contract with reasonable care in all circumstances. This principle may be seen in the case of *Lister v Romford Ice and Cold Storage Ltd* (1957), where the House of Lords re-affirmed the principle that an employee who breaches his or her contract by performing their obligations without reasonable care is required to indemnify the employer for any loss which follows. Mr Lister and his son drove a lorry for Romford. When Lister was injured as a result of his son's careless driving, he initiated a claim from his employers in terms of the principle of vicarious liability. Romford then invoked a subrogation clause within the contract, which utilized Romford's right to require Lister's son to perform his contract with reasonable care.

4

For the **employer** some of the implied duties may include the following:

☐ *The duty of mutual respect* – If the employee feels that he or she is not being treated with respect it may lead to a breakdown in the relationship as seen in *TSB Bank plc v Harris* (2000). The facts of the case involved Harris, an employee of the bank who, when applying for another position, cited the bank as a reference. Unbeknown to Harris, the bank indicated that a number of customers had made complaints about her conduct such that the prospective employers refused to process her application further. Harris resigned and brought a claim of constructive dismissal against the bank. The employment tribunal and the Employment Appeal Tribunal held that the employer had failed in its duty to demonstrate trust and confidence towards Harris as an employee.

☐ *The duty to provide work* – This duty is best illustrated in the famous quote set out in *Collier v Sunday Referee Publishing Ltd* (1940), "provided I pay my cook her wages regularly, she cannot complain if I take any or all of my meals out". The point held that the employee should be in no position to complain in situations where wages are paid but no work is provided.

☐ *The duty to pay wages* – In Turner v Sawdon & Co (1901) it was stated that an employer is under a duty to pay wages in return for the employee's service. Generally, the expectation is that a day's work should equate with an equal day's pay. For the most part the rate of pay and the regularity of payment will be included as an express term either within the contract or as provided for via section 1 of the ERA 1996 within the written statement.

☐ *The duty to provide references* – Generally, we can say that the employer owes a duty of care not to damage the employee's future career prospects. In *Spring v Guardian Royal Assurance PLC* (1994) the House of Lords held that Guardian Royal owed the purser a duty of care when they had provided a reference that claimed that the ex-employee had been in the habit of behaving fraudulently during the course of his employment. It was held a foreseeable consequence that he would suffer harm as a result of the negligent reference.

☐ *The duty to provide safe working systems and place of work* – This principle was established in *Wilsons and Clyde Coal Ltd v English* (1938), where the House of Lords held that an employer owed an employee a personal duty of care where the pursuer, a miner, had been injured as a result of an accident at work. Note that this duty extends to issues including the appointment of competent fellow employees and the provision of adequate equipment and materials. Modern day scenarios also reflect the duty to take care of an employee's emotional state as seen in the decision of *Walker v Northumberland County Council* (1995), where it was held that the council knew that the pursuer was vulnerable and were therefore responsible for failing to provide support where psychiatric injury was reasonably foreseeable.

Exercise

The law says that an employer must not damage the future prospects of an employee by providing a negative reference. Do you think this is fair, or should employers be allowed to be as brutally honest as they like?

4

Unfair dismissal

Section 94(1) of the ERA 1996 gives the statutory right to an employee not to be unfairly dismissed. If an employee is eligible to make a claim for unfair dismissal, and there has been a dismissal, the onus is on the employer to prove that the principle reason for dismissal was not unfair. An employee will be eligible for an unfair dismissal claim if they have been continuously employed for at least two years.

If an employee lodges a claim for unfair dismissal, an employment tribunal will be tasked with making the decision of whether it was fair or unfair. The ERA 1996 sorts dismissals into two categories: automatically unfair and potentially fair reasons. If a dismissal case is deemed automatically unfair, no further questions as to whether or not it was reasonable to dismiss the employee have to be considered.

■ Automatically unfair reasons

There are a number of reasons that are considered automatically unfair when dismissing an employee. If such a reason was used by an employer, they would be unable to claim that they acted reasonably. A number of the automatically unfair reasons include:

☐ *Dismissal on the grounds of pregnancy or childbirth* – The Maternity and Parental Leave Regulations 1999 protect employees from being unfairly dismissed if the principal reason is related to issues such as her pregnancy; the birth; that she took, or attempted to take ordinary maternity leave; that she took, or attempted to take additional maternity leave; or the fact the she declined to sign a workforce employment contract.

☐ *Dismissal for assertion of a statutory right* – A dismissal will be rendered automatically unfair if an employer has breached a statutory right of the employee, in connection with the dismissal. The relevant statutory rights that employees have are all those in the ERA 1996 and TULR 1992, including issues such as guarantee payments, time off for public duties or antenatal care, written statements of reasons for dismissal or redundancy payments.

Other automatically unfair reasons include: dismissal on transfer of undertaking; trade union membership or activities; protected industrial action and whistleblowing.

■ Potentially fair reasons

In dismissal cases that are not rendered either automatically fair or unfair, the employment tribunal must determine the outcome. The remit for such decisions requires the tribunal to consider whether the employer acted reasonably or unreasonably in the specific circumstances of the case. That is, the tribunal is not required to determine whether they think the dismissal is fair or unfair, they are only to determine whether the employer's actions were within the band of reasonable response (*Sainsbury's Supermarkets Ltd v Hitt* 2003). The five main categories of potentially fair reasons are now discussed in turn:

☐ *Capability and qualifications* – If an employee does not possess the 'skill, aptitude, health or any other physical or mental quality' required to perform the job then an employer may fairly dismiss them. Likewise, dismissal may be justified if an employee does not possess the 'degree, diploma or other academic or technical qualification' relevant to the position (*Shook v London Borough of Ealing* 1986).

☐ *Incompetence* – Incapability as a result of incompetence has a general rule that 'the employee's incapacity as it existed at the time of dismissal must be of such a nature and quality to justify dismissal'. It does not, however, need to be in connection to one incident, but may be in connection to several incidents. For example, the manager of shop is dismissed fairly for failing to manage stock and the cash register, and leaving the shop floor in poor condition (*Lewis Shops Group Ltd v Wiggins* 1973).

☐ *Misconduct* – Dismissal as a result of the conduct of an employee can be viewed in varying contexts. Disobedience of reasonable orders, for example, contradicts an important principle of the employment contract and may therefore justify dismissal. There must, however, be a serious breach of rules in order to justify dismissal, and employees must be giving warning (*Deeley v BRE Ltd* 1980).

☐ Another context in which misconduct is relevant is when an offence has been committed. The tribunals make a distinction between offences committed inside and outside of the workplace. If an offence committed outside the workplace is closely connected to the employment then it is likely that dismissal will be fair (*Securicor Guarding Ltd v R* 1994). Dismissal for an offence committed inside the workplace will be justified if it passes the test of reasonability. In cases of unfair dismissal, employers need only to have reasonable suspicion to justify fair dismissal (*British Homes Stores v Burchell* 1978).

☐ *Redundancy* – In order to justify redundancy as a reason for dismissing an employee, the employer must have settled criteria for the selection of employees to be dismissed. In *Williams v Compair Maxam* (1982) the criterion used was 'employees who in the opinion of the managers concerned would be able to keep the company viable'. The employer is not required to justify the declaration of redundancy itself. This is to ensure that the courts do not get drawn into making decisions on the economic viability of companies (*Moon v Homeworthy Furniture (Northern) Ltd* (1982).

☐ *Illegality* – This category refers to the condition where an 'employee could not continue to work in the position which he held without contravention (either on his part or on that of his employer) of a duty or restriction imposed by or under an enactment' (ERA 1996, s.98 (2) (d)). A practical example of illegality is an employee losing their driving licence when they must use a car for work. However, the test of reasonability may require the employer to offer the employee suitable alternative employment, such as a stationary job (*Appleyard v F. M. Smith (Hull) Ltd* (1972)).

4

Tip

To read more about the cases that have been mentioned throughout this chapter, you can access all of the details and facts online through Westlaw. Westlaw is an online legal research database that comprises case law, statutes, law journals and law reviews.

■ Remedies

If in a case at an employment tribunal there is judged to have been an unfair dismissal, the employee will be afforded a remedy for their loss. The remedies available for unfair dismissal include:

☐ *Reinstatement* – This is an order for the employer to treat the 'employee in all respects as if he would not have been dismissed', and provide wages lost for the period since dismissal. However, reinstatement will not always be granted by a tribunal if it is deemed to be an 'impractical' solution. For example, if it would lead to a 'poisoned' atmosphere there will be no reinstatement (*Coleman v Toleman's Delivery Service Ltd* 1972). Re-engagement is another remedy similar to reinstatement, except that the employee takes up a different post. This post, however, must be comparable and suitable to the previous post (*Artisan Press v Strawley and Parker* 1986).

☐ *Compensation* – Unfair dismissal compensations consist of two categories: the basic and the compensatory award. The basic award is calculated by taking the employee's age, years of service and average weekly pay to arrive at a figure. However, in the UK the maximum weekly pay figure is £464 and the maximum years that will be considered are 20. The pay is either multiplied by 0.5, 1 or 1.5 depending on the length of service and age of employee. Thus, the absolute maximum basic award is £13,920. The compensatory award provides what is just and equitable as compensation, having regard to the loss suffered as a result of the dismissal. The compensatory award is now capped at £76,574, or one year's gross pay.

Redundancy

Redundancy refers to the situation where the workforce is reduced by the employer. This is especially common where a business is running at a loss, and costs need to be cut to keep the company solvent. Another example of when redundancy might occur is in a merger of two companies. A merged company is unlikely to need both sets of staff to operate, and thus, redundancies are inevitable. For example, when UK console shops GAME and Gamestation merged in 2012, 2000 employees were made redundant and 277 stores were closed. Prior to the merger, GAME had entered administration and both companies were struggling to compete with the online giant, Amazon. The merger has however saved the companies, and 2013 saw the company record profits of £20million and expects new stores to open in the future.

In the UK, the provisions by which an employee will be classified as redundant are set out in the ERA 1996:

1) For the purposes of this Act an employee who is dismissed shall be taken to be dismissed by reason of redundancy if the dismissal is wholly or mainly attributable to –

a) The fact the employer has ceased or intend to cease -

i) To carry on the business for the purposes of which the employee was employed by him or

ii) To carry on that business in the place where the employee was so employed,

or

b) The fact that the requirements of that business –

i) For employees to carry out work of a particular kind, or

ii) For employees to carry out work of a particular kind in the place where the employee was employed by the employer,

Have ceased or diminished or are expected to cease or diminish.

■ Eligibility for redundancy

Employees will only have the right to redundancy payments if they have been continuously employed for a period of no less than two years (ERA 1996. S.155). There has been no age limit for redundancy payments since the introduction of the Employment (Age) Regulations 2006.

As seen above, the situations in which an employee can be dismissed for redundancy are set out specifically in s.139 of the ERA 1996. Despite this, the term 'redundancy' is often used differently in everyday language to include any type of dismissal. Clearly, this is not the case and redundancy is only applicable in certain situations. This chapter will now describe the situations in which redundancy is applicable in more detail.

■ Cessation of the business (ERA 1996 s.139 (1))

An employee of a business will be dismissed for reason of redundancy if they are dismissed on account of the employer either ceasing or intending to cease to carry on the business for the purposes of which the employee was employed. This situation is the most common type of redundancy and with which most people are familiar. For example, it is commonly reported on the news that a particular company is struggling and may be entering administration; to cope with this the company may have to make some or all of its employees redundant.

■ Cessation of business at place of employment

If an employee works at a particular office, factory or shop of a company, and it closes down, then there will potentially be a case for redundancy, providing that the company does not continue business elsewhere. This puts into focus the *place* of employment and, according to the courts, this does not mean the location of work but rather where under contract the employee could be required to work.

In the case in which the principle was established, *UK Atomic Energy Authority v Claydon* (1974), the employee was required under contract to work 'at any of their establishments in Great Britain or in a post overseas'. When the employee refused to go to a different location to work he was dismissed by his employer and redundancy was claimed. The court upheld the employer's contention that requirement for the worker had not ceased in the place where he was employed because it was in the contract that he could be required to go anywhere in the UK or overseas.

■ The employer sheds surplus labour

An employer's need to have a particular number of employees may diminish either because there is less work to be done or because the existing work can be done by a fewer number of employees. Advancements in technology and innovation have had a profound effect on the number of workers an employer needs to conduct business.

Problems in redundancy cases have been caused by the meaning of 'work of a particular kind', as set out in the ERA 1996 S. 139(2). Several different tests have been used by the courts in the past to establish the meaning of 'work of a particular kind'. In the case of *Safeway Stores Plc v Burrell* (1997) the Employment Appeals Tribunal established what is known as the 'statutory test'. The facts of the case involve a petrol station manager who was dismissed when Safeway carried out a widespread reorganization in which redundancies were inevitable. Safeway offered alternative employment, but the employee refused and claimed unfair dismissal. However, the court did hold that the employee was made redundant as the three stages of the 'statutory test' were established:

1 Was the employee dismissed? If so,

2 Had the requirements of the employer's business for employees to carry out work of a particular kind ceased or diminished, or were they expected to cease or diminish, if so,

3 Was the dismissal of the employee caused wholly or mainly by the state of affair identified at stage 2?

■ Redundancy payments

A payment for redundancy is calculated in the same way as a basic award for unfair dismissal, except the award cannot be reduced on account of the employee's contributory conduct. The employer must provide the employee with a written statement explaining how the redundancy payment was calculated. An employer may be fined if they fail to do this. A claim must be presented within 6 months of the effective date of termination. The employment tribunal can allow a claim to be made within 12 months if they deem it just and equitable to do so. The current maximum amount of statutory redundancy pay is £13,920.

Conclusion

This chapter has provided a comprehensive introduction to the subject of UK employment law for students. By reading this chapter, students will have gained an insight into the background of employment law and the various legal principles that underpin the common law, the law of delict and contract law. The institutions that govern UK law, namely the employment tribunals and the Employment Appeal Tribunal, have been discussed and their functions explained. Critical concepts to this area of law including employment contracts and employment tests have been examined and students will have gained an understanding of when individuals should be classified as employees or workers. In addition, the reasons why an employee may be fairly, or unfairly, dismissed from their job have been expounded. Finally, the laws relating to redundancy were discussed as was the payments that may be available to employees who have been made redundant. Overall, this chapter has presented a broad description of the main principles of employment law, however, students are encouraged to extend their reading beyond this chapter in order further improve their knowledge. Some recommended reading is provided below.

Recommended reading

Collins, H. Ewing, and K. McColgan, A., (2012) *Labour Law*. Cambridge University Press.

Honeyball, S., (2014) *Honeyball and Bower's Textbook on Employment Law*. 12th Edition. Oxford.

Lewis, D. and Sargeant, M., (2015) *Employment Law: The Essentials*. Chartered Institute of Personsel & Development.

Wylie, A. and Crossan, S., (2004) *Introductory Scots Law: Theory and Practice*. Holder Gibson: Paisely.

5 Research to Create Enterprise Value

Geraldine McKay and Linda Phillips

Understanding customers and gaining insight into the context in which the business is operating is key to creating a relevant, valuable offering. In order to secure funding, market research features prominently in business plans and is viewed as a necessity when setting up an enterprise or before the launch of a new product or service. For established businesses, continuous research helps keep abreast of turbulent business environments where new competitors emerge, customer tastes change and new opportunities develop. Research can help answer the following questions: who are the customers, where are they, what do they want, how can they be reached and why is this business different from others? This chapter will introduce some of the more readily available sources that can be helpful in discovering trends, and will evaluate a range of appropriate tools that can help improve business decisions.

Market or marketing research?

A common image of market research is that of a researcher armed with a clipboard approaching reluctant respondents whilst shopping in the mall. Although some research involves surveys administered in this way, its scope is much wider. Some practitioners refer to 'marketing research' and others use the term 'market research'. Market research investigates the macro and micro environment, the market and the customer. This information is relevant for all companies operating within the market. Marketing research includes market research but additionally considers the business offering and customer reactions to it. It is more tailored to the needs of a specific organization. Although a distinction is made here, many authors use the terms market and marketing research interchangeably.

The American Marketing Association (AMA) defines *marketing research* as:

> the function that links the consumer, customer, and public to the marketer through information....used to identify and define marketing opportunities and problems; generate, refine, and evaluate marketing actions; monitor marketing performance; and improve understanding of marketing as a process.

> Marketing research specifies the information required to address these issues, designs the method for collecting information, manages and implements the data collection process, analyses the results, and communicates the findings and their implications. (AMA,2004)

Marketing research is increasingly seen as a function that gathers 'evidence' using a diverse range of tools, techniques and skills to provide a more complete understanding of customers and their influences, to achieve evidence-informed decision making across the organization and value creation for customers (Keegan, 2005). Some of the questions that can be answered through research are given in Figure 5.1. This chapter will focus on customers, but the techniques can equally be used to gain insight from multiple stakeholders such as employees, funders, distributors, neighbours, interest groups and suppliers.

- Who are our customers and competitors?
- What creates value?
- What do customers think about a new idea?
- How should the product be promoted/packaged/distributed?
- How much can be charged?
- How much should be spent on advertising?
- How do customers navigate a website?
- Which creative advertising approach is most effective?

Figure 5.1: Marketing research questions

■ Is research always necessary?

Where the cost of doing research outweighs benefits it may be reasonable to act without a formalized research. The CEO of Amazon (UK) had reservations about the launch of the highly successful Kindle but realised that "bringing a 100 people together to ask them what they wanted" was futile as customers find it difficult to imagine something that does not yet exist (MacIntosh and Maclean, 2015). So the research decision depends on what needs to be achieved (research objectives), the resources available and any potential outcome or risk of a poor decision.

The research process

A systematic approach (Figure 5.2) ensures that all stages are considered and allows a company to refine their research question and evaluate alternative research methods.

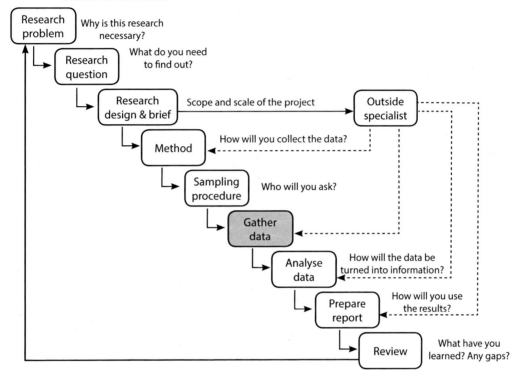

Figure 5.2: The systematic research process. Adapted from Stone and Desmond (2010).

Defining the research problem

Enterprises may struggle with the first step of the research process – defining the research problem and linking it to specific research questions. The problem could be broad and related to the macro environment, or more specifically business related.

■ Research design

Research can be designed to be exploratory, descriptive or causal depending on the purpose and outcomes expected.

Exploratory research uncovers background about the market, perhaps to indicate whether a business idea is worth exploring. Its aim is to raise, but not fully answer, further questions and should not be used to make decisions.

Descriptive research provides a fuller picture and might involve a systematic review of current information about the micro environment such as:

☐ A list of competitors sourced from web and printed directories

☐ Competitor prices and services

☐ Demographics and lifestyle data about customers.

Causal research tries to establish a connection between marketing activities, such as an increase in price and its effect on sales, or the impact of a new advertising message on customer perceptions.

Example: Paws-Play – defining the problem

Paws-Play is a fictional new business designed for pet owners who regularly work away from home. The initial problem is simply whether there is a market, which raises the potential research questions shown in Table 5.1.

Table 5.1: Research question

Research question	Research design
Which customers might benefit from the service?	descriptive
What macro environmental changes affect demand?	exploratory
How much does promotion influence interest in the service?	causal

Further research is then needed to assess the size and nature of the market.

1 Exploratory research

■ Dog control laws (macro environment).

■ Pet ownership figures and industry size reports.

■ Informal interviews with pet owners and professionals such as vets.

2 Descriptive research

■ Petcare spending worldwide will be $100billion, with $7billion spent in the UK (Davidson, 2015).

■ 10% of people who live in London spend over £2,000 p.a. on their animal (www.petplan.co.uk/petcensus, 2011).

■ In 2011, 20% of owners left their pet alone for 5-8 hours (op cit).

3 Causal research

■ Which of two advertising campaign is more memorable?

Question: What other type of causal research might Paws-Play need as it prepares for the launch of its services? How might data and insights be gathered?

Longitudinal data is gathered over time and highlights trends whereas **cross-sectional data** is gathered ad hoc and provides a snapshot of the current market. Once a clear idea of the service is established causal data might show how much a price affects demand or the effect of using social media on sales.

Research in action

Omnibus surveys are commercially run, continuous, longitudinal studies with large samples sizes allowing clients to share costs; e.g. the Arts Council (2013) include questions about attendance at cultural and artistic events on the British Market Research Bureau (BMRB) survey (29,000 interviews).

■ The research brief

The research brief is a written document that summarises what is already known, defines the problem and specifies the research questions. It indicates how the research will be used and by whom. Once complete, a decision on whether to complete the research 'in house' or use an outside specialist agency for some or all of the research is made. ESOMAR (2001) provide a guide to commissioning research.

Table 5.2: Benefits of external agency and in-house research

External research agency	In-house research
Objectivity	Opportunity to get first-hand knowledge of the market
Specialist skills	Work stays confidential
May elicit more candid answers	Can be cheaper
Likely to be completed	Questionnaire design and implementation software is available
Externally produced results seen as more credible	In-house researchers have better understanding of context

■ Research methods

A research project can be designed to include primary (or field) and/or secondary (or desk) research. Perhaps surprisingly, secondary research is considered first. Secondary research uses 'second hand' information that has already been published for another reason. It may fully answer the research questions. Primary research is new research, specifically undertaken for the particular project. Most research projects use a combination of primary and secondary research.

■ Secondary research

Secondary research may be available internally. Sources of internal data include:

- ☐ Sales, accounting and inventory records
- ☐ Profit and Loss statements
- ☐ Information provided by salesforce or distributors
- ☐ Customer complaints
- ☐ Marketing information systems
- ☐ Digital data such as Google analytics

There are numerous sources of freely available external research. For external secondary data a university library or the internet can be useful. Secondary information includes:

- ☐ Government statistics
- ☐ Trade association reports
- ☐ Journals
- ☐ Trade magazines and newspapers.
- ☐ Competitor annual reports
- ☐ Websites and specialist blogs
- ☐ Industry-wide research published by commercial research companies such as Mintel, Euromonitor and Keynote.

Whatever the source, reliability can be an issue. The Open University (2012) recommend that all sources are evaluated using the PROMPT framework

- ☐ **P**rovenance – Who is the author? If an academic piece has it been peer reviewed?
- ☐ **R**elevance – Does it cover the relevant sector/geographic area? Is it over-specialized or general for purpose?
- ☐ **O**bjectivity – based on opinion or fact? Web and newspaper articles may omit detail detracting from a good story
- ☐ **M**ethod – how was information obtained? Is the sample representative, the method rigorous and appropriate?
- ☐ **P**resentation – is the information clear?
- ☐ **T**imeliness – how old is the data? In some markets even recent information is out of date.

Exercise

Find government produced data available on the internet in your country. How might it be helpful for marketing? Apply the PROMPT framework to each source.

Research in action: Big data

Data from a number of sources (sales data, mobile and social media use) is combined and correlated to predict behaviour, choose promotions effectively and target new customers. Bravissimo, an online lingerie company, increased sales by investing in pay per click advertising at locations where the weather was forecast to be getting warmer (Treacy, 2015).

5

■ Primary research

Primary research can be either *qualitative* or *quantitative*, depending on whether detail and depth or quantifiable 'facts' are required.

Table 5.3: Comparison of qualitative and quantitative research

	Quantitative data	Qualitative data
Type of data	Objective: Measurement, numbers, facts	Subjective: Words, impressions, thoughts and feelings.
What questions does it help answer?	Descriptive: Who, what, when and how?	Diagnostic: Why?
Type of study	Causal and descriptive Spotting trends Segment comparison Correlating data about customer Describing behaviour. e.g. media use.	Exploratory and descriptive • Clarifies issues for investigation • Creative ideas for advertising and product development • Explains behaviour patterns Sensitive or personal studies
Main research tools (see page 89 ff)	Surveys and questionnaires, experimentation	Focus groups, depth interviews, projective techniques.
Results	Generalisable if sample large and representative	Results cannot be generalized but gives insight
Sample size	Large	Small

Quantitative methods are seen as scientific and highly valued but qualitative research is increasingly popular for its ability to delve more deeply and elicit findings that could not have been found using quantitative methods

Primary research tools

All primary research relies on the goodwill of respondents and one of the most important skills is designing research that will engage participants.

The choice of research tool depends on the research objectives and the resources available. Companies use a myriad of methods to research new ideas (Creusen, Hultink and Eling, 2012). Each method has limitations and some of the pitfalls are outlined below.

■ Questionnaires

Questionnaires are one of the most popular research tools. Crafting a questionnaire can be more difficult than it sounds and even professional companies sometimes get it wrong. When designing a questionnaire the following should be considered:

Question order and flow

☐ Keep opening questions broad, followed by more specific questions (known as a 'funnel technique') to ensure smooth flow and encourage customers to focus on the topic.

☐ Categorical questions such as age, income and gender can seem over-personal and are usually placed at the end of the questionnaire to put respondents at their ease.

☐ Including skip statements, such as "Go to question 5", will help guide respondents to the relevant question depending on their previous responses.

Question type

Questions can be **open** to allow the respondent to answer in their own words and provide richer detail, or **closed,** where a number of pre-defined categories are provided. Closed questions are quicker to answer and easier to analyse but can be restrictive. Providing an 'other' category allows for further responses.

Scaling questions using a five point scale will elicit strength of feeling responses. **Likert scales** allow the respondent to show the level of agreement with a statement and **semantic differential scales** permit respondents to indicate terms that matches their beliefs. Scales that ask for a number of factors to be ranked in importance can also be useful.

Example: Likert Scales

How much do you agree or disagree with the following statement?

I feel guilty about leaving my dog alone for more than 3 hours	
Disagree strongly	1
Disagree	2
Neither agree nor disagree	3
Agree	4
Agree Strongly	5

Completion time

Questionnaires should be as short as possible and should not usually take more than 10 minutes to complete, although more technical surveys may take longer.

5

Question wording

How questions are expressed is important, since this can influence the ways in which people respond on multiple levels. Therefore, it is suggested that:

☐ Language should be kept as simple as possible

☐ Focus on current attitudes and recent behaviour.

☐ Ensure that all questions are relevant.

☐ Avoid questions that lead the respondent. For example:

How would you describe the best-selling brand x?

The term "best" suggests positive responses should be given.

Example

The National Readership Survey question on newspaper readership is:

"Which of the following newspapers do your read regularly? By regularly I mean that you have seen the paper at least 4 days in the last week."

This explanation avoids any ambiguous interpretation of "read regularly"

Common questionnaire design pitfalls

There are many examples of poorly conceived questionnaire designs. These tend to include flaws such as:

☐ Ambiguous terms used in ways which could be interpreted in multiple, often contradictory, ways.

☐ Leading questions included

☐ Overlapping categories provided.

☐ Unclear instructions provided

☐ Language over complicated and filled with jargon.

☐ Questionnaire takes too long to complete and is not interesting.

To overcome these pitfalls, qualitative research could be used to develop the questions. The questionnaire is then piloted with between 5 to 10 respondents and refined where necessary.

Example: The wrong way to ask about age:

1   How old are you?

15-24   24-35   36-44   45 and over

Age categories overlap and the last category is too wide. An 80 year old is unlikely to respond in the same way as someone aged 45. In order to be sensitive, it is common to offer a "prefer not to say" category and rephrase the question to "Which of the following category do you fall into?"

Research tip

Quota sampling asks classification questions first so that respondents that do not fit the quota do not waste their time.

Exercise

Gather and critique examples of questionnaires from the market place. What is the overall research question? Would you change anything in the questionnaire?

■ In-depth interviews

In-depth interviews are semi structured or unstructured and may use projective techniques to open conversation.

☐ An interview guide should be available but questions should allow free flowing responses.

☐ Provides rich, in- depth and detailed information from a small number of respondents.

☐ Used in business-to-business environments.

■ Focus groups

Focus groups are used to discover opinions or gain initial feedback to marketing ideas, such as reactions to advertising ideas or brainstorming to help design new products.

- ☐ 5-8 group participants are recruited, to provide balanced views through interaction in a relaxed environment

- ☐ A skilled moderator ensures that no individual dominates the conversation (Henderson, 1992)

- ☐ Groups can be run online via Skype or through bulletin boards where highly flexible, 'asynchronous' discussion can take place across time zones and locations.

- ☐ Recruitment of the sample should ensure a variety of responses can be raised

- ☐ The small number of participants that take part in a group discussion limits the chances that any group will represent the whole population.

Research in action – New products

Co-creation of new ideas or crowdsourcing is being used by many businesses. When Nandos wanted to launch a new menu they asked the company's Facebook fans. Within a day of posting over 550 likes were recorded and more than 350 comments received. This technique is used widely to gain initial, fast reactions before further research and trials are undertaken.

■ Observation

Customers can be observed to see what they do in authentic situations such as shopping or navigating websites.

- ☐ Observation can be qualitative or quantitative.

- ☐ The observer may accompany the respondent on shopping visits (**participant observation**) or undertake **covert observation** (although this raises ethical and data protection issues).

- ☐ **Mystery shopper** exercises. Here the researcher acts as an ordinary customer and reports on service quality, process, and retail layouts.

Research in action – Observation Robocop style

Carlsberg, a European drinks company used ethnography and accompanied 250 people to bars and observed buying behaviour. Specially made eye glasses monitored eye movement and instantly fed back results indicating the impact of point-of-sale design on buying. (Barda, 2011).

■ Ethnography

Ethnography requires the researcher to immerse themselves into the lives of the respondent to discover behaviour within natural settings, activities and family routines.

☐ Outcomes from ethnography include slice-of-life advertising based around 'normal' families.

☐ These research tools can be useful for unearthing detail that a consumer may not report as important when responding to other methods such as surveys.

■ Projective techniques

Unstructured stimuli, objects or situations can be used to elicit the individual's way of perception of the world (Table 5.5).

Table 5.5: Projective techniques

Technique	Example
Sentence completion test	The person who leaves their dog alone all day is............
Word association tests	What words come to mind when thinking about Paws-Play
Cartoon/ picture Completion	Complete these thought boxes
Fantasy situations	If money was no object, describe the best pet day care.
Drawing	Draw a picture showing your feelings when you leave your dog alone.

■ Other methods

In pursuit of customer understanding, research is using ever more sophisticated techniques such as neuroscience, biometrics and digital observation methods (Web analytics). In reality many projects use more than one method.

■ Asking the questions

Traditional methods of data collection include face-to-face, postal, online and telephone interviews.

☐ Personal, face to face interviews give higher response rates and allow questions to be explained and responses clarified.

☐ Online and mobile surveys should be checked to make sure that the layout and instructions are clear on every device.

5

Sampling procedure: Who to ask?

Research is only useful if the right people are asked. For Paws-Play there is little point in asking those who do not own pets. It is impossible to question everyone and any sample should include opinions that *represent* as many customers as possible. Sampling aims to provide 'good enough' data in a cost effective manner. The most common methods will now be discussed.

■ Probability sampling

Random sampling

This requires a full list (sampling frame), of the population under study. Every person from the population has an equal chance of being chosen for the study. The choice can be made systematically (so every nth name on the list is chosen) or truly randomized (simple random sampling), equivalent to taking them out of a hat. Although this approach is statistically sound it does not in itself ensure that the sample necessarily includes all shades of opinion and marketing research tends towards quota sampling.

Stratified random sampling

The population is stratified or grouped according to criteria that might affect responses. For example a survey concerning attitudes towards a particular brand should include those who are frequent purchasers and those who are not. A random sample is taken from within each of the two groups.

Probability sampling requires the interviewer to interview the person selected, even if this requires repeated contact attempts or travelling long distances.

■ Non-probability sampling

For small research projects with no current sampling frame and tight resources, non-probability methods are used. It is a common approach for commercial market research. Steps to make the sample representative are necessary.

Convenience sampling

Easily accessible respondents are chosen (e.g. whilst shopping in a mall). Although convenient, this method is neither random nor objective (Denscombe, 2003). 'Snowball sampling' where respondents are recommended through social networks is a form of convenience sampling (Baltar and Brunet, 2012).

Quota sampling

To improve representativeness, a quota is set for certain groups replicating the proportion found in the total population such as gender, socio-economic status, full or part time working.

■ How big should the sample be?

A survey should ensure that shades of opinion are captured. If all customers think similarly then only one person needs to be interviewed. A census (every-one interviewed) gives maximum confidence but is not efficient. Free survey software often limits the number of respondents to 100 but this is insufficient for most research, particularly when this number is split into groups for comparison (e.g. male versus female opinions) as the initial sample is reduced to 50 within each subgroup. Splitting this further, perhaps by age, reduces numbers further so that inferences are unreliable. Hence sample size depends on population variability, the budget and time available but generally bigger is better.

Analysis and reporting: Turning data into information

Data by itself is not information. It becomes information when it has been transformed to be appropriate for, and understood by is intended audience. Each method brings challenges.

■ Quantitative data

Quantitative data is analysed by looking at the frequency of responses to each question and investigating whether there are any correlations between answers that can help provide deeper insight. It can seem a relatively easy process and some survey software will automatically summarise and output the data into readable charts and graphics. However it is very easy to make mistakes and so a systematic approach to analysis should be taken.

1 Check each response. Incomplete questionnaires should be excluded or respondents retraced.

2 Code each respondent, question and answer category so that it can be analysed using a relevant software such as SPSS.

3 Enter data and double-check the data entry. Any missing cases to be discarded.

4 Undertake descriptive analysis looking at frequency counts, ratios and mean results for each question.

5 Compare the results between groups to highlight relationships between answers using relevant statistical techniques.

A variety of graphical tools (e.g. pie and bar charts, histograms and graphs) alongside narrative explanation enlivens the report, but researchers should only report on the data that is relevant. The analysis should consider:

☐ Limitations of method, question design.

☐ Statistical significance of the results.

☐ Representativeness of the sample.

☐ Confidence levels that results could be reproduced.

Typical pitfalls when reporting quantitative data include:

☐ Assuming cause and effect.

☐ Small sample sizes in some of the sub groups.

☐ Failure to look at the result distribution and impact of outlying results on the mean.

■ Qualitative data

Qualitative data takes time to transcribe and analyse, even with the help of specialist software such as NVivo and Qualtrics. Qualitative research produces narrative (transcripts of interviews or reports of an observation) or photographic and pictorial evidence. The data needs to be reviewed several times until similarities, differences and themes start to emerge. The evidence will then be sorted into specific examples of each theme. Reports are enriched with video clips and sample quotes that illustrate main points. However, these should not be taken out of context. Qualitative research analysis may benefit from the services of a professional researcher.

■ The research report

Projects result in a debrief session with the marketing team. The job of the report or presentation is to reduce the volume of data into information that is true to the findings and yet can be understood. Every piece of information should pass the 'so what?' and 'now what?' test. This ensures that only significant and relevant data is highlighted. Less relevant detail can be moved to the appendix. Complex statistical techniques such as regression analysis or significance testing are not usually written in the main report.

Being ethical

The collection of data involving human respondents raises ethical issues. Research is intrusive and researchers must show empathy. This means:

☐ Being honest about the purpose and uses of research.

☐ Protecting anonymity of participants and confidentially of their views.

☐ Making it clear that taking part is optional and that opt is possible.

☐ Being truthful when reporting methods results and project limitations.

☐ Being sensitive to cultural needs.

☐ Safety of the researcher is paramount.

New methods of research raise new ethical questions, particularly with regards to privacy (Ochoa and Savin, 2015; Nunan and Di Domenico, 2013). The potential of online observation is clear but the right to privacy is a fundamental and universally recognised right. Legal frameworks have not kept up with technology such as smartphones and tablets which generate large volumes of personal information (Big Data). Fear that personal data will be used to compromise privacy reduces willingness to participate in research and will ultimately lead to poorer marketing decisions. Unethical marketers have used research as an excuse to make sales ('sugging' which is short for selling under the guise of marketing research or 'frugging' when it relates to fund raising organizations)

Ultimately, being ethical means that the researcher does the utmost to ensure that methods are based on the best evidence-based practice.

Conclusion

Marketing research aims to tell a story using data that gives consumer insight and improves marketing strategy. Research can reduce risk but it should not be used as a prop for bad practice or a substitute for decision-making. It is ultimately about providing information to create the best value for customers and other stakeholders. Research is a powerful tool to be undertaken systematically and ethically.

Further reading

Creusen, M.E.H., Hultink, E.-J. & Eling, K. (2012) Choice of consumer research methods in the front end of new product development. *International Journal of Market Research.* **55**(1): 81-104.

Useful summary of the methods, and also gives an example of how quantitative data can be reported.

Metcalf, L., Hess, J.S., Danes, & Singh, J. (2014). A mixed-methods approach for designing market-driven packaging. *Qualitative Market Research: An International Journal,* **15**(3): 268 -289.

Mixed methods research in packaging design.

Micu, A.C., Dedeker, K., Lewis, I., Moran, R. & Netzer, O. (2011). The shape of marketing research in 2021. *Journal of Advertising Research.* **51**(1): 212-221.

References

AMA. (2004). *Definition of Marketing Research.* Available at: https://www.ama.org/AboutAMA/Pages/Definition-of-Marketing.aspx [Accessed March, 2015].

Arts Council. (2013). *Taking part Survey.* Available at: http://www.artscouncil.org.uk/what-we-do/research-and-data/arts-audiences/taking-part-survey/ [Accessed March, 2015].

Baltar, F. & Brunet, I. (2012). Social research 2.0: virtual snowball sampling method using Facebook. *Internet Research*. **22** (1): 57 – 74.

Barda, T. (2011). Carlsberg. *The Marketer*. CIM 23 March, 2011.

Creusen, M.E.H., Hultink, E-J. & Eling, K. (2012). Choice of consumer research methods in the front end of new product development. *International Journal of Market Research*. **55** (1): 81-104.

Davidson, L. (2015). Britons will spend more than $7bn on their pets this year, *The Telegraph* 6 January. Available at: http://www.telegraph.co.uk/finance/ newsbysector/retailandconsumer/11327761/Pet-humanization-will-cost-Britons-7bn-this-year.html [Accessed September, 2015]

Denscombe, M. (2003). *The Good Research Guide: For Small-Scale Social Research Projects* (2nd edition). London: Open University Press.

ESOMAR. (2001). *How to Commission research*. Available at: https://www.esomar.org/ uploads/public/knowledge-and-standards/codes-and-guidelines/ESOMAR_Code-and-Guidelines_HowToCommissionResearch.pdf [Accessed March, 2015].

Henderson, N. (1992). Trained moderators boost the value of qualitative research *Marketing Research*. (June). **4** (2): 20-23.

Keegan, S. (2005). Emergent inquiry: The 'new' qualitative research. Paper given at the AQR/QRCA Bi-Annual Conference, Dublin.

MacIntosh, R. & Maclean, D (2015). *Strategic Management: Strategists at Work*. London: Palgrave Macmillan.

Nunan, D. & Di Domenico, M.L. (2013). Market research and the ethics of Big Data *International Journal of Market Research*. **55** (4): 2-13.

Ochoa, C. & Savin, F. (2015). *The Tracker, the technology that will change market research*. Available at: https://rwconnect.esomar.org/the-tracker-the-technology-that-will-change-market-research/ [Accessed March, 2015].

Open University. (2012). *PROMPT Checklist*, OU Library Services. Available at: http:// www.open.ac.uk/libraryservices/documents/prompt_checklist.pdf [Accessed March, 2015].

Stone, M. & Desmond, J. (2010). *Marketing Fundamentals*. Edinburgh: Heriot-Watt Management Programme.

Treacy, B (2015). Big Data – science fact or fantasy *The Marketer*. Available at: http:// www.themarketer.co.uk/analysis/in-depth/big-data-science-fact-or-fantasy [Accessed March, 2015].

6 Marketing to Create Value

Geraldine McKay

Entrepreneurs generally feel enthusiastic when discussing their product or service idea but less comfortable when asked about their marketing approach. Marketing can suggest advertising, selling or tricks to influence people to buy things that they do not need, at a price they perhaps cannot afford. Marketing does include advertising and selling, but it is not about manipulating customers. Fifty years ago the Chartered Institute of Marketing defined marketing as "the management process responsible for identifying, anticipating and satisfying customer requirements profitably" (CIM, 2007). It is both a way of thinking *about* and a function *within* business – an activity and a way of thinking. It is the part of an enterprise that thinks about the customer first; by taking a customer-centric view it better understands needs and wants. It can then actively use the resources available to provide the very best value goods and services and develop a long-term relationship with existing and potential customers. For many smaller businesses marketing can seem to be an expensive luxury but this chapter will consider how any new enterprise will benefit from both the ideas and actions of marketing.

Marketing and the enterprise

Not all enterprises claim profit as their main goal; some have other goals. Charities wish to create awareness, recruit volunteers and gather donations for their cause, while the health service works to cure illness and change behaviour to promote health. Even traditional, for-profit organizations may have other objectives requiring marketing thinking, such as recruiting the best employees or raising awareness of their corporate social responsibility activity. Multiple objectives and stakeholders necessitate a broader and more up to date definition:

> Marketing is…the strategic business function that creates value by stimulating, facilitating and fulfilling customer demand. It does this by building brands, nurturing innovation, developing relationships, creating good customer service and communicating benefits. With a customer-centric view, marketing brings positive return on investment, satisfies shareholders and stakeholders from business and community and contributes to positive behavioural change and sustainable business future. (CIM, 2007)

Marketing has been incorrectly criticised for being transactional, focussing on creating an initial sale. Good marketing strives to create longer-term relationships, where value is consistently delivered for mutual benefit.

Exercise

What are the differences between the two CIM definitions? Can marketing as a way of thinking and and as an action be separated? What other definitions of marketing are used across the world?

■ Which market?

This fundamental question should be tackled by every business. Defining the market determines who the customers and competitors are. It involves identifying influential macro environmental factors and drawing the boundaries within which the business operates. Levitt (1960) suggested that companies were myopic (short-sighted) when defining their business in narrow product terms. The railroads in the US failed to see the impact that air travel or motoring would have on their business. Had they identified their business as transportation they may have seen the threat posed by substitutes. Companies like Apple take a broad view and see their business as more than the design and manufacturer of computers. A growing 10% of their revenue is now generated from digital content through the App store, iTunes and iCloud (Dredge, 2014; Apple, 2015).

Value and exchange

Once an enterprise has determined which markets they wish to serve they need to think about how they can create value for customers. Fahy and Jobber (2012) identify four types of value:

☐ **Performance value** – the functional benefits achieved, i.e. what the product does, e.g. a mobile phone featuring new capabilities such as holographic projection. Competitors may be able to copy these tangible features relatively quickly.

☐ **Emotional value** – the intangible benefits based on consumer perceptions and how the product makes them feel. This is not easily copied. Luxury branded goods fall into this category.

☐ **Price value** – low prices and saving money. Aldi is an excellent example of a company benefiting from everyday low pricing (E.D.L.P.).

☐ **Relationship value** – developed between a company and its customers, evident in personal services such as hairdressing. Many physical goods also add value by developing customer relationships (e.g. Moonpig, the on-line greetings card retailer sends reminders of birthdays and anniversaries).

As we can see, tangible or intangible offerings are valued where benefits are clear. Value creation is a two-way process and both the customer **and** the organization must benefit. An organization must fulfil its own objectives to continue creating customer value. Value is about exchange; at the simplest level customers exchange money for products or services and the business profits from this transaction. But not all exchanges are about money and profit (see Table 6.1).

Table 6.1: The nature of exchange

Enterprise	Provides	For	Who exchange	Organization objective
Bakery	Bread and confectionary	Customers	Money	Profit
Bank	Salary/wages	Employees	Time and skills	Profit
Public hospital	Healthcare	Citizens	Taxes	Improved community health
Charity	Training	Volunteers	Time and skills	Widely available services

What does marketing do?

If every employee thinks about how they personally can add value for the customer, the part-time marketer is born and the marketing department becomes obsolete (Gronroos, 1990). But the professional marketer offers various skills in research, managing and running promotional campaigns, assisting sales force activity, pricing and forecasting. They act as:

☐ **Customer champions**, representing customers in all decision making and reinforcing commitment to customer value

☐ **Brand guardians**, protecting brand values when making decisions about the marketing mix.

Put simply, the marketing department combines a number of ingredients to provide customer value. The number and names of these ingredients has been debated over time, but the functions or activities of marketing are commonly referred to as the *marketing mix* (McCarthy, 1960) or the four Ps. The marketing mix includes:

☐ **Product** – what is offered, what are the benefits and value?

☐ **Price** – how much the company charges or the cost to the customer.

☐ **Promotion** – communication between the business and the consumer.

☐ **Place** – where and how the product is obtained, customer convenience created.

For a services market three additional Ps are generally included. These are:

☐ **Physical evidence** – the location and the look of the business.

☐ **Process** – how the service is organized and delivered.

☐ **People** – the service personnel who deal with the consumers.

Before examining the marketing mix in more detail the customer should be identified. A parent may buy goods (customers) used by the family (consumers) but all family members influence the decision. In a business-to-business (B2B) market, the influencers can include engineers, users, finance and specifiers. Where goods are sold through retailers or wholesalers, a priority is to ensure the product is available and marketing efforts need to be targeted towards the retailer. Marketers must therefore consider the needs of the whole decision making unit in determining the most appropriate marketing mix.

Segmenting the market

It can be difficult for an entrepreneur to understand that not everyone is in love with their product, brand or service idea. Not all customers are the same and this is why segmentation is important.

Segmentation is the essence of marketing. Levitt (1986) said: "if you're not thinking segments you're not thinking" (1986:128). Segmentation breaks up a larger market into smaller homogenous groups of people who share similar needs. People within each segment have similar characteristics but segments should be as distinctive as possible. Segmentation allows a business to get to know customers and concentrate efforts on using their resources to meet those customer needs. A segment that is not attractive to competitors could prove successful for a different business. Segmentation can assist location decisions and determine relevant communications messages.

This chapter identifies four methods used to segment the market, but additional methods are sometimes discussed in the academic literature (Baines, Fill and Page, 2013).

1 Demographics

Customers who share similar demographic characteristics (age, occupation, gender, life stage, socio-economic status or income) are relatively easy to identify. This segmentation method is the most frequently used with many examples of products that use demographic characteristics to group their markets. Consider toys aimed at girls or cosmetics marketed to mature women. Although popular, it is a crude method of segmentation.

2 Geographic

Customer location can affect the types of products and services needed and the capability to supply. Consider how population density might affect the size and type of home available and the impact on furnishing requirements, or the impact of nationality on preferred choices. Companies may initially operate locally but extend their geographical reach once established.

3 Lifestyle (psychographics) and benefits

This uses customer activities, interests and opinions to group customers. It is obviously useful when considering particular products used for a hobby and it is helpful in building up a richer picture of customers. A highly innovative energy saving product might appeal to three segments: those interested in environmental matters; those who seek frugality; and early adopters who just want the latest gadget.

4 Behavioural

Here, segments are formed according to:

- ☐ **Value and benefits sought by the consumer**. For example, confectionery bought as a gift will be packaged elaborately, acquired from specialist outlets, more expensive and promoted as luxury. The benefit for the customer is very different to a chocolate bar purchased as an everyday snack.

- ☐ **Users.** Regular and loyal purchasers are identified as a special segment and benefit from special discounts, loyalty points and upgrades; infrequent buyers are treated in a different way.

■ Hybrid methods

In reality, businesses find a mix of methods more meaningful. Geo-demographic segmentation, as the name suggests combines geographic location with other demographic factors such as socio-economic status. Companies such as Experian (http://www.experian.co.uk/marketing-services/products/mosaic/mosaic-in-action.html) and CACI (http://acorn.caci.co.uk/) use hybrid methods to give insight into consumer lives, allowing sophisticated tailoring of messages and access to potential customers with similar characteristics to those who already like the brand. Segment (2013) has used hybrid techniques across Europe to market sustainable transport systems.

Exercise

Draw up a list of brands that are targeted at younger, single audiences and those that are created for a more mature market. What are the differences employed in the marketing mix? Do marketers stereotype or patronise their consumers when segmenting using demographic characteristics?

For a business to implement suitable marketing plans the segmentation strategy must be compatible with company resources and know-how (Figure 6.1).

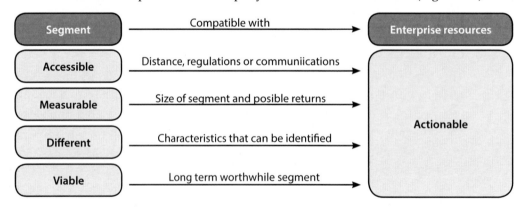

Figure 6.1: Successful segmentation criteria

■ Targeting

Once the enterprise has decided which segments actually exist in the market place it will decide how many of those segments will be served. There are four basic approaches to targeting (Figure 6.2):

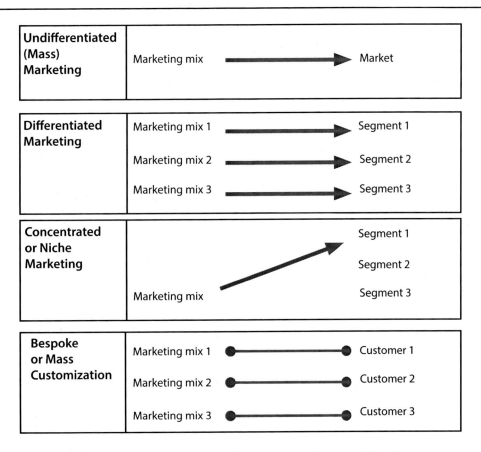

Figure 6.2: Target market selection. Adapted from Stone and Desmond (2010).

☐ **Undifferentiated or mass marketing** – the whole market is treated as homogenous and targeted with one offering and with no accounting for difference. Narrow product lines enable cost leadership and economies of scale. It is a production led, one-size-fits-all approach and rarely suitable for nascent enterprises.

☐ **Differentiated** – caters for the whole market with a variety of products. Car companies manufacture several car and truck models under numerous brand names to serve every segment. Although expensive it creates a balanced portfolio and reduces the risk of company failure when one segment declines.

☐ **Concentrated or niche marketing** involves specialist provision for one market segment. As the company becomes familiar with segment needs it ensures that exact needs are met. Reliance on one segment can be risky, particularly when competitors choose the same segment, but this can be a useful entry strategy.

Example

Hotel Chocolat is a niche marketer producing handmade confectionery. It has expanded to include retail outlets, cafes and a hotel, but it still targets the one main segment of chocolate lovers.

☐ **Bespoke or mass customization** – a totally bespoke, individually tailored service. Examples include personal services such as physiotherapy, architects and consultants. Technology allows companies to offer bespoke physical products to a number of customers. Freitag, (www.freitag.ch/) individually designs bags out of recycled materials. Prices tend to be high but the customer gets emotional value from knowing that their product is a one-off.

Target market selection will be internally influenced by resource availability, the potential to vary the product and stage in the product lifecycle. Smaller companies generally compete well by spotting a niche marketing opportunity and by serving the needs of those wanting something a bit different. External factors influencing the decision include variability between segments and the presence of competitors.

■ Positioning

Following segmentation and targeting the final step is to develop a clearly defined image of the product or brand in customer minds so it is seen as different from competing brands. The consumer takes cues from the marketing mix and what others say about the product to help them decide how it is positioned.

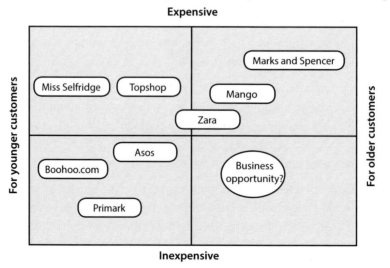

Figure 6.3: Imagined perceptual map for women's clothing retail

Market research can discover where competing products are positioned in the minds of customers and can visualise these results. In the sample positioning map (Figure 6.3) for ladies fashion there appears to be some potential for a mid-range, fairly inexpensive retail outlet for older consumers. If the enterprise has the capability to design an appropriate marketing mix then this opportunity would be stronger than trying to compete in the crowded upper quadrants.

Creating value through the marketing mix

■ Product – the offer?

At the heart of the marketing exchange is the product offered to the customer. Aimed at the consumer and/or the business market, products can be:

- ☐ **Physical goods** such as washing machines, yoghurts
- ☐ **Services** such as hairdressing or holidays
- ☐ **Ideas** such as management consultancy
- ☐ **Places** such as Malaysia or Dubai
- ☐ **People** such a celebrities or politicians.

Most products include an element of service and most services offer some physical aspects. Figure 6.4 shows the product made up of several layers. The core is the central essence of the product and the benefits it provides. The actual product includes the physical features, design, quality and packaging. The augmented product includes mainly intangible aspects such as the brand name and additional services such as guarantees, delivery, after sales and installation.

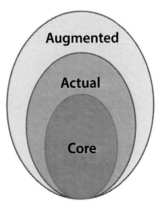

Figure 6.4: Levels of product

Along with product features, the name and augmented package of services, the range of products or the product mix needs to be determined. A wide range enables the company to serve several market segments. However, supporting each product requires resources and customers can find broad ranges confusing. Some corporations such as Unilever are trying to concentrate their marketing effort on core business and have reduced the number of products they sell, although they still manufacture over 400 brands bought by 2 billion customers each day (Unilever, 2015). Many businesses initially offer a single product but over time extend their portfolio to include a number of closely linked brand extensions or highly diversified products, covering the needs of many markets.

Products and services aimed at consumers can be:

☐ **Fast moving consumer goods** – as the name suggests these products are frequently purchased and include food or household cleaning products

☐ **Durables** – personal goods such as clothes, mobile phones or goods for households, e.g. refrigerators and furniture. Less frequently purchased and augmented elements such as guarantees and aftersales service are extremely important.

☐ **Luxury goods** – high-end items that are infrequently purchased by most people, including designer goods. An example might be Mulberry handbags or Porsche cars, which are often seen as an investment.

☐ **Services** – the number and types of services targeted at consumers are vast. The increased number of families where both parents work outside the home has meant great potential for household services such as gardeners, childcare, cleaners, grocery delivery and takeaways.

Exercise

As part of a university course a student must think about setting up a new business. Make a list of potential services that might be of interest to young couples and older empty-nesters (couples whose children have moved out). What skills are required to successfully offer those services?

■ Naming the product

A great name for a product can be protected. It can suggest product benefits, create emotional responses, boost awareness and raise interest. A name should:

☐ **Create associations**. Snuggle fabric softener has warm associations and says something about the brand. Many technical product names include numbers or X and Z to sound scientific, e.g. Xbox

☐ **Be easy to remember and say**. Names like Ikea or Nike are often pronounced incorrectly but appear to work because they have already achieved some recognition.

☐ **Be distinctive and not infringe copyright**.

☐ **Avoid unintended meaning(s) in other languages**.

Names can arise out of research but some names have occurred by accident. Apple is reputed to have been named by Steve Jobs because no alternative was suggested. Other names such as Hermes or Xerox have classical foundations. Today a number of name generators can be discovered online. Remember that the brand may eventual become global and so must work in different markets. If a name is too suggestive it may not be suitable for brand extensions.

Tip

Crowdsourcing a new business name through social media can lead to interesting ideas. The more popular names that say something about the brand will also register higher in search engines.

6

■ Managing products over time

Products may not be successful forever – this is known as the 'product lifecycle'. Sales may take off slowly, then accelerate and go into decline as the market matures and competition takes hold. Some products such as Chanel No. 5 have longevity. This perfume, launched in 1925 has many loyal customers. By contrast, fads have very short lifecycles. For example, Google glasses, a wearable technology, were launched in 2014, obtaining much press coverage. They were of interest to early adopters and innovators. Although hailed as innovative they were withdrawn from sale in January 2015, less than a year after launch (Cellen-Jones, 2015). Products die for a number of reasons and are withdrawn at different stages such as launch or when replacement products become available, or when profits start to fall.

■ Price

Setting prices can be challenging. Price signals the quality position and is influential in whether the product is worthy of consideration by a customer; from the business perspective this element of the mix creates revenue. Price is about the value created and equal to what the consumer is prepared to give up.

Pricing depends on the organization's objectives. To gain rapid market share or deter competition, low initial pricing (*penetration pricing*) might be successful where economies of scale benefits can be achieved (Tellis, 1986). If an enterprise aims to dispose of stock or generate cash flow then *promotional pricing* will be useful. *Market skimming* requires that a high initial price is charged (Dean, 1976, cited in Spann, Fischer and Telis, 2015) to suggest quality and enable research costs to be recouped before competitors are ready to enter the market. Prices fall as more consumers buy the product and production costs decrease. Price therefore varies across the life of the product (McDaniel, Lamb and Hair, 2013).

Example

Differential pricing is evident in the retail fashion market. Zara charge Japanese customers nearly 50% more because these customers recognise the brand's higher value (The Economist, 2011).

New businesses frequently undercut competitors to gain market foothold, but initial undervaluing signals poor quality and zero additional benefits to existing products. This pricing strategy is not recommended as competitors may undercut price in the short term and escalate a price war.

Ultimately, price must be set somewhere between the upper or ceiling price (no customers) and the lowest possible price (no profit). The price set will be influenced by customers, competitors and costs (Figure 6.5) and the focus of the organization.

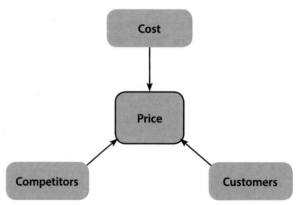

Figure 6.5: Influences on pricing

☐ **Cost focus** – Achieving a surplus at the end of the financial year requires costs to be covered. So price is determined by adding all costs with an extra amount for profit. This approach is more challenging that it sounds, as unit prices vary according to amounts produced and costs are affected by external factors such as inflation of raw materials. Keeping an eye on costs is important, but this method concentrates on creating value for the organization rather than the customer.

☐ **Competitor focus**. It is useful to know the *going rate*. Discovering this benchmark should be a research objective, but this approach assumes that competitors are pricing correctly. Undercutting may lead to a price war and a higher price assumes that consumers are willing to pay more for your brand.

☐ **Customer focus.** For marketers, the consumer is at the centre of pricing decisions and price charged should match customer perceived value. Intention to buy does not always equal action but an estimation of price sensitivity might be possible through dynamic pricing for on-line customers. Service industries will alter prices for certain segments to lift demand on quieter days.

Exercise: Dynamic pricing

How can Air Asia offer flights from Kuala Lumpur to Bangkok (a distance of 730 miles) for 100RM (around £20.00)? What costs are being covered within this fare?

6

Pricing is not always the most influential element of the marketing mix. The following section will consider the rest of the marketing mix.

■ Promotion – Communication

Communication should be a dialogue that fosters mutual understanding between the company and its customers and other stakeholders. Organizations must decide on relevant communication or promotional objectives, tools and messages. Much of what the consumer hears about the organization is unplanned and stems from non-company sources such as the press, employees and other customers. BP and Shell are well known but their reputation varies amongst stake-holding groups. Promotion can be expensive and money should be invested wisely. Figure 6.6 summarises influence on promotional mix choice.

Promotional goals

One method used to set promotional goals or objectives considers the stages a consumer goes through before they become loyal users of the product. A simple acronym for setting goals is AIDA

☐ **Awareness** – 50% of target market to know about us.

☐ **Interest** – 2000 click-through to the website.

☐ **Desire** – 200 potential customers saying brand is preferred choice.

☐ **Action** – Conversion to sale for 50.

Objectives extend beyond first purchase and should consider loyalty and relationship development, repeat purchase or encouraging recommendations.

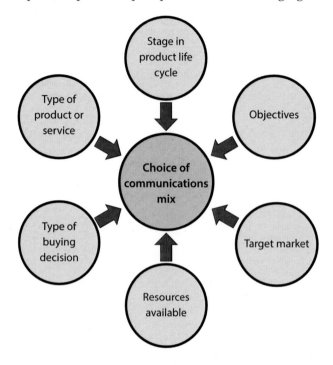

Figure 6.6: Influences on communication mix choice. Adapted from Phillips and Clews (2013).

■ Promotional tools

Traditional communication tools included advertising, direct marketing, public relations and sales promotion but the environment has changed and digital tools such social media are increasingly important (Figure 6.7). £15.7 billion was spent on promotion in 2014 (Sweeny, 2014) with over half spent on digital media. Facebook makes large sums in advertising revenue and has 936 million daily active users or with 1.25 billion accessing through mobile (Facebook, 2015). Vloggers (video bloggers) such as Zoella are earning large sums through product endorsement reaching millions of worldwide followers. Paradoxically, Facebook spent more than £6m on traditional media in the UK in 2014; a massive increase on the £16,000 spent in the previous year (Cookson and Kuchler, 2015).

Exercise

Why does Facebook spend money on traditional media?

Figure 6.7: The communications mix

Table 6.2 provides a summary of the promotional methods available.

Table 6.2: Main promotional tools

Promotional Tool	Examples	Good for
Advertising	Press, TV, radio, billboards	Raising awareness Brand positioning.
Public relations and sponsorship	Sports sponsorship, Press Releases announcing job creation.	Reaching multiple stakeholders Corporate social responsibility Creating interest.
Direct marketing and personal selling	Email, direct mail, personal selling. Avon cosmetics have c.5million sales people globally.	Developing customer relationships, Measure responses. Bespoke messages Sales generation
Events and Experiences	No make-up selfie for Cancer Research UK made £8million in 6 days	Customer engagement co -creation
Social media and digital	Facebook, Twitter, Pinterest, Snapchat. Airbnb uses social media to create community.	Viral messages Creating interest
Sales promotion	Competitions and price promotions such as buy one get one free (BOGOF).	Generates interest Stimulate purchase (often short term effect)

6

Example

O'Reilly and Lusch (2015) suggest that a 30 second ad in super bowl in 2015 will have cost $4.5million

Promotional tools are rarely used in isolation and communication methods must be integrated in order to complement each other and strengthen company messages. Generating communication about your product and creating a dialogue is insufficient and customers will be disappointed if they cannot access it. This is why distribution or *place* is important

■ Place

Where and how to get a product to market requires a compromise to be made between control and coverage (customer convenience). Before the advent of the internet, direct selling companies would require physical outlets, but now even relatively small organizations can reach distant locations. A hybrid approach, selling through direct channels and a number of intermediaries is popular. Even Google has a physical off-line presence, opening a retail shop where visitors can try the latest devices and experiment with applications, to create an immersive physical environment.

How many outlets?

☐ **Intensive distribution** – Many outlets, important for frequently purchased and impulse goods.

☐ **Selective distribution** – Strategy for durable shopping goods, bought occasionally where customers like to compare various brands and get retail advice.

☐ **Exclusive distribution** – Few distributors are given exclusive rights within a particular market (e.g. geographic region). The relationship between the manufacturer and the distributor is very well developed. Prada and other high end fashion brands adopt this approach.

Exercise

In the UK, Tesco have nearly 30% market share for fast moving consumer goods (FMCG).

Why should manufacturers seek to sell through Tesco? Are there any reasons why a company would not want a Tesco listing?

Channel length

Direct selling offers control but longer channels. Selling through wholesalers and retailers can be essential when trying to reach an unfamiliar market or resources are limited. Each member of the channel should support and promote the product to their customer – the next in the chain. This is known as a push strategy.

Manufacturer	End customer			
Manufacturer	Retailer	End customer		
Manufacturer	Wholesaler	Retailer	End customer	
Manufacturer	Agent	Wholesaler	Retailer	End customer
Channel length				

Figure 6.8: Channel length

A business cannot assume that all potential merchants will stock their brand. Distributors should be viewed as customers and offered a package of benefits to create long term value and partnerships. Distributors want to be reassured that any products will realise profit, will be supported by the manufacturer with promotional activity that stimulates demand and that enough inventory will be available. They may insist on exclusivity, point of sale materials, training and additional incentives.

Retailers hold a great deal of power over manufacturers and UK supermarkets have been criticised for acting in ways that are unfair, such as buying land and keeping it empty to prevent competition; delisting products at short notice; insisting on sale or return; or discounting brands too harshly. Care of distributor relationships should therefore be a priority for businesses.

Logistics management

Distribution or place is about getting the product in the right place at the right time to create value for the customer. This includes logistics functions such as order processing, warehousing, transport, delivery and inventory management. Forecasting demand is crucial to all of these activities. Retail chain Zara creates value through rapid logistics, with design and manufacture allowing ranges to be available in store within weeks. Unsold stock is removed, encouraging frequent customer return visits and encouraging loyalty.

Selling online requires a robust web presence, inventory holding, secure payment systems and the capacity to deliver in timely manner.

Example

Herschel Supply Co was set up in 2009 by two brothers in Vancouver, Canada. They design and manufacture backpacks, bags and travel goods using selective distribution. Products are available online (direct from Herschel or via e-tailers such as Amazon) and through bricks and mortar retailers, including department stores. Herschel chooses outlets that provide a suitable sales environment and decline distributors who do not match their own brand image.

The marketing plan

This chapter has introduced the main activities involved in marketing. Marketing needs to be planned and coordinated to create maximum customer value. This section presents an outline marketing plan, which feeds into the overall strategic planning document where overall mission and aims of the organization are stated. The objectives presented in the marketing plan should be achievable through the marketing actions outlined. Each element of the marketing mix will also have its own detailed activity schedule that feeds into the marketing document (Table 6.3).

Table 6.3: Outline marketing plan

Situation/ Context analysis	Internal strengths and weaknesses, external opportunities and threats, including market trends, competitors
Marketing objectives:	Quantified and timescales made clear
Target markets	Clear description of target markets using relevant segmentation criteria
The marketing mix	Product
	Price
	Promotion
	Place
Budget	How much to be spent, allocated to each part of the mix
Measurement	Linked to the objectives
Timescales and people	Responsibility for each activity – internal or using external specialists

■ Setting the budget

The main methods for deciding on the marketing budget are outlined in Table 6.4. Budgets will be allocated across the marketing mix and vary according to the industry, organizational goals and brand recognition.

Table 6.4: Setting the marketing budget

Method	Based on	Pros/cons
Objectives and task	What is required to achieve marketing goals	Regards promotion as an investment not a cost. The link between spend and outcome is not usually so clear.
Matching competitors	Assumes that the amount spent = customer impact and value.	Difficult to estimate competitors spend. Assumes competitors have same objectives.
Percentage of sales	Marketing is seen as a cost	Higher sales increase budget. Reverse approach might be more suitable.
Affordability	The company can only spend what it has	This strategy may limit growth.

Once a plan is ready, it becomes a working document, often referred to and checked to ensure the company is on track. Although a plan may be adapted, planning puts the organization in control and encourages a proactive approach to competitive environmental changes. The very act of planning does not ensure success but without a systematically researched and produced plan then failure is more likely.

Conclusion

Throughout this chapter the essential marketing activities have been discussed. However activities and actions alone are not enough. In order to produce continued, mutually beneficial relationships and create true value the organization must both act and think marketing. Only then can an organization be truly successful.

Further reading

Levitt, T (1960) Marketing myopia, *Harvard Business Review*, **38** (July-August 1960), pp. 24-47

Gronroos, C. (1994), From marketing mix to relationship marketing: Towards a paradigm shift in marketing, *Asia-Australia Marketing Journal*, 2, 1, 9–29.

The above articles are frequently cited and have contributed to change the way that marketing has been viewed.

References

Apple (2015). *App Store Rings in 2015 with New Records and Apple Reports Record First Quarter Results. Apple Press Info.* Available at: https://www.apple.com/uk/pr/library/ [Accessed January 2015]

Baines, P., Fill. C. & Page, K. (2013). *Essentials of Marketing.* Oxford: Oxford University Press

Cellen-Jones, R. (2015). Google Glass sales halted but firm says kit is not dead *BBC News*, 15 January. Available at: http://www.bbc.co.uk/news/technology-30831128 [Accessed May 2015]

CIM (2007). *Tomorrow's Word Re-evaluating the role of marketing.* Available at: www.cim.co.uk/files/tomorrowsword.pdf [Accessed April 2015]

Cookson, R. & Kuchler, H. (2015). Facebook turns to old-fashioned methods for advertising campaign. *Financial Times,* 12 April. Available at: http://www.ft.com/cms/s/0/689454c4-de07-11e4-ba43-00144feab7de.html#axzz3ok3raKRr [Accessed April 15 2015]

Dredge, S. (2014). Apple reveals iPhone and iPad owners spent $10bn on apps in 2013. *The Guardian,* 7 January [online]. Available at: http://www.theguardian.com/technology/2014/jan/07/apple-reveals-iphone-and-ipad-owners-spent-10bn-on-apps-in-2013 [Accessed April 2015]

Facebook. (2015). *Stats.* Available at: http://newsroom.fb.com/company-info/ [Accessed May 2015]

Fahy, J., & Jobber, D. (2012). *Foundations of Marketing.* London: McGraw Hill.

Grönroos, C (1990). Marketing redefined. *Management Decision,* **28** (8): 22-28.

Gronroos, C. (1994). From marketing mix to relationship marketing: Towards a paradigm shift in marketing. *Asia-Australia Marketing Journal,* **2** (1): 9–29.

McDaniel, C., Lamb, C.W. & Hair, J.F (2013). *Introduction to Marketing.* (12th International Edition). South Western: Cengage Learning.

Levitt, T. (1960). Marketing myopia. *Harvard Business Review.* July- August, 1960

Levitt, T. (1986). *The Marketing Imagination.* NY: The Free press.

McCarthy, E. J. (1960). *Basic Marketing, a Managerial Approach.* IL: Richard D. Irwin.

O'Reilly, L & Lusch, A. (2015). Watch all the 2015 Super Bowl ads here, *UK Business Insider.* Available at: http://uk.businessinsider.com/the-2015-super-bowl-ads-2015-1 [Accessed Feb 2015]

Phillips, L. & Clews, S. (2013). Marketing communications. In Gbadamosi, A., Bathgate,I.K. & Nwankwo, S. Eds. (2013). *Principles of Marketing: A Value-Based Approach.* London: Palgrave McMillan.

Segment (2013). *Segmented marketing for energy efficient transport*. Available at: http://www.segmentproject.eu/ [Accessed March 2015]

Spann, M., Fischer, M. & Tellis, G.J. (2015) Skimming or penetration? Strategic dynamic pricing for new products. *Marketing Science*. **34** (2): 235-249.

Sweeney, M. (2014). UK set to be first country in which more than half of ad spend goes digital, *The Guardian*. Available at: http://www.theguardian.com/media/2014/dec/01/gadget-obsessed-uk-top-digital-advertising-spend [Accessed May 2015]

Stone, M. & Desmond, J. (2010). *Marketing Fundamentals*. Edinburgh: Heriot-Watt Management Programme.

Tellis, G.J. (1986). Beyond the many faces of price: An integration of pricing strategies. *Journal of Marketing*. **50** (October):146–160

The Economist. (2011). Global stretch. When will Zara hit its limits? *The Economist*. Available at: http://www.economist.com/node/18333093/ [Accessed 24 March, 2015]

Unilever. (2015). *View our brands*. Available at: http://www.unilever.co.uk/brands-in-action/view-brands.aspx [Accessed May 2015]

6

7 The Human Resource Management Function

Kehinde Olowookere and Katherine Sang

Organizations come in different shapes and sizes, from small convenience stores to large multinationals. However, one common element found in any organization, regardless of size, shape or purpose is *people*, otherwise known as human resources (HR). Organizational success is largely dependent on such human resources (Petrone, 2014). As Petrone argues, a company is only as strong as its people. People construct organizational goals, bring creativity, skills and competencies, and largely make up the organization. Organizations, however, need to manage their people. Indeed managing HR is a fundamental part of the relationship between an organization and its people. The Human Resource Management (HRM) function is often given this responsibility in organizations. Torrington *et al.* (2005) define HRM as a continuous balancing act between fulfilling an organization's goals and objectives, and those of employees. Effective management of HR should merge the needs of individuals with the demands of the organization. This chapter will examine the particular ways through which the HRM function achieves these objectives.

Strategic role of HRM

The HRM function can be carried out at two levels, either operational or strategic. At the operational level, there is a heavy emphasis on the organization of everyday tasks, such as supporting line managers, recruitment, selection, training and development, serving as a channel for employees' concerns, personnel record keeping, and managing/negotiating collective bargaining agreements. For the strategic level, there is more emphasis on relating everyday tasks to organizational strategy (Golding, 2004). Activities will often include facilitating and managing employees in order to ensure that organizational goals are met, and aligning HRM goals with organizational goals. This, for instance, could mean ensuring that the necessary skills are evident within the workforce, or ensuring there is diversity and opportunities for career development. Most HRM tasks can be performed at both the operational and strategic levels, although in modern organizations emphasis is often on the strategic role of HRM. HRM tasks would, therefore, usually be incorporated into overall organizational strategy. The main objective is to develop HR practices, policies and strategies to deal with the employment and development of employees, and the relations that develop between employees and the organization.

The role of HRM in modern organizations has, thus, extended beyond functions such as recruitment and selection or personnel record keeping, to encompass equality and diversity, welfare, health and safety, employee relations, reward management, performance appraisal, training and development, and HR planning amongst other things. In addition, HR has the responsibility to conform to employment laws and legislation. The HRM role has therefore, come to be regarded as a 'specialist' role in organizations (Tracey and Nathan, 2002). It is nevertheless important to note that the HRM function is increasingly being outsourced and decentralized to line managers, in order to save costs. Beardwell and Claydon (2007) note that the majority of contemporary organizations have had to break down hierarchies and outsource several functions in order to save costs (e.g. we see catering and cleaning being outsourced within the National Health Service in the UK). These cost-cutting exercises yield short-term benefits, but they could result in the shortage of skilled staff. Even though the HRM function is increasingly being outsourced in organizations, it continues to play an important role in determining organizational success. Torrington *et al.* (2005) provide a simple illustration of the HRM function even further, suggesting that there are four major objectives for the function. The four objectives are illustrated in Figure 7.1, and discussed in the following sections.

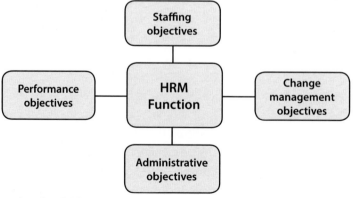

Figure 7.1: Strategic role of HRM

Exercise

Spend 5 minutes outlining what you think the role of HRM is within organizations.

Staffing objectives

There are three main tasks for the HRM function of an organization, in relation to staffing. The first relates to ensuring that the organization has the appropriate number of staff employed within it; second, the HR manager ensures that the organization employs staff suited to organizational goals, who will aid in competing effectively in the labour market; and third, the HR manager is in charge of writing contracts for staff. Making sure that the organization has the appropriate staff means assessing whether the workforce is of the correct size, and whether employees have the appropriate skills. HR managers can ensure an organization has appropriate staffing through the process of recruitment and selection. The recruitment and selection process comprises of four broad stages. These include:

- ☐ Carrying out a job analysis;

- ☐ Drawing up a person specification;

- ☐ Attracting/recruiting suitable applicants; and

- ☐ Assessing and selecting suitable candidates.

To begin, an HR manager will undertake a job analysis. This will require an assessment of the job, including whether it needs to be filled, and what the skills needs of that job are. This may comprise analysis of the work activities, the worker attributes required, and the work context (Sanchez and Levine, 2012). These are then used to build the person specification for the job, which sets out the type of applicant required, for example, does the job require a person with a specialist degree, or with line management experience? The person specification is then used to attract applicants to the role. This could include internal recruitment, such as promoting someone from within the organization. Alternatively, a decision may be made that the position requires external expertise. The job may then be advertised through websites, job centre boards, or professional trade journals. For senior positions, organizations may approach a head hunting company to secure a range of appropriate applicants. In addition, organizations may decide that they wish to recruit promising new trainees, resulting in a graduate recruitment scheme (Favell, 2008). Whatever the approach to recruitment, all applicants are then assessed in order to move to the process of selection.

7

Selection is the process by which the full list of applicants is assessed, eventually moving to the selection of the appropriate candidate to fill the vacant position. The complete list of applicants will be examined, possibly by the HR manager and the prospective line manager. This process may differ depending on the job to be filled. For senior positions, there may be a selection panel that will review all applications and identify a short-list. As Torrington *et al.* (2008) identify, a selection panel can reduce the chances that shortlisting decisions are made according to arbitrary criteria, such as the gender of the applicant. The shortlisting panel should select a shortlist based on those applicants who meet the agreed essential criteria of the position. A panel should then reach a consensus on the shortlist. Once the shortlist has been agreed, the HR team can then move to a detailed assessment of the shortlisted applicants. The recruitment and selection process is a key point at which equality and diversity should be considered (Analoui, 2007). Despite a range of equality legislation (covered later in this chapter), certain demographic groups are still discriminated against in the labour market. Holgersson (2013), for instance, revealed that managers prefer to recruit managers who are like them. This is called 'homosociality' and since most managers are men, this leads to a cycle of recruitment of men, by men. Women are thus excluded during both the recruitment and selection phases.

> As at 2014, the proportion of women aged 25-65 in the UK, who work is 69%, while for men it is 82% (Azmat, 2015).

The HR manager is also in charge of setting up the employment contract. The employment contract comes into existence when employment is offered by an organization and accepted by a prospective employee. Such contracts form the legal basis of employment relationships, and would usually be administered by the HR manager. Recruitment and selection processes are increasingly being aimed at diverse employees, with several options being made available. Employees could be part-time or full-time, temporary or permanent. Having employment contracts helps an organization manage these various terms of employment.

The relationship between an organization and its employees is therefore based on an employment contract. Basic terms and conditions of the job are set out, and where needed, can be applied in a court. Once agreed on, the terms of a contract cannot be modified without the consent of both parties. Employers, for instance, cannot decide singly to increase an employee's working hours, or reduce pay. Where this is necessary, both employee and employer need to be in agreement. When changes are made by employers without some form of agreement, either with union representatives or with employees themselves, there could be a legal case for unfair employment relations.

Exercise

List the methods that organizations could use to:

1   Recruit new employees

2   Select the appropriate employee.

What are the advantages and disadvantages of these methods?

Performance objectives

Ensuring that organizational performance objectives are met requires attention to three key areas:

☐ Staff motivation;

☐ Discipline of staff; and,

☐ Employee involvement.

Efforts to improve employee motivation are underpinned by beliefs that increased motivation will result in improved performance and reduced employee turnover or absenteeism. Managers and HR professionals may attempt to improve motivation through reward systems such as performance related pay. However, research provides weak support for a direct relationship between rewards, motivation and performance. Indeed, there is little evidence of a positive relationship between pay and performance (Gerhart and Fang, 2014). It may be that intrinsic motivation, such as the extent to which individuals perceive themselves to have mastery over the skills required for their job, has a positive relationship to performance, but this relationship is complicated and may change over time (Cerasoli and Ford, 2014). Increasing the motivation of staff may include training and development. In order to achieve performance objectives, it is necessary for line and HR managers to monitor the performance of staff. This can be achieved through an appraisal system. An individual's performance can be appraised according to three criteria set out by ACAS (Advisory, Conciliation and Arbitration Service, 2014) namely:

☐ The objectives which an employee should meet;

☐ The competencies needed for the individual to meet those objectives; and

☐ A discussion of the employee's personal objectives.

A performance appraisal may contain some regular informal meetings to discuss both personal and organizational objectives, and progress towards meeting agreed objectives. In addition, formal annual and possibly interim meetings should be held to identify employees' competencies, where there is partial performance, and how the organization can support the employee to develop further. DeNisi and Smith (2014) find no convincing link between performance appraisal and individual performance, although there does appear to be an indirect relationship between packages of HR practices and firm level performance. It is important that appraisers consider why performance may be partial, including sickness, poor interpersonal relationships at work or lack of necessary skills. Where performance continues to be below average, there may be need for disciplinary action. As noted by ACAS (Advisory, Conciliation and Arbitration Service, 2012), if an organization has tried unsuccessfully to support an employee's performance, there may be need for disciplinary action. Such action could involve writing to the employee first, followed by a meeting with the employee to discuss how performance objectives will be achieved within a specific period. These sorts of meetings, and whatever disciplinary action an organization decides to take, should not be aimed at punishing past performance, but rather it should be aimed at improving future performance.

Example

An employee makes a number of mistakes on invoices to clients. The organization brings the mistakes to the employee's attention, makes sure they have proper training, yet mistakes continue to occur. The organization may then invite the employee to a disciplinary meeting and an improvement plan is developed (ACAS, 2006).

Employee involvement has been identified as a route to improved organizational performance (Gruman and Saks, 2011). Involvement can take a number of forms, including formal routes such as trade unions or staff associations, and varies in the extent to which employees are involved in organizational decision-making (Marchington and Wilkinson, 2005). Employees may be involved in making decisions about how their work is organized, the development of new policies, or the strategic decisions of the organization. Evidence from large organizations suggests that involving employees in the design of staff well-being programmes can increase participation in training, and increased awareness of organizational policies (Gyi *et al.*, 2013). In addition, there is evidence that when increased employee involvement forms part of a package of HRM strategies, benefits may be observed in organizational financial performance (Akhtar *et al.*, 2008). However, it is important to remember that when organizations talk about employee involvement, this may take a number of forms: from the use of notice boards to inform staff of changes, to having formal meetings with employees. Therefore, claims of employee involvement must be taken with caution.

Change-management objectives

Organizations do not remain stable; change is inevitable and continuous. HR teams are key to supporting staff during change, while also remaining attentive to organizational objectives. Changes may occur due to external factors, including developments to legislation, which are discussed later in this chapter. In addition, changes may occur in the broader economy. Gyi *et al.*'s (2013) study demonstrates the dramatic impact the 2008 economic recession had on efforts to improve the health and well-being of employees. This included loss of key staff due to poor financial performance and relocation of occupational health professionals. Change may be predictable, as is the case with the introduction of new software, or unpredictable in the form of a natural disaster.

7

Example

Cigna Healthcare in the United States implemented a more focused production procedure in 2003 called the Six Sigma; this organizational change was needed in order to reduce operating costs and improve services. (Joseph, 2013)

However, change may be more incremental, and include the need to improve the internal culture of an organization. Whatever the driver of change, the successful adoption of new practices is key to its success. As discussed in the previous section, employee participation in the design of organizational change can result in increased staff buy-in (Gyi *et al.*, 2013). One often cited model of successful change is Kotter's (1996) 8-Step Process. The 8 steps are presented in Table 7.1.

This model is popular and provides an apparently discrete set of steps which organizations can adopt to increase the likelihood of a successful change process. Evidence from healthcare settings, for instance, suggests that adoption of Kotter's model can foster successful organizational change (Csont *et al.*, 2014). Yet, several argue that not all steps are relevant in all contexts (Gash *et al.*, 2011). Other models of change have been proposed including Lewin's (1958) 3-step model. Lewin's model is similar to Kotter's 8-Step Process, and proposes three different steps for effectively carrying out change in an organization namely unfreezing, moving, and refreezing. The success of any of these models is, nevertheless, largely dependent on how involved employees are during the change process. Employee involvement aids in encouraging employee acceptance. HR can ensure that employees are fully involved in the process of change by keeping them informed. More importantly, the employees in charge of the change process need to be adequately equipped with the appropriate skills for managing change.

Table 7.1: Kotter's (1996) 8-Step process

Kotter's 8 steps	Guidelines
Step 1: Create a sense of urgency	Identify and discuss any potential risks to the organization and key opportunities
Step 2: Build a guiding coalition	Assemble a team with the skills and competencies for leading the change effort
Step 3: Form strategic vision and initiatives	Create a vision for the change effort and develop strategies for realizing this vision
Step 4: Enlist a volunteer army	Utilise all possible avenues for communicating the vision, and disseminate the strategies developed for attaining the vision
Step 5: Enable action by removing barriers	Eradicate possible barriers to accomplishing the change
Step 6: Generate short term wins	Recognise and reward employees who contribute to the change effort
Step 7: Sustain acceleration	Reinvigorate the change effort with new plans, ideas, and tasks
Step 8: Institute a change	Articulate the relationship between the change effort and organizational success

Exercise

How can HR managers keep employees involved during organizational change?

Administrative objectives

Organizations should have all-inclusive and accurate information on their employees. Such information could range from personal details to contract terms, training experiences, or even attendance records (Torrington *et al.*, 2005). There are legal reasons for keeping employee records which could pertain to administering pay and pension funds, health and safety, provision of leave or tax contributions. More importantly, keeping such records aids in ensuring that organizational processes and systems run smoothly, and helps maintain credibility within organizations. The HRM function is often in charge of these administrative duties. While this HRM objective may be less related to organizational strategy compared to the other objectives discussed above, it does play a major role in organizational effectiveness and productivity. One of the major administrative roles of the HRM function revolves around 'pay'.

Pay

Pay and rewards refer not only to the monetary sum an employee is paid, but also encompass the nature of employment contracts. Pay represents the most visible transaction between an employee and the organization, and is negotiated as part of the employment contract, whereby organizations agree to pay certain benefits in exchange for employees' commitment, skills or time. Of particular significance, in the administrative role of HRM, is the need to manage and administer pay/reward legitimately and professionally. This is often achieved by making detailed monthly pay statements available for employees. According to Arnold (2005), pay is a dominant factor which an employee considers when deciding to work with an organization. Therefore, the HRM function may place importance into recruiting, selecting, training, developing and managing employee performance, but where issues exist with pay and rewards, the efforts could be in vain. If an employee, for instance, is employed by an organization, trained and developed, but receives unsatisfactory pay, such an employee may prefer to leave the organization. Several factors need to be considered when determining and managing pay, such as pension fund contributions, tax payments, National Insurance, Statutory Maternity Pay, and Statutory Sick Pay. It is HR's responsibility to ensure that all such factors are considered when determining the appropriate pay/reward for job positions. In addition, pay systems should be organized such that organizational and employee objectives are aligned. The aim should be to motivate and retain employees who are suited to organizational goals. There is, therefore, an inherent connectedness between adequate pay systems and the strategic role of HRM.

One of the major means for managing pay, and ensuring that there is a balance between pay and employee productivity, is the use of job evaluations. Job evaluations help in ensuring that pay systems are fair by linking particular pay rates to particular job prerequisites. It highlights how and why some jobs have more pay than others, and the value of jobs in relation to one another. With the use of job evaluation exercises, HR managers can ensure that pay is equitable, which aids in maintaining fairness in organizational reward systems. In addition, pay and reward systems need to be externally competitive. Job evaluations can help an organization maintain externally competitive reward systems. Arnold (2005) suggests having surveys of similar jobs in the labour market on an annual basis, in order to ascertain the competitiveness of an

7

organization's pay system. Furthermore, the method used for determining pay, and the manner in which pay is administered, is largely dependent on legal requirements, as well as a number of external factors. It is important that HR keeps up to date with ever-changing employment legislation, in order to ensure compliance with employment laws. Some of the legal requirements and external influences which influence pay and HRM will be examined in the next section.

Exercise

Rewards can either be in monetary or non-monetary form. Describe three non-monetary rewards, and how such rewards can be used for motivating employees.

External influences on HRM

Several external factors affect organizations to varying degrees, and can influence HRM practices and processes. With increasing globalization, labour markets are continually changing, and organizations need to be responsive and adaptive to these changes. These could be in terms of changing markets, evolving economics, legislations, or population demographics. There could be periods of boom, where there is plenty of work to go around, or recessionary periods, where organizations may need to make people redundant. The population is also becoming increasingly diversified; therefore, employers must consider the needs of different employees when designing and implementing policies. Diversity here could be with regards to age, gender, race, disability, or ethnic background, amongst other characteristics. There are, for instance, an increasing number of women in the labour market. Also, in countries with the ageing population, there is an increasing representation of older employees in the workplace. In the UK, the abolition of the Default Retirement Age (DRA) has made this particularly apparent; employees no longer have to retire at a set age, and as noted in an ACAS (Advisory, Conciliation and Arbitration Service, 2011) report:

> unless it can be objectively justified, it is no longer permissible to dismiss an older worker on grounds of retirement (pp. 5).

These are factors that impact on organizational processes in several ways. Employees in a similar age range, for instance, could have similar background experiences, and this could shape behavioural or attitudinal work characteristics (Beechler and Woodward, 2009). Differences in age could result in conflict, but could also be the source of organizational learning and development (Smola and Sutton, 2002). These factors need to be taken into consideration when developing HRM strategies. More importantly, HR managers need to stay up to date with changes in the external environment. Such knowledge aids in the formulation of fitting organizational practices and policies. The following sections provide an outline of the legislative framework in the UK regarding equality and diversity. Some of the major policies that impact on the HRM function are considered. Other countries may have similar legislation.

Employment legislation

Preventing discrimination, at any stage in employment relationships, is becoming imperative in the UK. Several policies, such as the Equal Pay Act 1970, Sex Discrimination Act 1975, Race Relations Act 1976, and Employment Acts 2002 and 2008, have been established over the years in order to prevent discrimination against 'minority' groups, and provide protection for vulnerable workers in the workplace. Organizations have a legal obligation to adhere to such policies. Some of these employment legislations are examined in the following sections.

☐ **Equal Pay Act 1970** – The first employment law in the UK to promote equality at work was the Equal Pay Act 1970 (Torrington *et al.*, 2005). This Act largely focused on preventing discriminatory practices on gender basis, with regards to employment conditions and rates of pay. The Equal Pay Act had a significant influence on the establishment of National Minimum wages, which at the time of writing stand at £6.50 for people aged 21 years and over, £5.13 for people aged between 18 to 20, £3.79 for people aged under 18 years, and £2.73 for apprenticeship positions (gov.uk, 2014). The scope of the Equal Pay Act was later extended to incorporate the Sex Discrimination Act.

☐ **Sex Discrimination Act 1975** – The Sex Discrimination Act was established in 1975. The Act focused on eliminating discrimination which occurred on non-contractual basis, such as during provisions of career development opportunities, or during recruitment and selection (Beardwell and Claydon, 2007). The Act protects all employees, including those not under contractual agreements and prospective employees. It is also applicable to both male and female employees, and applies to married individuals. Employees doing the same job should be paid on equal terms, regardless of their gender or marital status.

☐ **Race Relations Act 1976** – The Race Relations Act 1976 is the major Act in the UK that protects individuals from discrimination based on race. The precedents in the Race Relations Act are similar to that in the Sex Discrimination Act; both Acts prohibit 'direct' or 'indirect' discriminatory practices against certain groups. The Race Relations Act does extend

7

beyond discrimination based solely on race, to include ethnicity and nationality. Discrimination on the basis of nationality, for instance, against an Italian employee due to their nationality, is therefore, as prohibited as discrimination based on race.

☐ **Disability Discrimination Act 1995** – This is similar to the Sex Discrimination Act and Race Relations Act. It differs however with regards to its emphasis on direct forms of discrimination. According to the Disability Discrimination Act 1995 (s. 5(1)), "an employer discriminates against a disabled person if for a reason which relates to the disabled person's disability, he [sic] treats him less favourably than he treats or would treat others to whom that reason does not or would not apply". Emphasis is, therefore, on prohibiting direct discrimination against employees and job applicants with any form of impairment or disability. That is, legal cases can only be brought against employers where there is evidence of actual discrimination against disabled individuals. Hence, in the instance given by Hurstfield *et al.* (2004), where an employee on two months sick leave for depression was contacted by his employer that he had been made redundant, a Disability Discrimination Act case can be brought against the employer.

Other Acts have been introduced over time, some of which include the Employment Equality (Religion or belief) Regulations of 2003, the Equality Act (Sexual orientation) Regulations of 2007, and the Employment Equality (Age) Regulations of 2006. The current legislation which incorporates facets of all the afore-mentioned Acts is the Equality Act of 2010.

☐ **Equality Act 2010** – The Equality Act was established in 2010, and incorporates the afore-mentioned Acts. This Act is the major employment law in the UK, and legally protects employees or prospective candidates from discrimination, both in the labour market and the workplace. In addition to the afore-mentioned protected characteristics, the Equality Act prohibits discrimination based on age, unless there is 'objective' and beneficial justification, whereby there is good motive for differential dealings (Torrington *et al.*, 2005). The Act also expands facets of the Disability Discrimination Act to cover indirect discrimination against disabled individuals and makes it imperative that disability not be factored into screening processes. It restricts the conditions under which organizations can screen prospective employees, based on issues of health or disability. The Act expands to prohibit discrimination on the basis of gender reassignment, sexual orientation, marriage, maternity, pregnancy, religion/belief, and prevents discrimination by association or perception (Equality Act 2010), thus strengthening the power of employment tribunals.

Another major area of interest in employment legislations is the issue of health and safety in the workplace. This will be considered in the following section.

Health and safety at work

In the UK About two million individuals experience disability or injury related to work activities annually (Pilbeam and Corbridge, 2010). This results in the loss of numerous working days. For example, the rate of sick leave in the UK related to workplace injuries and impairments is approximately 19 million days per annum, which is about 40 times over the number of days lost due to industrial action (Price, 2004).

> Approximately 27,000 individuals leave work annually due to work-related injuries or disability (Price, 2004).

Employee well-being, and health and safety in the workplace are, therefore, increasingly important. HR has both the legal and moral responsibility to eliminate and minimise any risks to the health and safety of employees. Ensuring the work environment is psychologically and physically safe demonstrates the value placed on employees by organizations. Organizations can, through this, gain employees' loyalty and participation. Several legislations have been instituted with regards to Health and Safety, such as the Factories Act 1961, the Offices, Shops and Railway Premises Act 1963, the Fire Precautions Act 1971, and the Health Act 2006 (which bans smoking in enclosed spaces). The majority of these Acts in the UK have, however, been incorporated into the Health and Safety at Work Act of 1974 (HSW Act), which is the current major legislative Act governing health and safety issues in the workplace. Torrington *et al.* (2005) sum up the major objectives of the HSW Act as:

☐ To secure the well-being, health, and safety of people in the workplace;

☐ To prevent harm to the public from workplace activities;

☐ To minimise the usage and storage of dangerous materials; and

☐ To minimise the emission of potentially hazardous substances in the environment.

The HSW Act requires organizations to provide safe and healthy work environments, maintain an accident reporting book, take fire precautions, prohibit violence at work, provide safe working systems, maintain plant and equipment, and consult with trade union safety representatives, among other things

(Torrington *et al.*, 2005). All the afore-mentioned legislations change regularly and it is the role of the HR function to stay up to date with the changes.

It is important to remember that the size of an organization can play a major role in determining the makeup of its HRM function. In large organizations, the resources are more likely to exist to support the existence of a formal HR department, employing specialists in employment legislations, equality and diversity, occupational health and other areas of responsibility for HR. However, within smaller enterprises, these resources are less likely to exist. As the research by Cassell *et al.* (2002) demonstrates, HRM is often ad hoc and undertaken by non-specialists.

Conclusion

This chapter has examined the role of HR in organizations at a strategic level. The HRM function, as noted, requires ensuring that organizational staffing is appropriate for meeting organizational goals. This encompasses recruitment and selection, managing performance and change, ensuring the smooth running of the organization, and keeping up to date with relevant legislation. These functions occur across the operational (day-to-day) level, such as ensuring staff are paid, and the strategic level, where emphasis is on relating everyday tasks to organizational strategy. In modern organizations, the majority of HRM tasks would often be a part of the overall organizational strategy. The role of HR, in modern organizations has therefore, extended beyond operational roles to include strategic roles aimed at fulfilling both organizational and employee goals. However, the roles of the HRM function may differ based on organizational size. This has been illustrated in the afore-mentioned exemplar paper (Cassell *et al.*, 2002). Smaller enterprises may, for instance, lack the resources to employ dedicated HR specialists. Such companies may therefore adopt the principles and practices of HRM, but in less formalized ways than larger companies.

Exemplar paper

Cassell, C., Nadin, S., Gray, M. and Clegg, C. (2002). Exploring human resource management practices in small and medium sized enterprises. *Personnel Review*, **31**(6), 671-692.

This paper examines the HRM function in small and medium-sized enterprises (SMEs), and considers the impact of organizational size on HRM. The authors address the question: Can small companies be managed in the same way as large companies?

Summary

Surveys (n=100) and face to face interviews (n=22) with SMEs

- ☐ 20% have formal HR strategy.
- ☐ 64% have no HR strategy at all or have one but only use it a little.
- ☐ Commonly used practices – equal opportunities, appraisal, development/ recruitment and selection.

Interviews

- ☐ HR function – no key person – or the MD
- ☐ Doubling up of roles
- ☐ Informal systems

Findings

- ☐ Interview data suggests a reliance on informal HRM practices e.g. informal appraisals. Majority took a more creative and tolerant approach to equality and diversity.

- ☐ Majority had no dedicated HRM personnel. If work was done to formalise HR, it was often at the direction of the managing director and the role was usually given to someone else who already had a key task, such as the Managing Director's personal assistant. There was an acknowledgment of the vital role of HRM, but not necessarily as a separate function.

- ☐ Data suggests that smaller companies are adopting the principles and practices of HRM, but in less formalized ways than larger companies. Hence, HRM in such companies may not be at the strategic level (i.e. aligning their HRM policies with the organizational goals). Few SMEs adopt a strategic method of HRM; rather a more traditional small firm approach is often adopted.

- ☐ Larger organizations are more likely to have formal HRM, which is strategically aligned.

- ☐ The paper, therefore, presents evidence that size/age of organizations, and the prevalence of paid staff could play a role in shaping the HRM function in organizations.

- ☐ It is important to note that we cannot draw generalizations, given that there are a huge variety of organizations under the umbrella of SMEs. Also the birth and death rate of new firms is rapid.

Exercise

List five ways in which organizational size might affect the HRM function.

Who to read

Armstrong, M. (2012). *A Handbook of Human Resource Management Practice*. 12th ed., London: Kogan Page Limited.

Bratton, J., & Gold, J. (2007). *Human Resource Management: Theory and Practice*. London: Palgrave Macmillan.

Harrison, R. (1993). *Human Resource Management: Issues and Strategies*. Addison-Wesley: Wokingham.

Lawler, E. (1973). *Motivation in Work Organizations*. Monterrey, CA: Brooks.

Walters, M. (1995). *Performance Management Handbook*. London: IPD.

Taylor, S. (2002). *The Employee Retention Handbook*. London: CIPD.

Torrington, D., Hall, L., & Taylor, S. (2008). *Human Resource Management*. 7th ed., England: Pearson Education Limited.

References

Advisory, Conciliation and Arbitration Service ACAS (2006). Discipline and grievance at work. Available at: http://www.acas.org.uk [Accessed 21 June, 2015].

Advisory, Conciliation and Arbitration Service ACAS (2011). Working without the default retirement age. Available at: http://www.acas.org.uk/ [Accessed 9 April, 2015].

Advisory, Conciliation and Arbitration Service ACAS (2012). Managing performance for small firms. Available at: http://www.acas.org.uk [Accessed 21 June, 2015].

Advisory, Conciliation and Arbitration Service ACAS (2014). Advisory booklet – how to manage performance. Available at: http://www.acas.org.uk [Accessed 21 March, 2015].

Akhtar, S., Ding, D., & Ge, G. (2008). Strategic HRM practices and their impact on company performance in Chinese enterprises. *Human Resource Management*, **47**(1) pp.15-32.

Analoui, F. (2007). *Strategic Human Resource Management*. London: Thomson Learning.

Arnold, E. (2005). Managing Human Resources to improve Employee Retention. *The Health Care Manager*, **24**(2) pp. 132-140.

Azmat, G. (2015). *Gender Gaps in the UK Labour Market: Jobs, pay and family-friendly policies*. London School of Economics and Political Science: Centre for Economic Performance.

Beardwell, J., & Claydon, T. (eds.) (2007). *Human Resource Management: A Contemporary Approach*. 5th ed., Harlow: Prentice Hall.

Beechler, S., & Woodward, I. (2009). The Global War for Talent. *Journal of International Management*, **15**(3), 273–285.

Cassell, C., Nadin, S., Gray, M., & Clegg, C. (2002). Exploring Human Resource Management practices in Small and Medium sized enterprises. *Personnel Review*, **31**(6) 671-692.

Cerasoli, C., & Ford, M. (2014). Intrinsic motivation, performance, and the Mediating role of mastery goal orientation: A test of Self-determination theory. *The Journal of Psychology*, **148**(3), 267-286.

Csont, G., Groth, S., Hopkins, P., & Guillet, R. (2014). An evidence-based approach to breastfeeding neonates at risk for hypoglycemia. *Journal of Obstetric, Gynecologic, & Neonatal Nursing*, **43**(1) 71-81.

DeNisi, A., & Smith, C. (2014). Performance appraisal, performance management, and firm-level performance: A review, a proposed model, and new directions for future research. *The Academy of Management Annals*, **8**(1) 127-179.

Disability Discrimination Act (1995). Available at: http://www.legislation.gov.uk/ukpga/1995/50/contents [Accessed 10 December, 2014].

Equality Act (2010). Available at: https://www.gov.uk/equality-act-2010-guidance [Accessed 10 December, 2014].

Favell, I. (2008). Recruitment. In: Muller-Camen, M., Croucher, R., & Leigh, S. (eds.). *Human Resource Management: A case study approach*. London: Chartered Institute of Personnel and Development.

Gash, T., McCrae, J., & McClory, J. (2011). Transforming Whitehall departments. Evaluation Methodology. Available at: http://www.instituteforgovernment.org.uk/sites/default/files/publications/evaluation_methodology_for_whitehall_transformation_.pdf [Accessed 5 March, 2015].

Gerhart, B., & Fang, M. (2014). Pay, intrinsic motivation, extrinsic motivation, performance, and creativity in the workplace: Revisiting long-held beliefs. *Annual Review of Organizational Psychology and Organizational Behavior*, **2**(1).

Golding, N. (2004). Strategic Human Resource Management. In: Beardwell, I., Holden, L., & Claydon, T. (eds.). *Human Resource Management: A Contemporary Approach*. 4th ed., London: FT Prentice Hall, pp. 32-71.

Gov.uk (2014). National Minimum Wage rates. Available at: https://www.gov.uk/national-minimum-wage-rates [Accessed 20 December, 2014].

Gruman, J., & Saks, A. (2011). Performance management and Employee engagement. *Human Resource Management Review*, **21**(2) pp.123-136.

Gyi, D., Sang, K., & Haslam, C. (2013). Participatory ergonomics: Co-developing interventions to reduce the risk of musculoskeletal symptoms in business drivers. *Ergonomics*, **56**(1) pp.45-58.

7

Holgersson, C. (2013). Recruiting managing directors: Doing Homosociality. *Gender, Work & Organization*, **20**(4) pp. 454-466.

Hurstfield, J., Meager, N., Aston, J., Davies, J., Mann, K., Mitchell, H., O'Regan, S. & Sinclair, A. (2004). *Monitoring the Research Disability Discrimination Act (DDA) 1995*. Disability Rights Commission, Institute for Employment Studies.

Joseph, C. (2013). Factors that may cause change in an organization. Available at: http://smallbusiness.chron.com/factors-may-cause-change-organization-203.html [Accessed 10 December, 2014].

Kotter, J. (1996). *Leading Change*. Boston: Harvard Business Press.

Lewin, K. 1958, Group decision and social change, in *Readings in Social Psychology*, eds. E. E. Maccoby, T. M. Newcomb & E. L. Hartley. Holt, Rinehart and Winston, New York, pp. 197–211.

Marchington, A., & Wilkinson, A. (2005). Direct participation and involvement. In: Bach, S. (ed.). *Managing Human Resources*. 4th ed., Oxford: Blackwell Publishing pp. 398-423.

Petrone, P. (2014). The real reason companies are taking so long to hire. Available at: http://voiceglance.com/the-real-reason-companies-are-taking-so-long-to-hire/ [Accessed 10 December, 2014].

Pilbeam, S., & Corbridge, M. (2010). *People Resourcing and Talent Planning HRM in Practice*. 4th ed., England: Pearson Education Limited.

Price, A. (2004). *Human Resource Management in a Business Context*. 2nd ed., London: Thomson Learning.

Sanchez, J., & Levine, E. (2012). The rise and fall of job analysis and the future of work analysis. *Annual Review of Psychology*, **63**, 397-425.

Smola, K., & Sutton, C. (2002). Generational differences: Revisiting generational work values for the new millennium. *Journal of Organizational Behavior*, **23**(4) 363-382.

Torrington, D., Hall, L., & Taylor, S. (2005). *Human Resource Management*. 6th ed., England: Pearson Education Limited.

Torrington, D., Hall, L., & Taylor, S. (2008). *Human Resource Management*. 7th ed., London: FT Prentice Hall.

Tracey, B., & Nathan, A. (2002). The Strategic and Operational roles of Human Resources: An Emerging Model. *Cornell Hotel and Restaurant Administration Quarterly*, **42**(2) pp. 38-45.

8 Gender and Work-life Balance

Steven Glasgow and Katherine Sang

The concept of work-life balance is an increasingly important issue in today's society as a result of changing labour demographics. The traditional 9-5 working week cannot cater for all workers and many employers recognise this. Research from the CIPD (2012) indicates that 96% of employers in the UK offer some form of work-life balance practice, with part-time working (88%) and homeworking (54%) being the most common arrangements offered. Despite the increased interest in the work-life balance, there is ambiguity around what work-life balance is. Much of the confusion comes from a lack of agreement over what constitutes 'work', and what is 'life'. This chapter explains the concept of work-life balance, the measures organizations can take to support the work-life balance of its members and the potential benefits and barriers associated with their implementation. The chapter also considers the role of gender in work-life balance, as women are more likely than men to use a work-life balance policy, with 77% working flexibly in some way (CIPD, 2012).

What is work-life balance?

The relationship between employees' working lives and their non-working lives has been recognised as a concern at national levels across Europe (Crompton and Lyonette, 2006) and is driving policy at governmental level (Gregory and Miller, 2009). This relationship is often called: *work-life balance*, a widely used term with no set definition. It is usually taken by researchers and practitioners to refer to the balance between paid employment and child care. However, this perspective does not take into account other aspects of people's lives, for example, care of parents, partners, adult children or pets. In addition, it assumes that work-life balance is the interaction between paid employment and (unpaid) care work. Broader definitions may include other aspects of 'life', including leisure.

Researchers may consider how these different dimensions of an individual's life interact, referring to work/life conflict. This conflict can arise from the number of hours worked. Those early in their careers may feel pressure to work long hours in order to secure later career success (Sturges and Guest, 2004).

Employers are expressing an increasing interest in work-life balance due to changing labour market demographics. Data from the UK shows that women's labour market participation has increased over the last 40 years, with just under 70% of working age women in paid employment (ONS, 2013). Similar patterns are seen in other western countries but gendered divisions of household labour remain, with women undertaking most childcare work, and men more leisure time (Craig *et al.*, 2012). The gendered aspects of work-life balance are discussed in some detail later in this chapter. Further, patterns of work intensification across western countries is associated with poor work-life balance (Macky and Boxall, 2008).

An assumption underlying the development of work-life balance policies within organizations is that they will increase performance and reduce turnover and absenteeism, which are key aims of the HRM department. However, the evidence is mixed in this regard, with some suggestion that work-life balance can improve retention (Duffield *et al.*, 2011) or decrease engagement (Timms *et al.*, 2015).

Exercise

Suggest five measures an organization could put in place to support the work-life balance of its employees. How would these vary between employees who have/do not have young children?

■ Work-life balance practices

Work-life balance practices usually focus around the arrangement of working hours. This is called 'flexible working' and covers three core arrangements;

1   The number of hours worked by an employee,

2   When those hours are worked and,

3   Where those hours are worked.

Employees may work part-time, for example, a parent with a school age child may work between the hours of 10am and 3pm to accommodate the school day. Part-time working can also include working term-time only, or two employees 'job-sharing' one role. The timing of hours could mean that an employee is full-time, working a core working week of 37 hours, but these hours are condensed over four days. An employee would work longer hours on those four days. Alternatively, an employee may have an arrangement to work a certain number of hours over the course of a 12 month period (annual hours) and these are worked according to care needs. The location of hours can also be adapted in order to support an employee with their non-work needs. Working from home may be possible, for those whose roles permit. The work-life balance practices that can be used by employers include:

☐ Flexible hours,

☐ Home-working,

☐ Condensed hours,

☐ Job-sharing,

☐ Part-time working,

☐ Shift swapping.

It is important to recognise that the flexible working arrangements are dependent upon the job role, since some roles are less amenable to the kinds of flexibility to which employees may aspire. Someone working in the service sector, for example a waitress, is unlikely to be able to work from home, much like someone working in a traditional 9-5 occupation is unlikely to be afforded flexible hours. However, flexible arrangements can be more informal, such as, shift based employees swapping their working hours to accommodate responsibilities or other non-work issues, like attending a family wedding.

Work-life balance practices are designed to meet the needs of those with caring duties and such individuals are more likely to make use of them (Goni-Legaz and Ollo-Lopez, 2014), specifically for the care of young children, rather than older family members, spouses or pets. We can see here that 'work-life balance' often refers to the balance between paid employment and unpaid labour, such as childcare. Leisure hours are often neglected in the consideration of work-life balance, by employers and researchers. The relationship between the uptake of flexible work arrangements and employee engagement is complex, with evidence that use of policies is associated with decreased engagement in the long term (Timms *et al.*, 2015).

The approach taken to work-life balance practices is contextual amongst organizations, with each one having their own approach, whether that is formal or informal. A real world example is that of multinational retailer Marks & Spencer, who use a more informal approach. Employees are initially encouraged to raise work-life balance requests informally with their line manager

8

arguing that this both saves time and forges better working relationships (CIPD, 2012). Therefore students must be aware that practices deemed effective in one organization, may not be deemed effective in another.

Benefits of work-life balance practices

Employees with 26 weeks of continual employment have the right to request flexible working, and this right is not restricted to those with children. However, this is only a right to *request* flexible working and employers are not legally obliged to provide such flexible working practices. The adoption of work-life balance practices is not enforceable by Government legislation in the UK meaning for organizations to use these practices, they must be beneficial to the organization itself in some way. It is therefore important to look beyond what work-life balance practices mean for employees and focus on the business case for their implementation.

Advocates for work-life balance practices argue that they lead to an increase in organizational and employee performance. Beauregard and Henry (2009), in their review of literature linking performance with work-life balance practices, found evidence to suggest that employees have peak performance times, where they work more productively at certain times of the day. Employees working flexible hours could work at their peak performance times, which results in a greater output of work than that of a normal 9 to 5 week. Those working from home also report greater productivity, with workers often working longer days by factoring in time they would be away from the home (Kelliher and Anderson, 2009). However, it is important to remember that working from home can make it more difficult for employees to distinguish between working time and non-working time. Smartphones, tablets and home-based internet can all make it much more tempting, and easier, to stay in touch with work when out of the office. Better morale and greater job satisfaction are also cited as consequence of work-life balance practices which, although difficult to quantify, are argued to improve employee performance. A reduction in absenteeism is also proposed as a benefit from the practices (Joyce *et al.*, 2010). For employees with flexible working it is much easier for them to work from home if their child is home sick from school, for example, and therefore unauthorized absence is lower. However, De Menezes and Kelliher (2011) in a review of literature around work-life balance practices found the evidence for lower absenteeism is mixed.

Exercise

Taking the role of being the following employees' manager, discuss which work-life balance practices would be most suitable in accommodating:

- A website designer who has caring responsibilities for a young child.

- A construction worker who must provide round the clock care for an elderly relative, 3 days a week.

- A retail worker who has university lectures to attend 4 mornings a week.

Remember to justify your work-life balance practice decision.

Reiterating the point of fewer absences, the work-life balance has been found to have an impact on the occupational health of employees. Surveys like that of *Flexible working provision and uptake* (CIPD, 2012) reveal that staff reporting poor work-life balance report a range of concerns regarding their well-being, including difficulty sleeping and high levels of stress. This has significant implications for organizations, given that employees with poor work-life balance are also more likely to report a desire to leave their organization (Sang *et al.*, 2009). Further, these issues are starker for women who are more likely to report job dissatisfaction and poor work-related well-being arising from work-life imbalance (Sang *et al.*, 2007).

Another organizational reason for the use of work-life balance practices is that they are argued to retain staff. A new addition to a family or the sudden need to care for a relative can mean an existing worker is unable to perform to the same schedule that they used to. Use of a flexible working policy or a change to part-time hours in these instances would allow a worker to satisfy the demands of both work and care. Retaining staff is often preferable to replacing staff, the reason for which is because recruitment results in time and financial costs in the form of advertising and interviewing for the position, as well as additional training costs (Hinkin and Tracey, 2000). Instances of staff retention through work-life balance practices are not limited to workers whose personal circumstances have changed but also helps retain employees who look for employment elsewhere. Boheim and Taylor (2004) maintain that the availability of flexible work policies is a key reason for switching employment. The degree to which staff will be retained is partly dependent on the position held, with higher skilled workers more difficult to replace than those in low-skilled work. Again, it is clear that work-life balance policies and outcomes are different depending on the level within the organization someone is employed, and the nature of their work.

Tip

When answering questions relating to the benefits of work-life balance, remember it is context that matters. Some benefits are more applicable to certain people, jobs and companies than others. Use examples to better illustrate your response.

There are also reports suggesting that work-life balance practices can lead to increased discretionary effort from workers. Torrington *et al.* (2014) suggest that staff appreciate the measures taken by organizations to accommodate their flexible work needs and were inclined to input more effort beyond what their workload requires to repay employers. This suggests that the loyalty and effort made by organizations is shared by employees and as such reinforces the afore-mentioned increased productivity and staff retention.

Work-life balance practices can also result in outside skills feeding back into the workplace. For example, permitting an employee to switch to part-time work so they can enter part-time education can lead to that worker gaining new skills that an organization can benefit from without any cost to itself. Some jobs lend themselves better to this than others, with less skilled work being easier than highly skilled work to go part-time. Management consultancy firm Accenture recognise the potential benefits of outside skills, offering what they term 'Flexleave'. This is a voluntary sabbatical programme that offers employees partial pay in order to pursue their interests; in order to qualify there must be a recognised business need (CIPD, 2012). In summary, the supposed benefits of work-life balance policies are:

- ☐ Staff retention,
- ☐ Greater employee productivity,
- ☐ Reduced absenteeism,
- ☐ Outside skills feeding back into the workplace,
- ☐ Discretionary effort made by employees.

Exercise

As a manager of a small company with limited financial resources, discuss the ways in which you could use work-life balance policies to:

- Reduce costs,
- Attract and retain talented employees,
- Improve company performance.

Try to be innovative in your answers, there are various ways work-life balance policies can be operationalized.

Barriers to work-life balance practices

Despite the increased uptake of work-life balance practices by organizations (CIPD, 2012) and their subsequent benefits, there is still greater employee demand for their adoption than there are employers willing to implement them; this is known as the 'take-up gap'. To understand this phenomenon, the barriers that pertain to limit these practices being extended across all organizations need to be explored.

As previously mentioned in this chapter, the availability of work-life balance practices is partly dependent on the role itself (Wanrooy *et al.*, 2013). Part-time working and flexible hours can be easily incorporated into retail and service occupations but much professional work in the UK is still dependent on the established 9 to 5 work week. The UK labour market is notoriously rigid in this respect and those who cannot fulfil these hours may not be deemed suitable for continuing with a job on a part-time or flexible basis. Indeed, being visible in the workplace in these hours has been found to be necessitated by management in order for team integration and fears of 'slackers' working from home (Felstead *et al.*, 2003). Use of these policies in a 9 to 5 context can also cause a hostile response from those not afforded flexible working arrangements; Kirby and Krone (2002) reported that co-workers questioned whether those in the office were really doing their job or just 'shopping'. The implication of this is that management may be unwilling to adopt work-life balance practices and workers may choose to avoid them to limit hostile responses. Further to this, the use of flexible working – and in particular part-time working – has been linked with a lack of career progression which further limits the desire for their uptake; this is particularly prevalent with women and is discussed further on in the chapter. The established working week and the attitudes of management and other workers display a working culture in the UK labour market that is therefore resistant to work-life balance policies.

The previously discussed cost savings which can be achieved through work-life balance practices can be dependent on an initial outlay cost at the set up phase. Homeworking is a prime example of these costs as the creation of a homeworking environment necessitates the purchase of computing equipment and IT work establishing networks. The start-up costs incurred from work-life balance practices are often offset by the increase in productivity of the worker. However, organizations, especially smaller ones with fewer resources, may not look beyond the initial capital requirement. This is supported by Dex and Scheible's (2001) research into flexible working and small and medium (SMEs) enterprises which found that the cost of work-life balance practices dominated the thought process when dealing with their requests. Although the lack of

8

resources of SMEs can also cause them to become more creative with their benefits package to employees and therefore more inclined to offer work-life balance practices. Costs are not limited to the implementation stage of these policies but also include ongoing administrative and procedural time costs. Therefore, especially in situations involving homeworking, it can be difficult to convince an organization that there is a business case for work-life balance practices. Figure 8.1 shows the balance employers must make between the costs and benefits of implementing a work-life balance policy.

Tip

When discussing the barriers to work-life balance, give thought to how and if these barriers can be potentially alleviated. Doing this may help you demonstrate your critical thinking in exams.

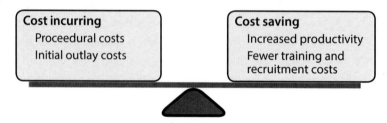

Figure 8.1: The cost savings versus the costs incurred by employers when establishing a work-life balance policy

Work-life balance practices are often introduced as a reaction to the needs of employees rather than part of proactive organizational strategy. What this means is that often work is arranged without the work-life balance in mind and so when these practices are needed by employees, they can be hard to implement. Not all organizations operate this way, with some who actively utilise work-life balance practices to better serve its customers. An example of an organization taking a strategic approach to work-life balance is the UK energy firm British Gas, an illustrative case study outlining their approach is presented below. Organizations need to be proactive in this regard – anticipating the needs of employees, rather than reactively attempting to address work-life balance.

Work-life balance practices can also lead to work intensification. Work intensification is where more is expected from an employee than was previously, with a greater workload in the worked hours. Those who transfer from full-time to part-time hours have been known to be most at risk. Kelliher and Anderson (2009) documented instances where workers found themselves working a full-time position but in reduced hours and for part-time pay. Such can be the case where work-life balance practices are mainly taken by employees out of necessity rather than preference, which limits their potential uptake and scope. In summary, work-life balance policies are often reactionary rather than strategic, and their disadvantages often relate to:

- ☐ The costs to employers of initial outlay and ongoing procedural costs,
- ☐ The difficulty for employees in balancing non-working life with increasing demands of employers (work intensification).

British Gas work-life balance case study

British Gas, the UK energy firm, states that work-life balance practices are a key element in the organization's business strategy. By offering employees various forms of flexible working, the firm claims to create total flexibility for its employees and 24/7 service for its customers. The flexible working provisions offered include allowing time for university students to study, letting people work longer or shorter hours, part-time and full-time roles, flexible hours to allow for childcare, remote working and on occasion, homeworking. British Gas state they offer work-life balance practices to attract and retain the best talent, regardless of background and responsibilities.

The organization believes the practices to be beneficial to its employees, arguing that offering flexible working increases employee loyalty to their brand and provides a great working environment. This is furthered with the HR Director Angela Williams stating:

> "We believe that happy, committed employees lead to a successful, flourishing organization. Offering benefits such as flexible working builds mutual trust between employer and employee. In return, our people reward us with great service and commitment to the business and our customers."

Source: Adapted from CIPD, 2012

Exercise

From reading the case study, outline both the benefits and drawbacks you would expect to see British Gas encounter through their strategic approach to the work-life balance. Would you make any changes to the policy?

British Gas is not the only employer to implement work-life balance policies. There are a range of orga nizations who are rated on their work-life balance policies and these can be found by researching lists of top employers. These lists (in the UK) include those run by Glassdoor, Employers for Work-Life balance, and Indeed.com.

> **Tip**
>
> The use of real world examples shows an examiner that you can apply academic theory into a practical context. Business case studies focusing on the work-life balance can be found at websites such as http://www.greatbusiness.gov.uk/flexible-working/

Gender and work-life balance

Earlier in this chapter, it was explained that the work-life balance is usually used by practitioners to refer to the balance between work and childcare. Research illustrates that men and women have differing experiences when it comes to their roles in the home and the workplace, with women often being the ones responsible for childcare. The feminist movement throughout 1960s and 70s in the UK opened the doors to employment for women, but their role as the main caregivers in the home has changed little. As a result, women are more likely to demand work-life balance practices (Hughes, 2002). It is therefore important to further understand how gender is related to work-life balance.

As there is no legal requirement in the UK for organizations to provide work-life balance practices, it is at their discretion to decide which circumstances constitute a valid reason for asking for them. Requests for work-life balance practices are viewed more favourably when they are for childcare rather than for other life-based needs. As it is women who are often responsible for childcare, it is they who are more likely to request a work-life balance practice. With more women than men taking up these practices, there is a danger that the work-life balance becomes a women's issue, something done to accommodate women with children (Atkinson and Hall, 2009). Indeed, a 'generic female parent' is constructed when work-life balance practices have been discussed in the workplace (Smithson and Stokoe, 2005). Being seen as a women's issue alienates those who wish to take up the practices but do not fit the social norm of someone who undertakes domestic work, men with care responsibilities for example. Indeed men who do care for children or older relatives can face severe penalties, and this is discussed later in the chapter (Sang et al., 2014).

Closely linked to the issue of alienation of other employees, as mentioned earlier, as a barrier to work-life balance practices, those who take these practices are often seen as having special privileges. Other members of the workforce can become resentful of flexible and homeworking practices being offered to women to help with childcare, as work-life balance practices are not universally available to all employees. Thoughts of special privileges can cause a hostile working environment for women with children and even the view that work-life balance practices are undeserved (Lewis, 1997). Examples of this can include dissatisfaction that when holiday allowances are taken up by those with children first, or when time off at Christmas is primarily reserved for parents. It is important for line managers to ensure that holiday time is equitably shared amongst employees.

Taking up a work-life balance practice has also been shown to be career limiting for women. In a study exploring the career paths of accountants and doctors, Crompton and Lyonette (2011) found that women in the mentioned professions felt they had to adapt their career paths in order to accommodate domestic responsibilities. The consequence being that women in these professions were crowded into family-friendly specialities which were viewed as less prestigious than those which necessitated more conventional working patterns. Part-time work in accounting was seen as particularly career limiting as the profession requires long hours in order to progress. Work-life balance practices with their career limiting effects create a view that they are for women with children who do not want a career. So, it seems that caring duties and a desire to have a good career are mutually exclusive – and since women remain responsible for the majority of care work and other domestic labour, this apparent incompatibility is maintained. Despite a few studies, little is known about men's work-life balance, namely, what are the experiences of those men who do engage in care work? This is an area in need of considerable further research to help to reveal the full gendered dimensions of the work-life interface. If research of this kind is not pursued, work-life balance will remain a woman's issue in both research and employment.

8

Tip

Think about how gender and the work-life balance may differ between countries/cultures. How might the UK differ from that of the UAE or Malaysia? Awareness of difference can aid in answering questions involving global organizations.

It is important to note that not all women have the same experience with work-life balance practices. Those in higher paying professions have the option to 'buy' their way out of domestic work through the purchase of childcare and other labour, and so can continue working without the need for these practices. For the women in positions that do not pay as well, they must either take a potentially career limiting work-life balance practice or attempt to negotiate domestic work outside of the office work week. Work-life balance practices are therefore not simply affected by gender but also interrelate with class. Class is not the only influence on women and the work-life balance however. Research by Rouse *et al.* (2013) details the work-life experiences of self-employed black women. The study found that these women had access to fewer economic resources to support their work-life balance, for example, they were less able to pay for a nanny. In addition, these women said they did not have access to social networks to support their childcare needs, and as such were working from 5 a.m. to prepare meals, going to work and then working again in the evenings. As such, ethnicity also needs to be accounted for when looking at the work-life balance. Gender, class and ethnicity are just a few elements that interrelate with work-life balance practices; evidence also suggests that religion and cultural expectations also affect work-life balance experiences (Kamenou, 2008). The intersection of gender with other social demographics is an area in need of further exploration, so organizations can fully understand the needs of their employees.

Despite the drawbacks to women taking up work-life balance practices, there are signs that some organizations are making efforts to implement work-life balance policies that can support women employees. In the UK, examples of this include Athena Swan (aimed to reduce gender inequality in science and technology departments of universities), and the Royal Institute of British Architects which supported the 50:50 campaign aimed at improving the gender balance in the architectural profession. However, the efficacy of such policy initiatives remains in doubt given the persistent gender inequality across the workforce.

Exercise

As an employer, discuss the steps that you could take to ensure that requests for work-life balance practices and those who use work-life balance practices were treated equally. Remember that equal treatment isn't simply affording both men and women flexible working but also concerns mitigating the negative effects workers may experience if using such a practice.

Conclusion

Work-life balance is an area of growing concern for employers, governments and individuals. With more women entering the labour market (while the household division of labour remains relatively static), the needs of women balancing work and caring duties will remain the focus of organizational initiatives. Organizations can benefit from increased retention, reduced unauthorized absence, higher morale and job satisfaction. However, employers must be proactive in managing these issues to help reduce the disadvantages related to financial cost, inter-team dynamics and patchy uptake of policies. It is key that employers do not penalise women for taking up flexible working through assumptions of reduced commitment to the employer.

Overall, it remains to be seen if work-life balance practices do indeed benefit workers. However, information regarding companies that are formally committed to 'fully embracing' work-life balance practices can be found at workingmums.co.uk. The website topemployersforworkingfamilies.org.uk also have awards for companies who supposedly excel in work-life balance practices.

Exemplar paper

Sang, KJC, Dainty, A.R.J & Ison, S. G. (2014). Gender in the UK architectural profession (re)producing and challenging hegemonic masculinity. *Work, Employment and Society.* **28**(2) pp. 247-264.

This study of architects' work-life balance adopted a novel approach, by examining the experiences of men with caring responsibilities. The existing literature has revealed the difficulties women architects report balancing a demanding full-time role as an architect with caring for children. In the Sang et al study, in-depth interviews with male and female architects revealed that work-life balance was problematic for both men and women. However, for male architects who were caring for children or ill parents, the issues were particularly complex. These men were seen to be transgressing societal gender norms, and experienced considerable penalty within the workplace as a consequence. Specifically, the men reported mental health concerns including major depressive episodes. Importantly, the working conditions that made combining paid employment with care work impossible for these men, were perpetuated by women managers. The study reveals that not all men experience the workplace in the same way, and for some men, failure to meet up to the expected standards for men had serious implications for their health and careers as architects.

8

Further reading

Armstrong, M. (2006). *A Handbook of Human Resource Management Practice.* 10th ed., London: Kogan Page Limited.

Bratton, J. & Gold, J. (2007). *Human Resource Management: Theory and Practice.* London: Palgrave Macmillan.

Harrison, R. (1993). *Human Resource Management: Issues and strategies.* Addison-Wesley: Wokingham.

Lawler, E. (1973). *Motivation is Work Organizations.* Monterrey, CA: Brooks.

Taylor, S. (2002). *The Employee Retention Handbook.* London: CIPD.

Torrington, D., Hall, L. & Taylor, S. (2008). *Human Resource Management.* 7th ed., England: Pearson Education Limited.

Walters, M. (1995). *Performance Management Handbook.* London: IPD.

References

Atkinson, C., & Hall, L. (2009). The role of gender in varying forms of flexible working. *Gender, Work and Organization,* **16**(6), pp.650-666.

Beauregard, T. A., & Henry, L. C. (2009). Making the link between work-life balance practices and organizational performance. *Human Resource Management Review,* **19**(1), pp.9-22.

Böheim, R., & Taylor, M. P. (2004). Actual and preferred working hours. *British Journal of Industrial Relations,* **42**(1), 149-166.

CIPD. (2012). *Flexible Working: Provision and uptake.* London: CIPD.

Craig, L., Powell, A., & Cortis, N. (2012). Self-employment, work-family time and the gender division of labour. *Work, Employment and Society,* **26**(5), 716-734.

Crompton, R., & Lyonette, C. (2006). Work-life 'balance'in Europe. *Acta Sociologica,* **49**(4), 379-393.

Crompton, R., & Lyonette, C. (2011). Women's career success and work–life adaptations in the accountancy and medical professions in Britain. *Gender, Work and Organization,* **18**(2), 231-254.

De Menezes, L. M., & Kelliher, C. (2011). Flexible working and performance: A systematic review of the evidence for a business case. *International Journal of Management Reviews,* **13**(4), 452-474.

Dex, S., & Scheibl, F. (2001). Flexible and family-friendly working arrangements in UK-based SMEs: business cases. *British Journal of Industrial Relations,* **39**(3), 411-431.

Duffield, C. M., Roche, M. A., Blay, N., & Stasa, H. (2011). Nursing unit managers, staff retention and the work environment. *Journal of Clinical Nursing,* **20**(1-2), 23-33.

Felstead, A., Jewson, N., & Walters, S. (2003). Managerial control of employees working at home. *British Journal of Industrial Relations,* **41**(2), 241-264.

Goñi-Legaz, S., & Ollo-López, A. (2014). Factors that determine the use of flexible work arrangement practices in Spain. *Journal of Family and Economic Issues,* **36**(3), 463-477.

Gregory, A., & Milner, S. (2009). Editorial: Work–life balance: A matter of choice? *Gender, Work and Organization*, **16**(1), pp.1-13.

Hinkin, T. R., & Tracey, J. B. (2000). The cost of turnover: Putting a price on the learning curve. *The Cornell Hotel and Restaurant Administration Quarterly*, **41**(3), 14-14.

Hughes, C. (2002). *Key Concepts in Feminist Theory and Research*: Sage.

Joyce, K., Pabayo, R., Critchley, J. A., & Bambra, C. (2010). Flexible working conditions and their effects on employee health and wellbeing. *The Cochrane Library*.

Kamenou, N. (2008). Reconsidering work–life balance debates: challenging limited understandings of the 'life'component in the context of ethnic minority women's experiences. *British Journal of Management*, **19**(s1), S99-S109.

Kelliher, C. and Anderson, D. (2010) Doing more with less? Flexible working practices and the intensification of work, *Human Relations*, **63** (1), 83-106

Kirby, E., & Krone, K. (2002). "The policy exists but you can't really use it": Communication and the structuration of work-family policies. *Journal of Applied Communication Research*, 30(1), 50-77.

Lewis, S. (1997). 'Family friendly' employment policies: A route to changing organizational culture or playing about at the margins? *Gender, Work and Organization*, **4**(1), 13-23.

Macky, K., & Boxall, P. (2008). High-involvement work processes, work intensification and employee well-being: A study of New Zealand worker experiences. *Asia Pacific Journal of Human Resources*, **46**(1), 38-55.

ONS. (2013). *Women in the labour market. UK*: Office for National Statistics.

Rouse, J., Treanor, L., Fleck, E., & Forson, C. (2013). Contextualising migrant black business women's work-life balance experiences. *International Journal of Entrepreneurial Behavior and Research*, **19**(5), 460-477.

Sang, K. J., Dainty, A. R., & Ison, S. G. (2007). Gender: a risk factor for occupational stress in the architectural profession? *Construction Management and Economics*, **25**(12), 1305-1317.

Sang, K. J., Ison, S. G., & Dainty, A. R. (2009). The job satisfaction of UK architects and relationships with work-life balance and turnover intentions. *Engineering, Construction and Architectural Management*, **16**(3), 288-300.

Smithson, J., & Stokoe, E. H. (2005). Discourses of work–life balance: Negotiating 'genderblind'terms in organizations. *Gender, Work and Organization*, **12**(2), 147-168.

Sturges, J., & Guest, D. (2004). Working to live or living to work? Work/life balance early in the career. *Human Resource Management Journal*, **14**(4), 5-20.

8

Timms, C., Brough, P., O'Driscoll, M., Kalliath, T., Siu, O. L., Sit, C., & Lo, D. (2015). Flexible work arrangements, work engagement, turnover intentions and psychological health. *Asia Pacific Journal of Human Resources*, **53**(1), 83-103.

Torrington, D., Hall, L., Taylor, S., & Atkinson, C. (2014). *Human Resource Management*, 9th ed: Harlow: Pearson.

Wanrooy, B.V., Bewley, H., Bryson, A., Forth, J., Freeth, S., Stokes, L. & Wood, S. (2013). *Employment Relations in the Shadow of Recession: The 2011 Workplace Employment Relations Study: First Findings*. Palgrave Macmillan

9 Porter's Five Forces and Generic Strategies

Norin Arshed and Jaydeep Pancholi

Competition is what keeps organizations and industries alive. Harvard Business School Professor, Michael Porter, was keen to understand the drivers of success in commercial organizations. His research indicated that industry structure mattered more than individual firm behaviour and his Five Forces model (1979) offers his explanation of the sources of competition at industry level. The model is based on the theory of determining the competitive intensity and attractiveness of a market. The five forces within the model include: competitive rivalry, threat of new entry, supplier power, buyer power, and threat of substitution. The model has been widely used by firms to analyse the external environment and specific external forces like competition, government policies, and social and cultural forces (Vining, 2011). Furthermore, to overcome such fierce competition created by the Five Forces model, and to ensure successful survival, Porter (1985) also introduced competitive strategies to gain a competitive advantage. By combining price and market type, Porter suggests these competitive strategies: cost leadership, differentiation, and market segmentation (or focus) to enable a competitive environment to prosper. This chapter concentrates on establishing and understanding the Five Forces model and the generic strategies.

Porter's Five Forces

Porter (1980, p.80) argues that "understanding the competitive forces, and their underlying causes, reveals the roots of an industry's current profitability while providing a framework for anticipating and influencing competition (and profitability) over time." When Porter introduced the five forces model it "propelled strategic management to the very heart of management agenda" (Grundy, 2006, p.213). Over the years, Porter's model has offered the following insights and attributes into competitive industries:

☐ It implied micro-economic theory into just five major influences.

☐ It effectively and before its time applied 'systems thinking'.

☐ It showed how 'competitive rivalry' is very much a function of the other four forces.

☐ It helped predict the long-run rate of returns in a particular industry.

☐ It went beyond a more simplistic focus on relative market growth rates in determining industry attractiveness.

☐ It helped combine input-output analysis of a specific industry with industry boundaries via entry barriers and substitutes.

☐ It emphasized the importance of searching for imperfect markets, which offer more national opportunities for superior returns.

☐ It emphasizes the importance of negotiating power and bargaining arrangements in determining relative market attractiveness.

☐ It focused managers on the external environment far more than traditional 'SWOT' analysis. (Grundy, 2006, p. 215).

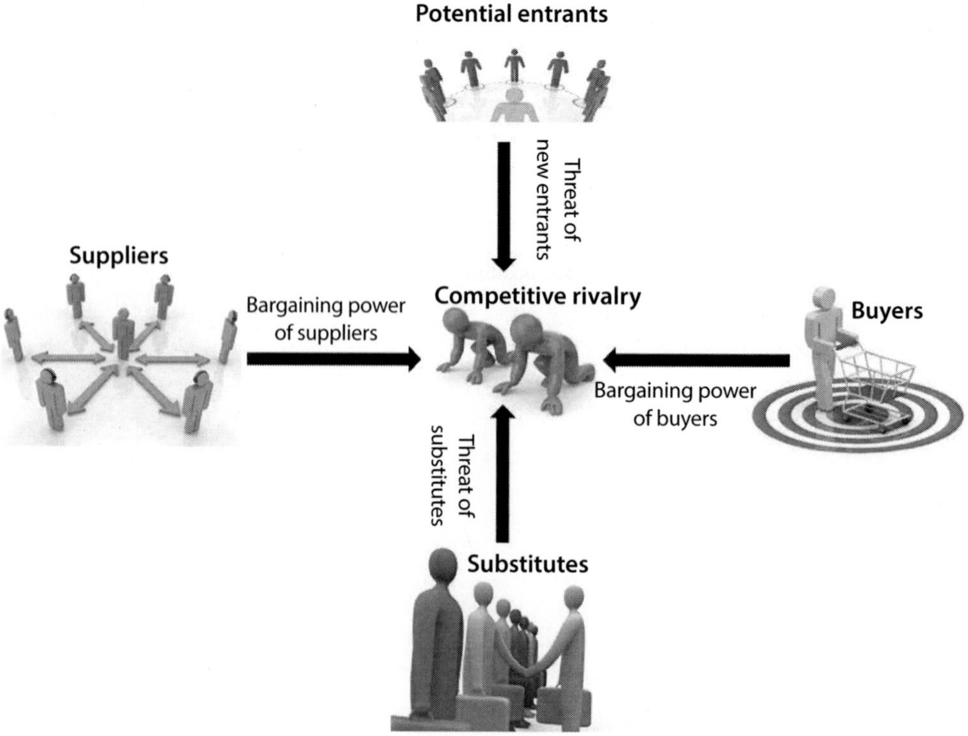

Figure 9.1: Porter's Five Forces Model

As such, to ensure competitive advantage, strategists and organizations need to understand the forces that determine the state of competition in any given industry. The key five forces involve (Figure 9.1):

1 The **ease of entry** (dependent upon entry barriers),

2 The power of **buyers** and,

3 The power of **suppliers**, whereby the bargaining power of each group influences profitability,

4 The availability of **substitutes**, which could potentially include alternatives for consumers, and,

5 The degree of **rivalry** among competitors.

■ Airline industry example

In order to facilitate understanding of these five forces in practice, this chapter will examine each of these forces in relation to the airline industry. Before discussing each force it is important to provide an overview of the airline industry.

The airline industry has evolved over the last 60 years, with more than 8 million people flying daily (IATA, 2015), and 3.3 billion passengers flying in 2014 (equivalent to 44% of the world's population); the global airline industry turnover is estimated at $743 billion in 2014 (IATA, 2014). Despite this ever-growing increase, in 2012 airlines made profits of only $4 for every passenger carried (*The Economist*, 2014). This has been due to the intensive competition and de-regulation (Wang *et al.*, 2015) within the industry, causing price wars that have affected the industry as a whole.

9

Competitive rivalry

Competitive rivalry has been described as the one of the most important of the five forces because it describes the degree of competitiveness amongst companies. If there are companies competing with each other, pressure leads businesses to change prices; this in turn may lead to price wars. Consequently, further investments into research and development may be made, while an increase in the drive for promotion, such as sales and marketing, might be warranted. Given this, organizations will need to increase their costs, in turn lowering their profits. There are a number of factors that determine the intensity of competitive rivalry (Table 9.1).

Table 9.1: Factors affecting competitive rivalry

Factor	Information
Number of competitors in the market	Competitive rivalry will be higher in an industry with many current and potential competitors – all businesses looking to strive for market leadership.
Market size and growth prospects	Competition is always most intense in stagnating markets.
Product differentiation and brand loyalty	The greater the customer loyalty, the less intense the competition. The lower the degree of product differentiation the greater the intensity of price competition.
The power of buyers and the availability of substitutes	If buyers are strong and/or if close substitutes are available, there will be more intense competitive rivalry.
Capacity utilization	The existence of spare capacity will increase the intensity of competition.
The cost structure of the industry	Where fixed costs are a high percentage of costs then profits will be very dependent on volume. As a result there will be intense competition over market shares.
Exit barriers	Even if companies are receiving low or negative returns on investments, it is often difficult or expensive to exit an industry. The major barriers include: Specialized assets Fixed costs of exit Strategic interrelationships Emotional barriers Government and social restrictions

Source: Adapted from Porter (1988)

Intense competitive rivalry has three main benefits. The first benefit involves companies differentiating themselves from one another to gain a larger market share. In such cases they will invest in research and development, allowing innovation to flourish. Second, they will lower prices because of the many choices available to their consumers. The fear of losing a customer to a competitor will mean that not only will prices change but companies will make an effort in understanding and meeting the consumers' demands and tailoring them in accordance. Lastly, competition also drives economic growth where technological advances, such as the introduction of computers and robots, may mean a reduction on the minimum efficient scale of enterprise.

Airline industry example

Competition is intensive amongst rivals in the airline industry. Today, there are many options to get from A to B with different routes offered by different airlines. The airlines all offer different service levels to potential customers. For example, quality of service, food, availability of entertainment, legroom, fare price and so forth. The introduction of privatization and de-regulation within the industry has led to a host of low-cost carriers entering the industry, i.e. Easyjet, RyanAir, AirAisa, Jetstar, etc.

Exercise

Looking at Emirates and British Airways, list the product advancements to consumers that have resulted from competitive rivalry within the airline industry.

■ The threat of entry

The threat of entry involves organizations entering into an industry whereby they will gain market share and competition will intensify. Porter (1979) argues there are six barriers to entry.

1 **Economies of scale** – as the organization produces more, their average costs fall. This makes it more difficult for new and smaller firms to enter the market and be competitive.

2 **Product differentiation** – organizations are forced to increase their spending to overcome customer loyalty to a certain brand. Loyalty is considered as a barrier to entry because some organizations have high degrees of brand loyalty and their consumers stay loyal to a product and their chosen organization. The consumer becomes attached to the brand over time (Shugan, 2005).

3 **Capital requirements** create barriers because to operate organizations require financial resources, such as infrastructure, employees, research and development, advertising and sales. Larger organizations often have the financial support but for smaller organizations this makes it very difficult to enter certain industries, such as technology, manufacturing etc.

4 **Cost disadvantages** – independent of scale, this includes factors such as access to raw materials, favourable locations, government subsidies, experience curve and so forth. These will allow existing organizations to have a competitive edge because those trying to enter the industry's marketplace will not be able to replicate the cost advantage.

5 **Access to distribution** channels is a potential barrier if the new organization has not secured distribution of their product or service.

6   The **government** is a key player because the government is the formal
institution which has substantial and unrivalled power to limit or prevent
entry to industries with various controls (Grimm, 2006).

The attractiveness of an industry will be the main reason why new entrants
will try and enter, alongside the size of the customer base to support the new
entrants' product or service.

Airline industry example

Due to the fact that an airline requires a phenomenal amount of capital to be invested,
the threat of new entrants is low. An existing airline such as British Airways thrives on the
credibility of their reputation, a loyal customer base, routes available all over the world
(both short and long-haul), high standards of safety, etc. making them more attractive to
customers than an emerging company. Also, government regulations within the airline
industry, such as security, health and safety, licenses required for new routes, etc, often
make it difficult for new entrants because of regulations.

Exercise

Think of an industry that a start-up business would find easy to enter. Why does this
industry have low barriers to entry?

■ Buying power

The buying power within the Five Forces model involves those customers who
collectively become a group, powerful enough to exert pressure to either drive
down prices or increase the quality of a good or service for the same price,
therefore reducing profits in an industry. An example of such extreme buying
power in the UK is seen in the dominant supermarkets, Tesco, Sainsbury's,
Morrison's and Asda (known as the 'Big 4'). The Big 4 are able to exert great
power over their suppliers, for example, what food is grown and how it is processed and packaged (Consumers International, 2012). Further to this, several
factors determine the bargaining power of customers:

☐ The purchase of the good or service is bought in large volumes or
quantities.

☐ The product or service being purchased is standard or undifferentiated.
This allows consumers to 'shop around' and then play suppliers off each
other to get the best deals, especially if there are fewer buyers and many
more suppliers.

☐ The buyer is large and the supplier is small, which typically means that the supplier has much more to lose than the buyer.

☐ There are substitutes available from another related industry and supplies are readily available.

☐ Threats of vertical integration – if demands are not met by the suppliers, buyers threaten to provide their own supplies. These demands often include lowering the price of the products and services. Furthermore, buyers can also threaten to backward integrate where they buy the producing firm or its rivals (Porter, 2008).

Airline industry example

When customers make a choice about who to fly with, they often prioritise their time and their financial costs – who will transport them from A to B in the fastest time? In other words, the customer wants the fastest route at the cheapest rate. However, customers also take into account where they can buy the tickets (online versus travel agent), what class of flight they are looking for (economy, business or first) etc. Each airline has different unique selling points, for example EasyJet prides itself in low cost fares whereas Emirates is renowned for the food it offers on its flights. Therefore the bargaining power of buyers is a low threat to the airline industry.

Exercise

Think of a company that has acquired rivals from the same sector. How did they do this and why?

9

■ Supplier power

The power is not only with the buyers but also with the suppliers. The suppliers have power to sell their products at higher prices. An interesting example of supplier power is seen in fast food restaurants. Fast food restaurants depend heavily on their suppliers for the basics of making their business successful – food products, packaging, furniture, napkins, crockery, etc. Given this, potential new entrants to the fast food industry should consider the level of influence and bargaining power of their suppliers; if the suppliers have high levels of influence in the industry, then future projections and growth strategies need to be accounted for due to the likelihood of price increases. There are a number of factors that determine the power of suppliers (Figure 9.2).

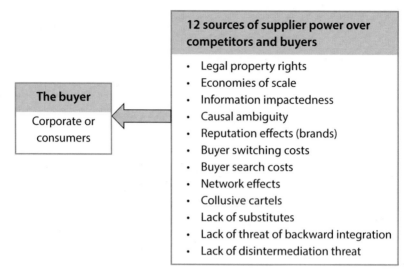

Figure 9.2: The fundamental bases of supplier power over buyers.
Source: Cox (2001, p. 3)

Airline industry example

There are only two firms that supply the airline industry – Airbus and Boeing. This makes it very difficult for airline companies to switch suppliers. Most firms have long term contracts with their suppliers.

Exercise

Given the strength of supplier power within the pizza delivery industry, research and analyse the pros and cons of buying a known franchise or setting up as a sole trader.

■ Threat of substitutes

The threat of substitutes is where "a substitute performs the same or a similar function as an industry's product by a different function … [and] limit an industry's profit potential by placing a ceiling on prices" (Porter, 2008, p. 84). The extent of the threat depends on the:

☐ **Switching costs**: if there are no switching costs – moving from one supplier/buyer to another, then the chances of moving to a more attractive substitute increase. For example, if a consumer wants to replace buying hardcopies of books to reading books online, they will be able to do so without any additional fees or costs for the switch.

☐ **Product price**: if substitutes are priced cheaper or at a fairer rate, this can then attract buyers.

☐ **Product quality**: if the substitute is of higher quality than that of any other product in the market then the chances are that consumers will pay attention to this and switch to the competitor.

Case study – Coca-Cola

Threat of new entrants/potential competitors: Medium pressure

■ Entry barriers are relatively low for the beverage industry: there is no consumer switching cost and zero capital requirements. There is an increasing number of new brands appearing in the market with similar prices to Coke products

■ Coca-Cola is seen not only as a beverage but also as a brand. It has held a very significant market share for a long time and loyal customers are not very likely to try a new brand.

Threat of substitute products: Medium to high pressure

■ There are many kinds of energy drinks/soda/juice products in the market. Coca-Cola doesn't really have an entirely unique flavour. In a blind taste test, people can't tell the difference between Coca-Cola and Pepsi.

The bargaining power of buyers: Low pressure

■ The individual buyer has no pressure on Coca-Cola

■ Large retailers, like Wal-Mart, have bargaining power because of the large order quantity, but the bargaining power is lessened because of the end consumer brand loyalty.

The bargaining power of suppliers: Low pressure

■ The main ingredients for soft drink include carbonated water, phosphoric acid, sweetener, and caffeine. The suppliers are not concentrated or differentiated.

■ Coca-Cola is likely a large, or the largest, customer of any of these suppliers.

Rivalry among existing firms: High pressure

■ Currently, the main competitor is Pepsi, which also has a wide range of beverage products under its brand. Both Coca-Cola and Pepsi are the predominant carbonated beverages and committed heavily to sponsoring outdoor events and activities.

■ There are other soda brands in the market that become popular, like Dr. Pepper, because of their unique flavours. These other brands have failed to reach the success that Pepsi or Coke have enjoyed.

Source: Valuation Academy (2015)

9

Airline industry example

People who are travelling to domestic destinations, for example Glasgow to Aberdeen, have a variety of substitutes to choose from – train, car, aeroplane and bus. Each will have different journey times and costs will vary. However, when travelling to international destinations or long distances there are fewer options available. It may be that to achieve an alternative route, passengers would have to switch mode of transportation, possibly several times, increasing both travel time and cost to a point where the alternative route is so unattractive as to be unviable. Airplanes in this context surpass other modes of transport on cost, convenience and more often quality.

Exercise

Think of three products or services you have substituted (even though the outcome from them is similar) over the past two years. Why was the switch made?

Criticisms of the Five Forces

As with any model, Porter's Five Forces model is not without flaws. Over the years the model has received numerous criticisms. First, the Five Forces model does not assist firms to identify and leverage unique sustainable advantages (Speed, 1989), neither does the model incorporate complementary products. Porter himself argued that competitive forces are not a this sixth force but rather they are factors that act via the original five forces (Miller, 1988). A sustainable advantage might include a unique process, a patent, or specialist skills permitting the business to dominate their industry and push out and exclude competitors. Second, the model focuses on what makes some industries more attractive (cross-sectional problem – *understanding what underpins a competitively advantageous position in an industry*) and not on why some firms are able to get into advantageous positions (longitudinal problem – *getting to an advantageous position again and again*). Third, it overemphasizes competition to the detriment of cooperation. But with cooperation, organizations would become stronger rather than weaker. Fourth, given that the Five Forces model does not adapt to the ever-changing and evolving environment, a snapshot of the industry in one given time period may no longer be the appropriate tool for formulating strategy. For example, the recent downturn in the global economy or the natural disasters effecting Japan, America, Nepal, etc. have caused a shift in politics and economics for many governments. Last, the primary focus of the strategic analysis is the business unit. This unit of analysis is adequate if corporate strategy is seen as a portfolio strategy, but less appropriate if the corporation is viewed as a bundle of resources (Bridoux, 2004).

Given these criticisms it is worth mentioning that it has been suggested that "each of Porter's five forces offers a useful 'window' onto industry dynamics" (MacIntosh and MacLean, 2015: 64). Further to this, academics such as Wernerfelt (1984) and Barney (1986) introduced the resource-based view (RBV) in the 1980s. RBV is a contrasting view to Porter's Five Forces; the RBV approach has become dominant in sustaining competitive advantage because it concentrates on organizations themselves (rather than an industry in the case of Porter), where these organizations compete on the basis of their resources and capabilities (Peteraf and Bergen, 2003a). The RBV adheres to "look within the enterprise and down to the factor market conditions that the enterprise must contend with, to search for some possible causes of sustainable competitive advantages", holding constant all external environmental factors (Peteraf and Barney, 2003b, p. 312). It is useful to take note of the RBV view of competition.

Tip

In 1996 Porter addressed many of the criticisms of his in paper titled "What Is Strategy?" published in the *Harvard Business Review* (Porter, 1996).

Exercise

In small groups, discuss the relevance and viability of applying Porters Five Forces if you were to create a start-up enterprise. Provide a balanced view.

Adopting Porter's generic strategies

9

Given the competition within an industry created by the Five Forces model, for organizations to survive and succeed they need to adopt a competitive strategy. Organizations can choose to follow one of Porter's competitive strategies to gain a competitive edge. In his seminal work, Porter (1980) identifies three main strategies on the basis of the competitive advantage of a firm in relation to its competitors (Garau, 2007): cost leadership, differentiation, and focus/differentiation focus strategies. Both cost leadership and differentiation are relatively broad in market scope whilst the market segmentation is narrow in scope (Figure 9.3). Porter's (1980) framework of generic strategies is not only the dominant paradigm in the corporate strategy organizations and business policy literature (Murray, 1998; Gurau, 2007) but also amongst organizations within industry (Kumar and Subramanian, 2011). Porter's generic strategies have previously been seen as "useful, because (1) it builds on previous findings and (2) it is appropriately broad, but not vague" (Hambrick, 1983, p.688).

Furthermore, White (1986, p.220) noted that Porter's generic approach to business strategy incorporated "a few critical dimensions yet have strong theoretical underpinnings".

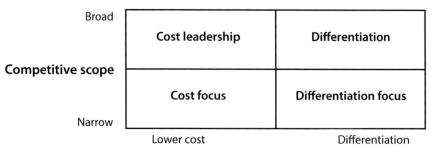

Figure 9.3: Porter's generic strategies. Adapted from Porter (1985: 12).

Porter argues that there are two decisions to make when choosing which strategy is the most suitable. First, whether competition is to be based on cost or value added, and second, whether competition is based towards a broad market (mass market) or whether a narrow market (niche) is to be served. Miles *et al.* (2012, p. 777) highlight that "Porter's framework integrates the firm's choice of competitive approach (cost leadership or differentiation) with the choice of product/market the firm plans to address (broad or narrow) to describe generic strategies that should, if implemented properly, lead to profits that exceed industry averages."

■ Cost leadership

The way to gain cost leadership is ensuring the lowest cost in the industry. The aim of the organization is to serve a mass market and a successful cost leader will have products or services of a quality comparable to their competitors. There are many ways to achieve cost leadership such as mass production, mass distribution, economies of scale, technology, product design, input cost, capacity utilization of resources, and access to raw materials (Akan *et al.*, 2006). The mass market often has many competitors as well as products and services on offer, increasing the competition. However, because the cost leader is supplying to the mass market, they lack a specialism and/or technology, they are likely to be average (rather than grow), as are profits (but not always).

If we look at Ikea (a Swedish company) selling homeware and accessories, we can see that the products sold are not catered to small segments of the market but rather to the mass market. The prices are reasonable, the furniture is displayed and ready to be picked up on site and the varieties of products available cover many styles and tastes.

Examples of cost leadership

- Wal-mart
- Easyjet
- Primark
- Ford Fiesta
- Ikea

■ Differentiation

This strategy also serves the broad market but the organization concentrates on providing a unique product or service, developing a unique selling point (USP) to ensure they are different from their competitors. Product differentiation satisfies the consumers' need and involves tailoring the product or service to the requirements of the individual customer (Akan *et al.*, 2006). Given that the product or service is offering uniqueness (this may include extra features, better quality etc.), the customer must be prepared to pay more, which allows the organization to achieve superior profits (otherwise the added cost is lost).

Examples of differentiation

- **Marks and Spencer's -** Middle - high age group, luxury food products
- **British Airways -** Quality, reliability
- **Topshop -** Young to middle age group, cheaper and high variety clothing line
- **Volkswagen Golf -** Engineering, style
- **Homebase -** DIY for homeowners
- **Nike -** Sport, athlete
- **Apple -** Sophistication, design, high price position

Exercise

Compare two companies in the technology industry that have applied a differentiation strategy. Bullet-point why and how the company have achieved this and what effect this has had on their consumers.

■ Focus/differentiation focus

This strategy *focuses* on a select few target markets or seeks *differentiation* in its target segment with the aim to gain a competitive advantage through effectiveness rather than efficiency. These strategies concentrate their efforts on being clear in their differences from other market segments – customers are often expected to pay much more for the product and service because of its niche status.

Examples of focus

- Waitrose
- Chartered private jet
- Rolls Royce

'Stuck in the middle'

Some organizations will attempt to adopt all three of these strategies and by adopting all three Porter (1980, 1985) calls them 'stuck in the middle' (Pertusa-Ortega *et al.*, 2009). Being 'stuck in the middle' highlights that the organization has not made a choice about how to compete within the industry. It also illustrates a lack of clarity in their strategy, as they have decided to occupy a middle position involving both costs and differentiation with respect to their competitors (Spanos *et al.*, 2004). A classic example of 'being stuck in the middle' is the large, international airline companies, whereby many of them are now bankrupt (Dostaler and Flouris, 2006), for example Malaysia Airlines (Topham, 2015).

Although Porter's generic strategies have provided a solid base for organizations and industries with respect to addressing competitiveness, Garau (2007, p. 373) outlined the main criticisms of Porter's theory of generic strategies (Table 9.2).

Table 9.2: Criticisms of Porter's generic strategies

Criticism	Explanation
Theoretical shortcomings	Generic strategies are too general
	Strategic approach is too simplified
Fit with reality	Generic strategies do not fit with empirical reality
	Generic strategies' model is based on an invalid epistemological approach
	Limited market knowledge
	Generic strategies do not consider the evolution of the competitive environment
Limited applicability	Generic strategies are not applicable for small firms
	Generic strategies are not applicable in fragmented markets
	Generic strategies are not applicable to retailers
	The generic strategies are not alternative solutions, but can profitably coexist in the strategic approach of a firm
Alternative theoretical approaches	The strategic analysis should apply a resource-based approach
	The strategic process is a flexible and emergent, being based on trial and error
	Generic strategies do not consider the necessity for collaborative strategies

Source: Adapted from Garau (2007, p. 373).

Exercise

As a student consumer, present a list of brands/products that you feel would fall under the 'stuck in the middle' category, providing a short explanation for each. Recommend one solution that could provide the company with a clearer direction.

The criticisms of Porter's generic strategies typically allude to the linear approach, which an organization takes towards competition, i.e. it is inflexible, limited and lacks specificity. It is important to note that Porter established his strategies in the 1980s, when the industry was stable, but markets, economies and organizations have since evolved in response to recent changes in technology, globalization and government regulations. However, the merit of Porter's work cannot be denied in discussing strategy and competitive advantage, where his work has played an important role in strategy formulation.

Further reading

Porter, M.E. (1985). *Competitive Advantage*. New York: Free Press.

Porter, M.E. (1998). *Competitive Strategy*. New York: Free Press.

Porter, M.E. (1996). What is strategy? *Harvard Business Review,* **74**(6), 61-78.

Porter, M.E. (2008) The five competitive forces that shape strategy. *Harvard Business Review,* **86**(1), pp.25-40.

Tip

Michael E. Porter's biography is available at the following link:

http://www.hbs.edu/faculty/Pages/profile.aspx?facId=6532

9

References

Akan, O., Allen, R. S., Helms, M. M., & Spralls III, S. A. (2006). Critical tactics for implementing Porter's generic strategies. *Journal of Business Strategy,* **27**(1), 43-53.

Barney, J. (1986). Strategic factor markets: expectations, luck, and business strategy. *Management Science* **32**, 1231-1241.

Bridoux, F. (2004). A resource-based approach to performance and competition: an overview of the connections between resources and competition. Luvain, Belgium Institut et de Gestion, Universite Catholique de Louvain. Available at: https://www.uclouvain.be/cps/ucl/doc/iag/documents/WP_110_Bridoux.pdf

Consumers International (2012). The relationship between supermarkets and suppliers: What are the implications for consumers? www.consumersinternational.org/

Cox, A. (2001). Understanding buyer and supplier power: a framework for procurement and supply competence. *Journal of Supply Chain Management*, **37**(1), 8-15.

Dostaler, I. and Flouris, T. (2006). Stuck in the middle revisited: The case of the airline industry. *Journal of Aviation/Aerospace Education and Research*, **15**(2), 6.

Garau, C. (2007). Porter's generic strateies: a re-interprettion foma realtiosnship marketing perspective. *The Marketing Review* **7**(4), 369-383.

Grimm, H. (2006). Entrepreneurship policy and regional economic growth: Exploring the link and theoretical implications. In Rihoux, B. and Grimm, H. (eds.) *Innovative Comparative. Methods for Policy Analysis Beyond the Quantitative-Qualitative Divide* USA: Springer.

Grundy, T. (2006). Rethinking and reinventing Michael Porter's Five Forces model. *Strategic Change* **15**, 213-229.

Hambrick, D.C. (1983). High profit strategies in mature capital goods industries: A contingency approach. *Academy of Management Journal* **25**, 687-707.

IATA (2014, 2015) International Air Transport Association, http://www.iata.org/Pages/default.aspx [Accessed April 2015].

Kumar, K. and Subramanian, R. (2011). Porter's strategic types: Differences in internal processes and their impact on performance. *Journal of Applied Business Research* **14**(1), 107-124.

MacIntosh, R. and MacLean, D. (2015). *Strategic Management: Strategists At Work.* London: Palgrave Macmillan.

Miles, P., Miles, G. and Canon, A. (2012). Linking servicescape to customer satisfaction: exploring the role of competitive strategy. *International Journal of Operations &Production Management* **32**(7), 772-795.

Miller, D. (1988). Relating Porter's business strategies to environment and structure: Analysis and performance implications. *Academy of management Journal* **31**(2), 280-308.

Murray, A.I. (1988). A contingency view of Porter's 'Generic Strategies'. *Academy of Management Review* **13**(1), 390-400.

Pertusa-Ortega, E.M., Molina-Azorín, J.F. and Claver-Cortés, E. (2009). Competitive strategies and firm performance: a comparative analysis of pure, hybrid and 'stuck-in-the-middle' strategies in Spanish Firms. *British Journal of Management* **20**(4), 508-523.

Peteraf, M. and Barney, J. (2003a). Unraveling the resource-based tangle. *Managerial and Decision Economics* **24**, 309-323.

Peteraf, M. and Bergen, M. (2003b). Scanning dynamic competitive landscapes: a market-based and resource-based framework, *Strategic Management Journal* **24**, 1027-1041.

Porter, M.E. (1979). How competitive forces shape strategy. *Harvard Business Review* **57**(2), 137-145

Porter M.E. (1980). *Competitive Strategy*. New York: Free Press.

Porter, M.E. (1985). *Competitive Advantage*. New York: Free Press.

Porter, M.E. (1998). *Competitive Strategy*. New York: Free Press.

Porter, M.E. (1996). What is strategy? *Harvard Business Review* **74**(6), 61-78.

Porter, M.E. (2008) The five competitive forces that shape strategy. *Harvard Business Review* **86**(1), 25-40.

Shugan, S.M. (2005). Brand loyalty programs: are they shams? *Marketing Science* **24**(2), 185-193.

Spanos, Y.E., Zaralis, G. and Lioukas, S. (2004). Strategy and industry effects on profitability: evidence from Greece. *Strategic Management Journal* **25**,139–165.

Speed, R.J. (1989). Oh Mr Porter! A re-appraisal of competitive strategy. *Marketing Intelligence and Planning* **7**(5/6), 8-11.

The Economist (2014). Why airlines make such meagre profits. *The Economist* (February 2014).

Topham, G. (2015). Malaysia Airlines 'technically bankrupt' as new chief seeks to shed 6,000 jobs. *The Guardian*: http://www.theguardian.com/business/2015/jun/01/malaysia-airlines-technically-bankrupt-christoph-mueller-cuts-boss

Valuation Academy (2015). http://valuationacademy.com/porters-five-forces-in-action-sample-analysis-of-coca-cola/ [Accessed 1 March 2015].

Vining, A.R. (2011). Public agency external analysis using a modified "Five Forces" framework, *International Public Management Journal* **14**(1), 63-105.

Wang, J., Bonilla, D. and Banister, D. (2015) Air deregulation in China and its impact on airline competition 1994–2012. *Journal of Transport Geography*. (in press) http://dx.doi.org/10.1016/j.jtrangeo.2015.03.007

Wernerfelt, B. (1984). A resource-based view of the firm. *Strategic Management Journal*, **5**(2), 171-180.

White, R.E. (1986). Generic business strategies, organizational context and performance: An empirical investigation. *Strategic Management Journal* **7**, 217-231.

9

10 Operations Management

Umit Bititci and Stavros Karamperidis

Operations management is the activity of managing products, processes, services and supply chains. By managing these activities, an organization creates and delivers services and products that clients/customers want. Essentially, operations management is responsible for translating and executing an organization's objectives, policies and strategies into day-to-day operations. In other words, operations management is responsible for delivering the performance objectives of the organization.

In this chapter we present operations management in two parts. The first section provides a detailed account of the development of the field since its inception during the early 1900s through to the modern day. In doing so we introduce various concepts, methods, tools and techniques that are commonly used in operations management. In the second section a more detailed account of key concepts in operations management is provided. Some are covered in greater detail (e.g. process management) and others just introduced but covered in detail in other chapters (e.g. supply chain management).

Operations management: evolution and key concepts

The fundamental principles of operations management are rooted in a discipline that is historically referred to as industrial engineering, which started during industrialization (1750-1850). Prior to this period, the world's economy was largely based on craft-based industries where craftspeople, such as ironmongers, tailors and carpenters made products and provided services customized to individual people's requirements. In this craft production model, everything was produced from scratch, the costs were high and many products and services were only accessible to the wealthier members of society.

The industrial revolution was born of technological advances which helped to make everyday products more accessible to the masses, hence the birth of the term *mass manufacturing*. The early stages of mass manufacturing are epitomized by the Ford Motor Company's first product, the Ford Model-T, which you could buy in "any colour as long as it was black" (i.e. there was no choice for the consumer). These early stages of industrialization also led to development of management, and particularly operations management as a scientific discipline, as captured in F. W. Taylor's book *Principles of Scientific Management* in 1911 (Taylor, 2006).

Today, the Toyota Production System is heralded as the best example of modern operations management, as described by the books entitled *Machine That Changed the World* (Womack, Jones and Roos, 2008) and *Lean Thinking* (Womack and Jones, 2010).

Figure 10.1: From mass manufacturing (Ford Model-T) to lean manufacturing (Toyota production systems). Source: Toyota GB (2015) and Wikimedia Commons (2015).

■ Early developments (1900-1940)

During the early stages of industrialization and mass manufacturing, power lay largely with producers rather than customers. Firms produced what they thought would be appropriate for the market. Consumers had little if any choice; the norm was that you simply bought what was available. Taylor (2006), who undertook research into early factories and mass manufacturing, identified a key change in manufacturing processes, known as the **production line** concept. While in the pre-industrial revolution era, one person would produce the whole product, this new approach enabled the product to flow at a constant speed down the production line, where people with specialized skills and equipment would build a small and very specific part of the product. A production line allowed specialization of labour on one task (such as hanging a door on a car, sprinkling cheese on a pizza, sticking a label on a product). Specialization of labour was achieved by breaking complete jobs into smaller, repetitive component parts, which Adam Smith (1776) called "the division of labour". This enabled people to get really good at doing a very specific task and led to huge productivity gains, at the price of more satisfying and skilled work.

The main purpose of industrial engineering was to maximise the flow of work through the production line, i.e. make as many products as possible out of the same production line by improving the **productivity**[1] of the production line. In order to achieve that, production engineering aimed to get as much **value added work**[2] as possible from every unit of resource. For that reason, techniques such as **work measurement** and the **method study** were developed. Work measurement is concerned with the measurement of time needed to perform a job. It typically classifies tasks or activities in to **value-adding** or **non-value adding activities** and attempts to eliminate or minimise the non-value-adding activities. Method study is concerned with how various activities are organized, sequenced and integrated to ensure that the product is produced in the most efficient way. Method study and work measurement are often referred to collectively as **work study**. Work study helps to ensure the minimization of wasted time, by minimising non-value adding activities, thus increasing productivity.

Exercise

If you were managing a factory how would you measure production performance, and why?

■ Increasing variety and competition (1940-1980)

As the industrial era progressed further into the 20th century, the world economy started to improve; consumer buying power increased and some producers began to offer more choice as a means of securing an advantage. In contrast to the example of the single Model T Ford, General Motors sought to develop a product for every type of customer, through options that would allow customization. With increased choice, greater levels of uncertainty and complexity were introduced to the once simple production lines. Now production lines had to be designed to deal with a variety of products. This had a negative affect on both efficiency and productivity. Attention began to focus on **layout planning** to ensure that products flowed efficiently from one production area to another within the same factory. Layout planning is concerned with the organization of the production resources (i.e. machines, equipment, tooling and

10

---

1 Productivity is a measure of the efficiency of a production system. It can be expressed as the ratio of output to inputs used in the production process.

2 Value added work are the activities conducted by an organization in order to generate an output which is considered as more valuable by external customers than the inputs needed for its production.

people) on the factory floor. Whilst the **production line layout** was considered to be most effective for producing a single product in large quantities with little or no variation (i.e. mass manufacturing), it proved less effective in dealing with increased variation, uncertainty and consumer choice. Alternative forms of shop floor organization emerged that included **functional/process layout** and later **group technology** (sometimes referred to as **cellular manufacturing**). Descriptions and illustrations for these alternative forms of shop floor organization are provided below.

A **Production/flow line layout** is one where resources are organized in a line to enable the products to flow through the production system as efficiently as possible with minimum interruptions. Here, the focus is on the maximization of flow and thus productivity by balancing the work content of each work-station (**line-balancing**) along the production line. Typically, the production line lay out is suitable for low-variety high-volume manufacturing (Figure 10.2).

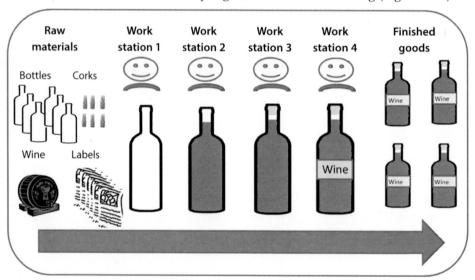

Figure 10.2: Flow line production

Functional/process layout is where similar resources, activities or skills are grouped together into departments, such as welding department, painting department, machining department, finishing department. Here different products are routed through different departments according to their production requirements. Although highly flexible, these layouts do not have the productivity characteristics of flow line production as products have to travel from one resource to another. In operations management any unnecessary travel is considered as non-value adding and waste. Typically, functional/process layout is more suitable for small batch manufacturing normally characterized by high-variety and low-volumes.

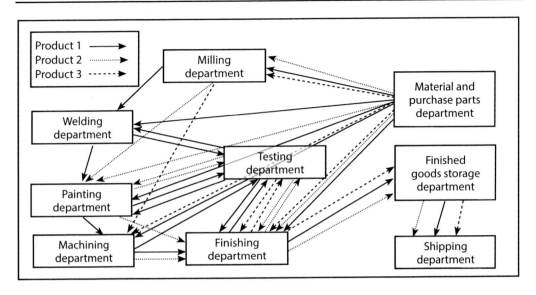

Figure 10.3: Functional or process layout

Group technology or a **cellular layout** is a hybrid of the functional and production line layouts described above. Here, products with similar production requirements are grouped together (group technology) and small manufacturing cells (cellular manufacturing) are created in order to mimic production line characteristics as closely as possible within each cell. In other words, each cell is optimized to produce a group of products with similar manufacturing requirements thus resembling a mini production line. Typically cellular layout is suitable for medium batch manufacturing, usually characterized by medium-variety and medium-volumes.

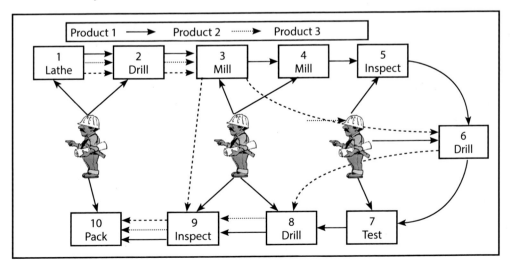

Figure 10.4: Cellular layout

10

With the introduction of greater product choice and verity, manufacturers had to find new ways of dealing with **uncertainty** and **complexity**:

☐ **Uncertainty:** is the inability to accurately predict the exact nature of customers demand. (For example, you may be able to guess that you will sell 200 cars next month but it would be more difficult to predict their exact specification, such as colour choice, until the customer order arrives).

☐ **Complexity:** is the number of different components, parts, manufacturing processes and assembly operations that needs to be planned to produce a product.

Consequently **simplification** and **variety reduction** techniques were developed to help manufacturers to deal with this complexity and uncertainty.

☐ **Simplification**, in this context, deals with product complexity reduction through design and production engineering.

☐ **Variety reduction** is usually associated with standardization of parts, components and subassemblies used in different products. (For example, today you will find many common parts used in products which are branded as distinct. Cars from Volkswagen, Audi, Seat and Skoda use of a relatively small number parts and components to produce a relatively large number of different end-products).

A key driver of productivity was the **quality** of the products produced. Poor quality is normally associated with rejects, scrap and rework (**internal quality**), as well as customer dissatisfaction and complaints (**external quality**). Whilst early **quality control** techniques solely focused on sorting bad parts from good ones, more sophisticated quality control techniques were developed that attempted to assure quality (i.e. **Quality Assurance**) by controlling the characteristics and capabilities of the manufacturing processes, thus **Statistical Quality Control (SQC)** and **Statistical Process Control (SPC)** techniques were developed.

Exercise

In small groups, choose a product and assess which style of layout might be most appropriate to produce that product. What trade-offs does this production system face in terms of flexibility and productivity?

As industrialization spread around the word, Japan emerged as a major industrial economy and began to make dramatic improvements in productivity using new approaches to management. With the globalization of Japanese products, particularly automotive products, such as Datsun (now Nissan),

Toyota and Mitsubishi, new industrial management concepts started to emerge, which further improved quality and productivity.

The term **'Just in Time (JIT) manufacturing'** emerged from the lessons learned from Japanese manufacturing methods, where products or components were produced just before they were needed. If product is produced early it would be sitting in the warehouse, which has to be heated, and where the product could be damaged or it could perish.

Another concept that emerged from similar kind of thinking was the **Optimization Production Technology (OPT)** (Goldratt and Cox, 2004) which focuses on maximising the **flow of production** and identifies **the bottlenecks** or **constraints** that prevent the process from flowing better. For example, a chain is only as strong as its weakest link, i.e. the bottleneck or constraint. By finding this weakest link and strengthening it, we would increase the strength of the chain. Thus, the idea of optimized production technology is to identify the key constraint in a production system and how other resources could start synchronising in order to work with each other and improve the flow through the production system. The OPT concept was extended to include all types of system (not just manufacturing) where work flows through the system. Today it is commonly referred to as the **Theory of Constraints (ToC)** (Goldratt, 1990) and it focuses on three performance measures that are fundamental to management of operations: **maximum throughput** (i.e. flow), **minimum operating expenses** and **minimum inventory**.

Over the same time period the importance of **maintenance management** to productivity was recognised. The purpose here was to ensure reliable operation of key production equipment, as breakdowns inadvertently cause loss of valuable production time. Maintenance management replaced responsive maintenance (i.e. waiting until a machine breaks down to repair it) with planned/ scheduled maintenance practices. Rather like regular servicing of your car, the argument is that productive operation of complex equipment depends critically on the time invested in preventative repairs. An evolution of this way of thinking is the approach known as **Total Preventative Maintenance (TPM).**

Another concept developed through this period was **Materials Requirements Planning (MRP)** (Plossl and Orlicky, 1994) which used the **Bill of Materials**[3] (product structure) to compute the quantity and timing of materials required to meet the actual and predicted demand. With MRP materials management started to become a science, as it enabled all the parts to come together at the right time and the right place.

10

---

3   A bill of materials is a comprehensive document which lists all the raw materials, parts, sub-assemblies, intermediate assemblies, sub-components and the quantities needed of the aforementioned materials for manufacturing an end product.

■ Modern times – Maximization of quality and minimization of waste (1980- today)

The global recession of the late 80s and early 90s caused a lot of organizations to re-examine their approach to managing productivity. This, together with the emergence of new manufacturing and work place organization techniques emerging from Japan, moved the focus on to **managing waste**. In this context **waste** is defined as any activity that does not add value to the final product or service. Major sources of waste are considered to be:

☐ Defects;

☐ Overproduction;

☐ Transportation;

☐ Waiting;

☐ Inventory;

☐ Unnecessary motion;

☐ Unnecessary processing.

This led to increased adoption of **cellular manufacturing,** together with other methods for reducing waste such as the **Single Minute Exchange of Die (SMED)**. SMED is a technique used to reduce the time taken to change over a production line from one product to another. The time taken to change over a line is considered waste because during this exchange the cell production facility is unproductive. For example, if a bottled water producer with a production line which makes one-litre bottles changes to 500 ml bottles, it has to modify its production line accordingly. This would require changes to tooling, labels, caps and the bottles used. Typically this changeover would take two to three hours changeover time. Today, using SMED techniques, the same changeover can be done in about 15 to 20 minutes. Whilst this is not a single minute change over, it nonetheless results in significant increases in productivity.

Example: Formula 1 pit stops

More extreme examples of SMED techniques can be found in Formula 1 racing cars. A driver in everyday life might need 20-30 minutes to change a wheel if the tyre is flat. But in Formula 1 the tyres are changed by the racing team within seconds. In the race environment the rewards for time saved are huge. Racing teams train extensively using video recording to identify opportunities to save fractions of seconds from the change-over time allowing the car to rejoin the race as soon as possible.

Visit YouTube and compare videos of the first F1 pit stops (1950s) with some of the most recent.

This line of thinking, which focuses on minimization of waste, is known as **lean thinking** or **lean management**. It is based on further evolution of quality management; from managing the quality of the process and the products, to managing the quality of the entire organization, i.e. **Total Quality Management (TQM).** Through TQM the same principles of lean management can be applied to an office environment, to production and to the entire organization. For example, if a secretary types a letter that contains a spelling mistake and prints it out, they have to repeat the process in order to correct the spelling mistake and reprint the document. Several resources are wasted: paper, ink of the printer and the secretary's time. If traditional typewriters were being used, the waste would be far higher but even with modern word processing software, reprinting is necessary. Getting things right first time in every task leads to greater productivity and this is the central tenet of total quality management.

As quality management evolved into TQM, several models emerged around the world. For example in Japan the Deming (1986) model is common, the Malcolm Baldridge model emerged in the US (National Institute of Standards and Technology, 1995) and in Europe the EFQM (European Foundation for Quality Management) (1994) model evolved. Each model come with an award that rewards excellence in the way an organization manages its processes, people and products. For example, the EFQM model depicted below (Figure 10.5) (reading from right to left) focuses on achievement of key performance results, which is a function of satisfied people, satisfied customers and a positive impact of society. In turn, all these results are a function of processes that are aligned to strategy, operated by appropriately skilled and qualified people with the right partners and resources, all facilitated with the right kind of leadership. Today, these models have developed to be recognised as business excellence models.

10

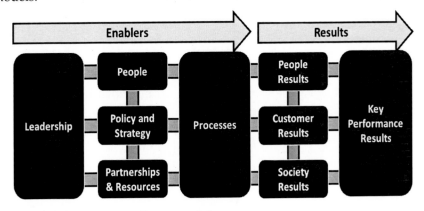

Figure 10.5: The EFQM business excellence model

In parallel with the development of the business excellence models, more scientific approaches to quality management also developed from Statistical Process Control. The Taguchi method and the Six Sigma methods both use statistical methods to analyse, and improve the variation in a process, thus increasing the reliability and repeatability of a process.

A vital part of achieving quality and productivity is how we organise our workplaces; **5S (Sort, Straighten, Shine, Standardize, and Sustain)** is a key technique developed to help workplace organization, whether a manufacturing facility, office space or a personal work place. The principle of that technique is to keep your workspace clean and tidy; by doing that you minimise losses. For example, if you are keeping several papers on your desk there is a higher chance of losing or mixing-up pages; filing everything in advance could minimise this.

Exercise

Demonstrate through examples which of the 5S you use in order to organise your workplace. Exchange the practices that you have found useful with your friends and try to apply those which you think that are useful to your everyday work.

The approaches identified above were developed in order to minimise mistakes. As in the early stages of operations management, the human element was considered as a necessary evil. Thus creativity and thinking were not involved in the production process. Over the years, a key change in the perception of operations management is that today we see people as a valuable asset, as they solve problems and innovate.

Through this period, materials requirement evolved to **Manufacturing Resources Planning (MRP II),** which goes beyond planning of materials and includes all resources, including: manpower, tooling, money, machines and other necessary resources. Today this is known as **Enterprise Resource Planning (ERP).** The extension of the ERP is the **e-Supply chain** which is all about collaborative planning with customers and suppliers enabled through modern communication technologies.

As outlined at the start of this section, operations management is responsible for delivering the performance aspirations of the organization. In this respect operations management links closely with the strategy of the organization because it integrates organizational goals and objectives to day to day operations through performance measurement. Thus, some strategic management tools and techniques such as management by objectives, policy deployment, balanced scorecard and triple bottom line (focusing on business performance, impact on the environment and the society) have become increasingly common in operations management.

In summary, although the origins of operations management is rooted in industrial engineering and manufacturing industries over a century ago, (see Figure 10.6), operations management techniques are commonly and widely applied to a wide variety of sectors and processes today.

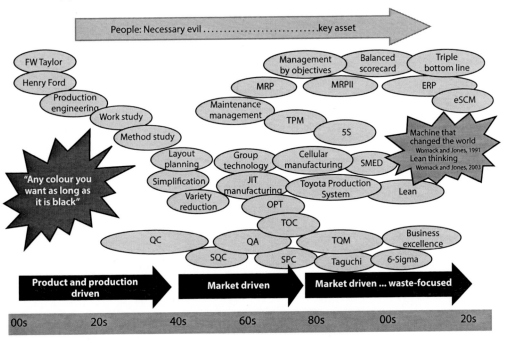

Figure 10.6: Evolution of the operations management field

Operations management and the organization

Operations management integrates seamlessly with **tactical management** and **strategic management**, as it not only executes strategic and tactical decisions but also informs strategic and tactical decision making. For example, operations management has an important input to make when making strategic decisions about infrastructures, services, supply chain configuration/design, supplies, customer service and so on. Similarly, tactical decisions concerning factory layout, shift patterns, operating times, maintenance policies and operational budgets are important considerations where operations management input is central.

According to the statistics on the business management consulting, market operations management accounts for approximately 35% of management consulting activities (Poor, Milovecz and Kiraly, 2012). This further demonstrates the critical role of the discipline in the overall management of organizations.

10

In our modern world, operations management is not only concerned with efficient and effective use of machines to manufacture products, it is also concerned with effective use of knowledge, people and external resources (partners, suppliers, customers) to diagnose conditions in patients, create solutions for the customers and creatively present ideas and markets' real needs.

Operations management is central to other business functions and it works closely in collaboration with these functions as illustrated in Figure 10.7.

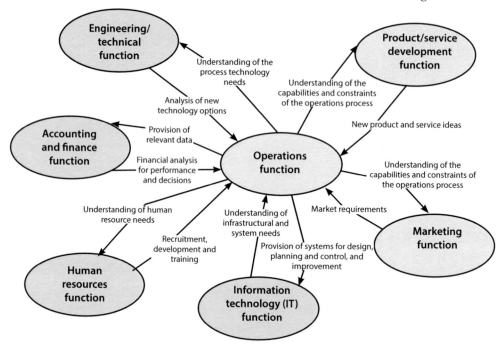

Figure 10.7: Inter-functional relationships between operations and other functions

Products/services and operations management

Operations management is about delivering products and services efficiently (i.e. productivity) and effectively (i.e. customer service). Those products and services are derived from both transformed resources (such as technical information, market information, time information and materials), and transforming resources (such as test and design equipment and design and technical staff). During the process the **performance is measured** by the following key performance criteria: **quality** of product or service, **speed** of response, **dependability** of product and/or service, **flexibility** of response and **cost**. These criteria apply to every sector and business: public, service and manufacturing. The output of the process is a fully specified product or service that meets customers' requirements.

All products and services have a life cycle and each one behave differently. For example, some fashion products have a short life-cycle (just few weeks or months) while some manufacturing products have longer life-cycle (tens of years). The product process life-cycles have four phases, as illustrated below.

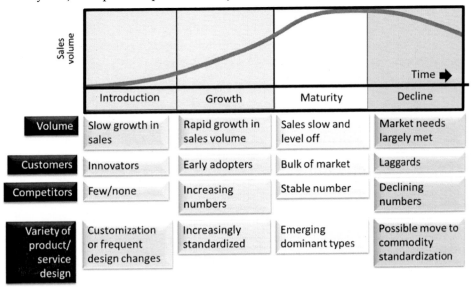

	Introduction	Growth	Maturity	Decline
Volume	Slow growth in sales	Rapid growth in sales volume	Sales slow and level off	Market needs largely met
Customers	Innovators	Early adopters	Bulk of market	Laggards
Competitors	Few/none	Increasing numbers	Stable number	Declining numbers
Variety of product/ service design	Customization or frequent design changes	Increasingly standardized	Emerging dominant types	Possible move to commodity standardization

Figure 10.8: Characteristics and phases of the product lifecycle

In the **introduction phase** a slow growth in sales is observed; customers buying (or testing) the product are innovators and at this early stage the product could change according to feedback received. At this stage only few or no competitors exist. The **growth phase** takes place with rapid growth in sales volume a key characteristic of this phase. Some early adopting customers exist, and there is increased competition in terms of suppliers. At that stage the product is standardized. By that time the **stage of maturity** appears, with sales slow and level-off occurring, while companies are selling in a bulk market. Competition stabilises and a few firms start to dominate the market. The final stage is the **decline phase,** where the markets' needs are largely met, with only a few customers looking for products/services. At that stage the number of competitors is declining and the product/service is becoming a standardized commodity.

10

Exercise

1 Identify four different products and services, one at each phase of the product life-cycle (please justify your answers).

2 In which phase do you think that the smartphones are in and why?

In operations management, it is important to understand at which point of the lifecycle our organization actually operates, as each stage has different criteria and complexities which need to be managed. Organizations cannot always operate as stable high volume manufacturing businesses producing standard product/services because changes will take place. Two variables could affect the lifecycle of products and the manufacturing process: the volume of the product and the variety of the product. Various combinations of those variables lead to different products and manufacturing processes. With very low volumes (e.g. one-off) and high variety (where each order is different), such as ship building, a **projects** approach is more appropriate. **Jobbing** deals with slightly less variety combined with low volumes. **Batch manufacturing** is when medium variety and medium volume products are produced and **mass manufacturing** for low variety and high volume production. Finally, **continuous manufacturing** is when a very low variety of products (typically one standard product) are continuously produced. This relationship between production volume, variety and manufacturing process is illustrated below (Figure 10.9).

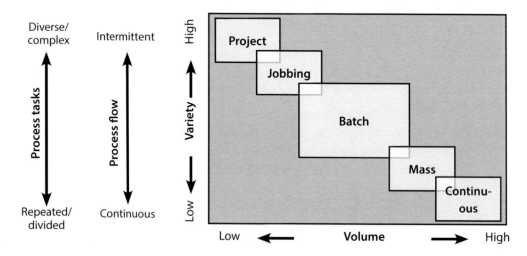

Figure 10.9: The relationship between production volume, variety and manufacturing processes

The same model could be applied to services, as illustrated in Figure 10.10. There are some **professional services** where clients' needs are significantly different. This means that variety is high and volume is low, as each case is unique. **Service shop** services provide medium variety and medium volume of services, as your services could be used from various people according to some customization. Finally, a **mass service** could be offered when the volume is high and the variety is low.

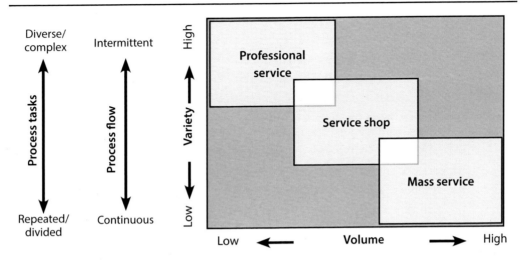

Figure 10.10: The relationship between production volume, variety and service processes

Balancing supply and demand

Balancing supply and demand is a key challenge for operations management. This can be achieved through accurate forecasting of demand; accurately forecasting resource availability (will supplier deliver on time or late; will people go off sick; will machines break down?) and accurate planning and scheduling of demand and resources. In order to deal with this challenge of balancing supply and demand, a number operations management approaches have been developed.

Materials and inventory management is a concept of operations management which deals with the management of stocks. These are mainly consumable materials (e.g. coco powder that goes in to making a chocolate bar), but sometimes could also be tooling, test equipment and services. Usually excess inventory is generated when supply exceeds demand. On occasion, having some excess inventory may be beneficial, but usually it is associated with risk and waste. Thus, operations management aims to minimise inventory without running out. Inventory could be split into two categories: **perishable** and **non-perishable**, with those two categories describing the product that has been placed in inventory. Perishable products have to be sold or proceed up to a specific day; if that is not the case then the opportunity to be sold is lost. Non-perishable products are more flexible in terms of time. In most cases service inventory is considered to be perishable, e.g. if an airplane seat, hotel room or a consultant's time is not sold, it is lost forever, because it is not possible to turn back time and sell yesterday's empty hotel room.

10

Tip

The first inventory management software has used barcodes to track inventory. Nowadays RFID (radio-frequency identification) tags have replaced barcodes for the tracking of large parcels, while Bluetooth technology is tested as a more effective option.

Several strategies exist to balance demand and supply, including: operational efficiency, time compression, postponement, Just-In-Time (JIT), e-business, online business transaction, information sharing, information sharing with customers and suppliers using electronic means, channel alignment and empowering suppliers to manage inventory. But the most important consideration for balancing supply and demand is communication; being able to minimise and manage uncertainty and complexity through continuous and open communication with customers, suppliers, employees, and other key resources. Operationally, organizations that reduce complexity and minimise uncertainty tend to perform better. However, it is impossible to completely eliminate uncertainty, particularly when it comes to events outside our control. For example, we may have selected the best suppliers but this does not prevent the ship carrying our raw materials from sinking in the middle of the ocean. So, no matter how good we are at forecasting and planning in operations management, we need to be able to deal with uncertainties up and down our supply chains.

Supply chain management is an important sub-set of operations management that has been developed to deal with the uncertainties and the complexity of our operations from customers' customers to suppliers' suppliers. It is primarily concerned with achieving a balance throughout the supply chain through collaboration, information and knowledge-sharing, where extensive use of modern information and communication technologies is made to enable free flow communication. The subject of supply chain management is more extensively covered in Chapter 11 of this book.

Supply chain management comprises a number of concepts, which include:

☐ **Purchasing and supply management** deals with the first and second tier suppliers providing materials and services. This is also known as *supply side* or *up-stream supply chain.*

☐ **Physical distribution management** involves management of inventory levels, inventory locations, warehousing and physical distribution of goods and services to first and second tier customers. This is also knowns as *demand side* or *down-stream supply chain management.*

☐ *Logistics* is the term used to describe the management of the material flow from the first tier supplier to the final customer.

❑ *Materials management* is usually the term used to describe the management process from the first tier suppliers to the first tier customer.

The scope of these concepts is illustrated in Figure 10.11 below. However, it is worth noting that, in practice, some of these terms are used interchangeably. Thus, when having conversations and discussion on the subject it is worth clarifying exactly what is meant by the terminology that is being used.

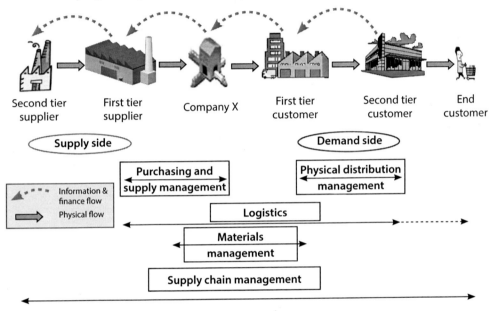

Figure 10.11: Various concepts used in supply chain management

Quality management and continuous improvement

As introduced earlier in this chapter **quality management** is an important concept within operations management. Here quality is defined as meeting customers' requirements/expectations/specification. The concept of quality is equally applicable to products as well as services. Two main principles underpin quality management. *First* is that quality of a product or a service can be managed by managing the process which delivers that product or service, thus assuring that the resulting product or service meets expectations (i.e. quality assurance). *Second* is to continuously look for opportunities, however small, to improve the performance of the process, i.e. continuous improvement.

Figure 10.12 illustrates what happens when quality is improved. Essentially, whichever way you look at it, improvement in quality usually results in a combination of reduced costs, increased sales and increased profits, i.e. improved performance.

10

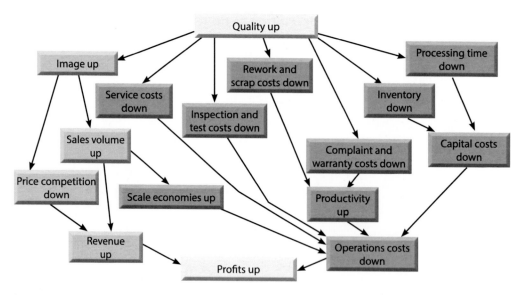

Figure 10.12: Business impact of improved quality

Tip

The British Standard (BS) 5750 for quality systems was published in 1979, while the first ISO 9000 quality standard has been developed in 1987 (http://www.dti.gov.uk/quality/evolution and http://www.iso.org/iso/about/the_iso_story.htm#12)

Continuous improvement is at the core of today's modern operations management. Whether it is an administrative process of how customers' orders are received and processed, a financial process of how credit is checked, how a particular product is shipped, or the manufacturing of a product that needs to be improved, the following five step **DMAIC (Define, Measure, Analyse, Improve, Control)** cycle can be followed to improve the process and the product or service it delivers.

Exercise

How you could use the DMAIC process to improve your action to get out of bed and come to university? In order to tackle the question please:

1 Define all the steps,

2 Explain how you will measure it,

3 Analyse each step,

4 Demonstrate how you will improve it,

5 Explain how you will control it.

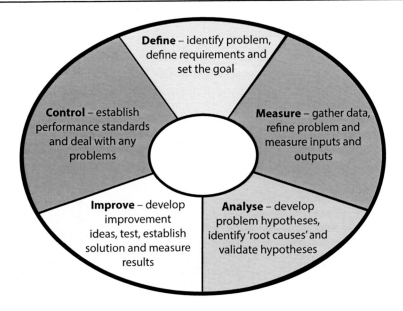

Figure 10.13: DMAIC cycle for continuous improvement

Process management

In the preceding section we have already intimated that **business processes** are an important concept in operations management. In this section we will argue that operations management is all about managing processes and thus improving the performance of the operations.

Within organizations (industrial, commercial, public sector) people do things (with other people, with machines, computers, etc.) that lead to results (good or bad). When you string what people do end to end you get a process. For example, a customer order fulfilment process may comprise of receiving the customer order, checking the customer's credit, planning the order, producing the order, delivering the order and finally invoicing the customer and collecting payment. Typically each one of these steps will be carried out by a different person in a different part of the organization (e.g. sales, finance, planning, production, shipping, etc.). Thus the performance of the process (customer satisfaction, quality of the product, productivity, etc.) is a function of the process.

In short, in operations management we can conceptualise everything an organization does as a process. That helps us to manage the performance of our operations, and indeed the overall business, by focusing on getting the people and process components right. In summary: *operations management is about realising organizational goals and objectives through business processes.*

10

A **business process** is a series of continuous or intermittent (it does not have to be continuous, it might be once a week, once a month, but it is still a process) cross-functional (so it covers more than one department) activities that are naturally connected together, with work flowing through these activities for a particular outcome/purpose.

All processes have inputs (materials, information and customers), they use resources (machines, employees, computers, time, money, etc.) to transform these inputs into outputs (products, information and customers) operating within the controls (policies, procedures, rules and regulations) of the business. Furthermore, the performance of the process can be measured in two dimensions: *effectiveness* (i.e. quality – does the process meets expectations/requirements/specification) and *efficiency* (i.e. how much resources the process consumes in delivering the output).

The most important thing about a process is the **flow of work** through it. If everything goes right first time and the work flowing through the process is at the right rate then an efficient and effective process is achieved. The process is divided into its activities when analysis and improvement of its performance is needed. In this way a process can be divided down to any level of detail as required by the analyst, as illustrated in Figure 10.14.

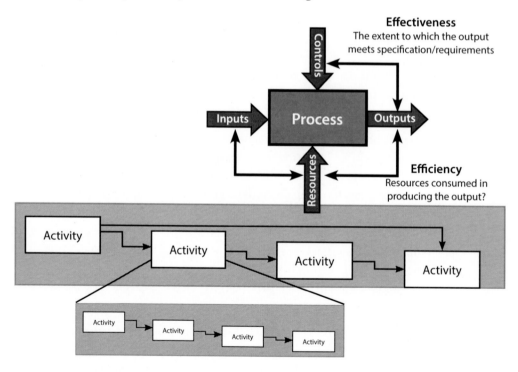

Figure 10.14: Structure of a business process

In general, the business processes of any organization (industrial, commercial and public sector) can be categorized as:

Operational processes – deal with the competitiveness of the organization here and now. These underpin the organizational competitiveness in the short to medium term. If an organization is better in all these processes than its competitors it will be in general more competitive than them. These processes are:

☐ **Developing products** and services that customers want;

☐ **Getting orders** for these products and services;

☐ **Fulfilling orders** for these products and services;

☐ **Supporting product**s and services after sales, including warranty, servicing, spare part and information provision.

Managerial processes – deal with maintaining the future competitiveness of the organization. These processes are:

☐ **Scanning the horizon** – being aware of what is happening in the operating environment, i.e. customers, competitors, suppliers, technologies, politics, economics, etc.;

☐ **Setting direction** – creating a clear and concise direction for the organization so that everyone can work towards a common objective;

☐ **Managing strategy** – planning for how you are going to sustain and develop your competitive advantage;

☐ **Managing performance** – monitoring and managing how the organization is performing against these plans;

☐ **Managing change** – changing to new ways of doing things.

Support processes which exist to support operational and managerial processes. These include:

☐ Supporting in HR;

☐ Supporting technology;

☐ Supporting finance.

With the use of operations management, the organization could be supported to achieve its aims and objectives by managing the efficiency and effectiveness of these processes.

In managing these processes it is also important to understand the characteristics of different types of processes. According to their characteristics, at the broadest level, business processes are classified as **scientific** and **artistic**

10

processes. The **scientific process** is rational, logical, codifiable process. In other words it can be written down and explained fully. In contrast, an **artistic process** is cognitive, creative and difficult to codify. It cannot be written down as it is experiential (e.g. riding a bicycle – no matter how much you can write down and explain how to ride a bicycle, unless the learners experience the sensation and fall off a few times they will not be learn to ride). In business, an example of an artistic process is the new product development process that starts with a creative idea, which is then developed, tested and finally implemented. As illustrated in Figure 10.15, this process is artistic at the start, as it is difficult to codify how to come up with a good idea. As the idea develops and is implemented, it becomes more mechanical and the process can be managed as a project.

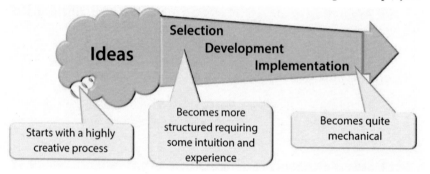

Figure 10.15: The artistic and scientific nature of the new product development process

However, as intimated earlier, all processes are affected by people's skills, capabilities and behaviours. An organization may have an excellent process but if the employees involved are demotivated, performance will suffer. However, if an organization has good processes that are operated by motivated people, who are appropriately skilled and educated, performance results are likely to be positive. Indeed, a great deal of operations management is also about managing people. In fact, in many organizations, the largest proportions of people are usually employed in operational functions. Thus, management of process and people performance becomes a central concern for operations management.

Performance measurement and management

Performance is defined as the efficiency or effectiveness of an action, activity or process. A **performance measure or indicator** is a quantitative or qualitative expression of the performance of a process. A **performance measurement system** is a set of performance measures that is used to manage the performance of an activity, a process or an entire organization. **Performance management** is the process in which uses the performance measurement system to manage the performance of an activity, process or the organization.

In measuring the performance of processes **flow** becomes a central concept. In order to manage the flow of work through a process **leading** and **lagging** **indicators** are used as illustrated in Figure 10.16. As demonstrated, whilst supplier on-time delivery is a *leading* indicator for customer satisfaction (i.e. it provides advance warning that customer satisfaction may suffer in the future, if our on-time delivery performance is not good today), it is a *lagging* indicator for on-time delivery (i.e. by the time we know that our supplier on-time delivery is 70% it is too late to do anything about it).

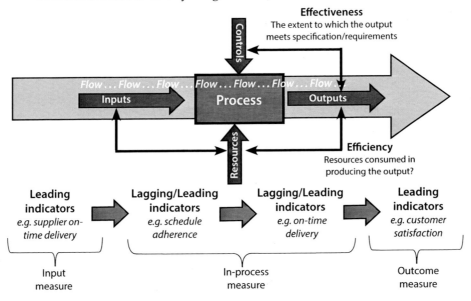

Figure 10.16: Leading and lagging indicators for a business processes

In many organizations performance measures are reported on performance scorecards, cockpits and dashboards. This attempt to bring all pertinent performance information together into one place enables a mature conversation about the performance of the organization, which usually include s information on; financial (are we meeting our financial objectives), customer (are we satisfying our customers), process (are our processes running efficiently and effectively) and learning and growth (are we continuously striving to improve our process, customer and financial performance) performance of the organization. Performance measurement systems organized around these four perspectives of an organization are known as Balanced Scorecards.

Exercise

Take a process that you are familiar with. Identify its key steps, its flow and the leading and lagging indicators that could enable you to control the process.

Conclusion

Operations management is a very broad term covering several areas such as material management, quality management, inventory management, supply chains, etc.

On the one hand, operations management is a very broad discipline of management; it is all about the efficient and effective organization of the firm's resources that are fundamental to the organization's goals and objectives. It can involve complex global supply chains, where management of people is a key element of managing the performance of operations. On the other hand, operations management is all about managing performance of business processes, where people are a key component of any process. Processes can be simple and within one firm, or complex, joining several firms together in global supply chains.

However you look at operations management, it is about the efficient and effective organization of resources, to deliver high level goals and objectives. It is important to recognise that operations management is about balancing process management with management of people, to maximise the performance outcomes for the organization.

Further reading

Bititci, U.S. (2015). *Managing Business Performance: The Science and the Art*. Chichester: John Wiley and Sons.

Bititci, U.S., Garengo, P., Dörfler, V. and Nudurupati, S. (2012). Performance measurement: Challenges for tomorrow. *International Journal of Management Reviews*, **14**(3), 305-32.

Bititci, U.S. *et al.* (2011). Managerial processes: an operations management perspective towards dynamic capabilities. *Production Planning and Control*, **22**(2), 157-173.

References

Deming, W. (1986). *Out of the Crisis*. Cambridge: Massachusetts Institute of Technology Press.

European Foundation for Quality Management (1994). *The European Quality Award (1995) -Application Brochure*. Brussels: The European Foundation for Quality Management.

Goldratt, E. M. (1990). *Theory of Constraints*. Great Barrington, Massachusetts: The North River Press.

Goldratt, E. M. and Cox, J. (2004). *The Goal: A Process of Ongoing Improvement*. 3rd ed. Great Barrington, Massachusetts: The North River Press.

National Institute of Standards and Technology (1995). *The Malcolm Baldrige National Quality Award*. Gaithersburg, MD: US Department of Commerce, Technology Administration.

Plossl, G. W. and Orlicky, J. (1994). *Orlicky's Material Requirements Planning* (2nd Ed). New York: The McGraw-Hill Professional.

Poor, J., Milovecz, A. and Kiraly, A. (2012). *Survey of the European Management Consultancy 2011/2012*. Brussels: FEACO (European Federation of Management Consulting Associations). http://www.feaco.org/sites/default/files/sitepagefiles/Feaco%20Survey%202011-2012.pdf [Accessed 24 July 2015].

Smith, A. (1776). *An Inquiry into the Nature and Causes of the Wealth of Nations*. London: W. Strahan and T. Cabell. http://www.econlib.org/library/Smith/smWN.html [Accessed 22 September 2015].

Taylor, F. W. (2006). *The Principles of Scientific Management*. New York: Cosimo Classics.

Toyota GB (2015). Andon – Toyota Production System guide. http://blog.toyota.co.uk/andon-toyota-production-system [Accessed 26 April 2015].

Wikimedia commons (2015). Ford model T. Thttps://commons.wikimedia.org/wiki/File%3ARestored_Ford_Model_T.jpg [Accessed 24 July 2015].

Womack, J. P., and Jones, D. T. (2010). *Lean Thinking: Banish Waste and Create Wealth in Your Corporation*. New York: Simon and Schuster.

Womack, J. P., Jones, D. T., and Roos, D. (2008). *The Machine that Changed the World*. New York: Simon and Schuster.

10

11 Logistics and the Supply Chain

Christine Rutherford and Christian König

Critical to the success of any business is a supply chain capable of serving the end customer more effectively and more efficiently than the competition. Central to this premise is an understanding that in today's global marketplace it is supply chains that compete, not individual firms. We explore the central role of logistics and the supply chain in gaining competitive advantage in a volatile global market by first defining the key principles of a market-responsive supply chain. Second, we discuss different supply chain strategies to improve the match between supply and demand, before dedicating two sections to the important subjects of logistics outsourcing and global sourcing. But first we begin by defining the supply chain, logistics and supply chain management.

Logistics and supply chain management

Supply chains are rarely simple chains, but rather complex networks of interconnected and interdependent companies. The end-to-end supply chain may comprise several tiers of organizations, each contributing in some way to the value of the chain as a whole. The interconnectivity of networks invariably means that competing firms are likely to have overlapping networks and may share suppliers and compete for the same customers. Figure 11.1 illustrates this idea showing two competing firms that are embedded within two interconnected and competing supply networks.

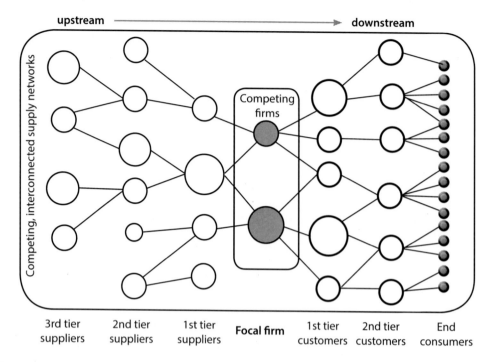

Figure 11.1: Interconnected competing supply networks

The success of the two focal firms indicated in Figure 11.1 is, to varying degrees, dependent on the combined abilities of all the companies that contribute to their respective value chains. If a critical node in the network fails then the whole network could be at risk. It is this understanding of network interconnectivity and interdependence that leads to the conclusion that supply networks compete, not individual firms. Christopher's (2011) definition of supply chain management reflects this understanding.

Supply chain management: the management of upstream and downstream relationships with suppliers and customers to deliver superior customer value at less cost to the supply chain as a whole. (Christopher, 2011, pp5)

This definition underlines the importance of supplier and customer relationship management, as well as the need for an integrated enterprise view, focused on the final consumer and not just first tier customers and first tier suppliers.

If supply chain management is about managing relationships in the supply chain then what is logistics management? Some may argue that supply chain management is simply a new name for logistics, but logistics is a narrower discipline, focused on the movement and storage of materials through the supply chain. Christopher (2011) provides the following definition:

Logistics: the process of strategically managing the procurement, movement and storage of materials, parts and finished inventory (and the related information flows) through the organization and its marketing channels in such a way that current and future profitability are maximized through the cost effective fulfilment of orders. (Christopher 2011, pp4)

The goal of logistics management is to find the optimal trade-off between a number of often conflicting costs including: inventory holding costs, transportation costs, warehousing facility costs and batching and information processing costs. We might consider logistics to be part of the wider field of supply chain management; the two subjects together addressing the science and the art of managing supply networks.

Using the supply chain to compete

Competitive advantage over industry rivals is often won through innovation in supply chain design and not necessarily by product or service innovation alone. A great product delivered by an ineffective and inefficient supply chain will ultimately fail; to succeed, companies must recognise the critical role that the supply chain plays in achieving and sustaining market share. Without an effective supply chain strategy and without efficient supply chain management, companies will struggle to respond to changes in customer demand and shifts in consumer behaviour. Refer to Christopher (2011) for a more in-depth understanding about how logistics and the supply chain can be leveraged for competitive advantage.

Zara's innovative supply chain

The fashion retailer Zara (owned by Inditex) is an example of a company that effectively leveraged logistics and the supply chain to gain competitive advantage over other fashion retailers. Zara's success is not due to innovation in fashion design, but rather in the innovative design of their supply chain. Zara chose not to employ expensive fashion designers but rather young unknown designers keen to reflect the latest fashion trends in their designs. Using several supply chain strategies such as postponement of design, product differentiation and immediate use of real-time demand (discussed in the following section), Zara reduced the time it took to turn strategic stocks of raw materials into fashionable items of clothing in their stores from the standard 12 to 18 months, typical of the sector, down to just 3 weeks. This exceptionally short supply pipeline meant that Zara could completely refresh their product range every few weeks, enabling them to keep up with changing fashion trends whilst the competition continued to suffer the consequences of long, expensive supply chains.

Source: Zara: Responsive, high speed, affordable fashion, 2005, The Case Centre, Ref No. 305-308-8

11

Exercise

What is innovative about Zara's supply chain and how has this helped Zara gain competitive advantage?

Market-responsive supply chains

To create a market-responsive supply chain, companies can adopt a combination of different management concepts that together increase supply chain efficiency, as well as effectiveness in the marketplace. The aim is to match supply chain type with market requirements and, wherever possible, delay adding value to a product until the last possible moment before true demand is realised. Five key concepts are explained in the following sections.

■ Product differentiation

Central to achieving a market-responsive supply chain is an understanding that not all products or customers are equal. Managers must select the right supply chain to meet different market requirements, whilst considering different economic and non-economic product characteristics. In his seminal work, Fisher (1997) advises that managers should carefully consider the nature of demand for their products before devising a supply chain strategy. Fisher argues that products typically fall into two categories as described in Table 11.1. (The reader is referred back to Chapter 9, which also discusses product differentiation).

Table 11.1: Functional versus innovative products: differences in demand

Aspects of demand	Product type	
	Functional	Innovative
Demand	Predictable & steady	Unpredictable & variable
Product lifecycles	> 2 years	3 months to 1 year
Contribution margin	5% to 20%	20% to 60%
Product variety	low	high
Forecast error at time production committed	10%	40% to 100%
Average stock-out rate	1% to 2%	10% to 40%
Average end-of-season markdown (% full price)	0%	10% to 25%
Lead time required for make-to-order products	6 months to 1 year	1 day to 2 weeks
Management focus	*Physically efficient*	*Market responsive*
Supply chain strategy	*Lean*	*Agile*

Source: Adapted from Fisher, 1997, pp.107

Functional products tend to have long product lifecycles and predictable demand patterns; examples include every day commodities such as shampoo, washing powder, or 'functional' items of clothing. Innovative products such as electronic items, fashionable clothing and seasonal items have less predictable demand and short lifecycles. Fisher argues that managers should select a physically efficient and lean supply chain for functional products and a market-responsive supply chain for innovative products. When dealing with innovative products, the aim is to reduce market mediation costs (lost sales, forced mark-downs) through increased supply chain velocity and agility. To become more market-responsive there is the need to focus aggressively on reducing lead-time; hence managers should consider local sourcing, rapid modes of transport and other supply chain concepts such as postponement. The aim with regards to functional products is to supply the product at minimum cost, utilising economies of scale in manufacturing and transport. Lead-time should only be reduced if there is little impact on cost.

Exercise

New innovative products often mature into functional products later in the life-cycle. Explain how and why the supply chain would need to evolve as the lifecycle progresses.

■ The material decoupling point

The second principle involves identifying the best position in the supply chain to decouple or separate lean and agile strategies with a buffer of inventory. The decoupling point is the point where push meets pull in the supply chain (Figure 11.2).

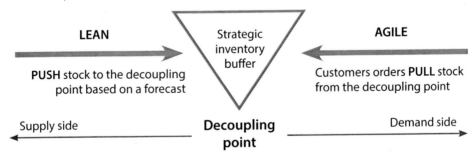

Figure 11.2: Decoupling the supply chain

On the supply-side of the decoupling point, product is pushed based on a forecast of demand; on the demand-side product is pulled from inventory held at the decoupling point in response to customer orders. As a rule of thumb, managers should position the decoupling point as far upstream in the supply chain as the customer will allow. If customers are prepared to wait two weeks for a particular product then the decoupling point should be positioned two weeks upstream in the supply chain process. However, if products need to be available for same day delivery to customers then the decoupling point will need to be physically within 12 hours of the customer, e.g. stock would need to be pushed to a regional distribution centre in easy reach of customers.

■ Postponement

To postpone is simply to delay adding value to a product wherever possible in the supply chain. In essence there are two types of postponement:

1 **Form postponement** involves delaying the final configuration of the product until customer orders have been received. This may involve delayed manufacturing and final assembly or simply delayed packaging and labelling.

2 **Place postponement** involves holding product back in a central location and only distributing to regions once customer orders have been received. This policy takes advantage of 'riskpooling', where the centralization of finished product in a single location allows us to reduce the total inventory required to serve customers in different market locations. However, the drawback is that it may take longer and cost more to serve distant customers.

■ The lead-time gap

The problem with long lead-times is that we end up having to carry more inventory to fill the operational pipeline (manufacturing and logistics) and to mitigate our increased uncertainty in future demand. The more inventory we carry, the greater the risk of obsolescence (by the time the stock gets to market it may be out of date), the higher the costs associated with managing inventory (storage, damage, insurance costs) and the more cash is tied up in stock that could be better invested in new technology, new product design or simply paying off debt. For these reasons companies should work with their supply chain partners to reduce process lead-times and hence compress the lead-time gap (Figure 11.3).

The lead-time gap: The time difference between the customer order cycle time (the time the customer is prepared to wait for a delivery once an order is placed) and the total supply chain lead-time (the time to source, make and deliver a product to a customer.)

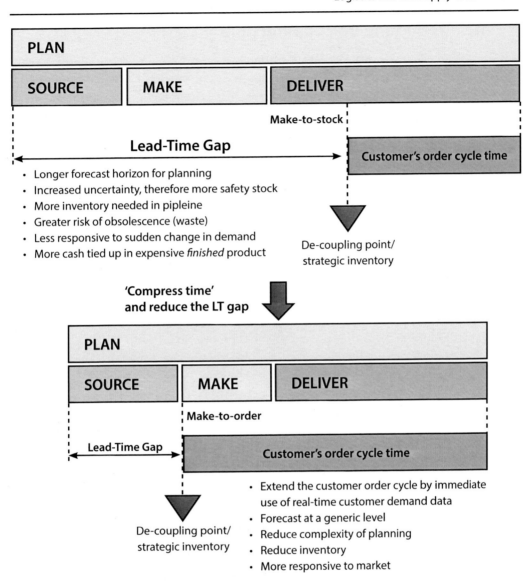

Figure 11.3: Reducing the lead-time gap

The aim is to do as much 'value-adding' activity as possible during the order cycle time, i.e. after the customer order has been received. In other words, we should aim to postpone adding value until we have received the customer order. To focus on adding value, it makes sense to eliminate or reduce time spent on non-value adding activities using 'time compression', a technique that employs the principles of Lean to reduce waste and increase the velocity of critical path processes. Managing the lead-time gap goes hand-in-hand with the concept of de-coupling; the shorter the lead-time the further upstream we can position the de-coupling point and still meet the customer order cycle time.

11

■ The information de-coupling point

A key characteristic of market responsive supply chains is their ability to capture and use real-time data upstream in the supply chain. The information decoupling point is a location, or perhaps several locations, in the supply chain that receive real-time data about market and consumer demand. This decoupling point is usually immediately upstream of the material decoupling point so that strategic inventory is always available to meet fluctuating demand. Visibility of true demand is vital if the supply chain as a whole is to work together to meet changes in demand whilst dealing with the challenges of supply. Today it is relatively easy to share electronic point of sale (ePoS) data collected by retailers with upstream suppliers so that they can respond sooner to changes in demand and not wait for retail replenishment orders that may lag several days or weeks behind. Increasing the visibility of data increases trust between supply chain partners; this in turn helps to reduce uncertainty and the need to carry excessive safety stocks. The immediate use of customer demand information upstream in the supply chain in effect extends the customer order cycle time (illustrated in Figure 11.3), giving the supply chain more time to carry out value adding activities instead of waiting for the order signal to be passed up the chain in the form of periodic batched orders.

Supply chain planning

The principle aim of supply chain planning is to match consumer demand with the timely supply of the right product in the right place. If we overestimate demand we risk ending up with excess or obsolete stock; if we underestimate demand we suffer poor customer service and the costs associated with lost sales.

Striking an affordable balance between these two opposing costs is no easy task. As products proliferate and markets diversify, producing an accurate forecast of future sales becomes more difficult. Manufacturers of fast–moving consumer goods (FMCG), including products such as laundry detergent and everyday grocery items, will typically have to deal with forecast errors greater than 20% for at least three quarters of their product range and higher than 80% errors for 10% of their products. This is in part due to the increasing number of slow moving items that cram the shelves of retail outlets; slow moving items such as speciality cooking ingredients, books or white goods that sell infrequently in small quantities are notoriously difficult to forecast – hence the risk of over- or under-supply is significant.

Although the volatility of the marketplace makes it difficult to match supply and demand, the root of the problem is lead-time (Christopher, 2011).

The longer the supply lead-time, the further into the future we must forecast demand. Hence the greater the risk of poor forecasts; it is much easier to forecast how much we might sell tomorrow than it is to forecast sales for one day six months from now. In six months' time the marketplace will probably be very different. For these reasons, companies have rightly placed much emphasis on the need to improve their supply chain planning. The approaches used are often quantitative, involving best-fit statistical forecasting and inventory optimization methods, but more often companies have come to realise that the best solution is in fact to become less dependent on a forecast, and this can be achieved through collaborative planning and increased agility in the supply chain. These approaches applied together can significantly improve the match between supply and demand.

Best-fit forecasting

Managers should begin by generating a baseline forecast using best-fit statistical algorithms and clean historic sales data. Modern planning software packages incorporate a suite of statistical forecasting algorithms from a simple moving average to exponential smoothing techniques and more sophisticated autoregressive integrated moving average (ARIMA) models. These algorithms are pitched against each other in a 'forecasting tournament' and the software identifies the best-fit (lowest forecast error) algorithm which can then be adopted by the planning manager to forecast next period sales.

However, this approach to forecasting assumes that the future is simply a projection of the past, i.e. any patterns in historic sales will be repeated in the future. So, although a best-fit projective forecast is an excellent baseline for building a forecast, product proliferation and the volatility of the marketplace ensure that a quantitative approach alone has very little chance of producing a good match between supply and demand.

Collaboration

There are two forms of collaboration that can significantly improve upon the accuracy of a projective best-fit statistical forecast. The first is cross-functional collaboration within the company between different planning functions. An increasingly popular process for achieving this is Sales and Operations Planning (S&OP) or, in its newest form, Integrated Business Planning (IBP). The traditional S&OP process brings together marketing, sales and operations functions to agree a single aligned supply and demand plan. The demand plan is based on a projective forecast, adjusted by marketing and sales personnel to take into account latest market intelligence. The supply plan considers production and material constraints and may not always match the expectations of the demand plan, for example there may not be enough capacity in production to meet an ambitions demand plan for a new product promotion.

The S&OP process is designed to identify these mismatches and find solutions to align both plans. Typically the process culminates in a monthly Executive level S&OP meeting attended by functional Directors. The purpose of this meeting is to make the consensus decisions to align the plans and importantly, to ensure that the plan supports the strategic objectives of the company. The recognition that financial planning is an essential part of sales and operations planning has led to a fully integrated approach, IBP, which brings all planning functions together to agree one aligned and achievable plan.

The second form of collaboration is cross-organizational, between trading partners in a supply chain. The simplest form is Vendor Management Inventory (VMI) where the vendor (supplier) takes responsibility for managing stocks of their products at a customer's location. The vendor simply monitors customer stock levels, replenishes stock as required (keeping levels between agreed minimum and maximum levels) and invoices the customer periodically for the stock delivered. The advantages are well documented and companies that successfully introduce VMI can expect up to a 50% reduction in the overall inventory held jointly by both parties, thus increasing on-shelf-availability.

With the invention of the internet and systems to support data sharing such as Electronic Data Interchange (EDI), VMI soon evolved into a more data intense collaborative approach in the mid 1990s called Collaborative Planning, Forecasting and Replenishment (CPFR) where two or more trading partners, (usually a large retailer and a significant FMCG supplier e.g. Wal-Mart and Procter & Gamble) work collaboratively to agree a joint plan for the forecasting and replenishment of a particular range of products. With the development of Cloud computing, data sharing between companies is expected to become much easier and hence CPFR agreements should become more accessible and less expensive to implement. Despite the need to share different data sets including ePoS data, sales forecasts, inventory data, etc., successful CPFR requires close cooperation between planners and managers from both companies. The most cited reason for failed collaborative relations between companies is a breakdown in trust between managers and a reluctance to share sensitive data.

■ Agility

Ultimately the root cause of poor forecasts is long lead-times, so to reduce the risks associated with forecasts, organizations should make every effort to become more agile by removing wasted time and shortening lead-times wherever possible. Reducing the lead-time gap and employing strategies such as postponement and immediate use of real-time demand can significantly improve supply chain agility and allow companies to become less dependent on the forecast of finished product sales. For further reading about agile supply chains refer to Christopher (2000).

Exercise

What are the main obstacles to the successful implementation of collaborative planning processes such as S&OP and CPFR?

Outsourcing and the role of logistics services

Trends toward globalization and offshore sourcing have been growing rapidly during the last decades. Manufacturers, producers and retailers across different industries pursue outsourcing practices as a part of their overall strategy. Outsourcing per se, however, is not considered as a strategy itself but can be perceived as a strategic decision that helps organizations to achieve their long-term goals and visions by sub-contracting non-core and peripheral products or services.

■ Core competences and outsourcing

A central question in defining a firm's strategy is what product or service is the firm's unique selling point and what it can do best? These so called 'core competencies', according to Porter (see Chapter 9) and other strategy scholars, must be a firm's only concern; all other supporting or peripheral functions should be delegated to and sourced from external suppliers or third parties. Such outsourcing practices ultimately results in a buyer-supplier relationship, which represents the smallest unit in today's business environment of supply networks.

At this point, a theoretical basis for outsourcing decisions can be introduced. The resource-based view (RBV) of the firm (Barney, 1991) and the theory of transaction cost economics (TCE) (Williamson, 1985) are widely accepted amongst scholars to explain the phenomenon of outsourcing relationships.

Since we now know that firms outsource products or services for competitive reasons, we can furthermore state that a firm achieves the following strategy-, finance- and operations-related benefits from outsourcing the logistics function in particular:

11

☐ **Strategic benefits** of logistics outsourcing refer to increasing customer satisfaction, due to the exploitation and access to national and international distribution networks. It also enhances flexibility in terms of responding to market changes and demand fluctuations.

☐ **Financial benefits** of logistics outsourcing refer to the cost savings that can be achieved through the reduction of capital-intensive assets (i.e. turning fixed costs into variable costs), and the reduction of labour and maintenance costs. Also, the unit prices for distribution, warehousing, delivery or any other logistics function are lower due to the logistics provider's ability to achieve economies of scale.

☐ **Operational benefits** of outsourcing the logistics function refer to the reduction of inventory levels, shorter transportation lead times, and shorter order cycle times. Overall, these benefits contribute to the improvement of the focal firm's customer service level.

Logistics outsourcing, however, increases the likelihood of the following relationship-, asset- and competence-related risks that have an impact on both the focal firm's business operations and the overall supply chain performance:

☐ **Relationship risks** refer to the lack of understanding, the possibility of opportunistic behaviour and the assumptions of information asymmetry or goal incongruences. A poor buyer–supplier relationship therefore results in the loss of control over the previously outsourced activities.

☐ **Asset risks** refer to the increasing costs that occur if a focal firm cannot monitor or supervise employees or physical assets anymore. Also, poor outsourcing management arrangements result in costs and efforts related to gaining information about the operations, as well as negotiating with and switching suppliers.

☐ **Competence risks** refer to the reduced customer satisfaction and loss of strategic competences. Third parties might not be able to deliver the requested and required performance in terms of quality, speed, and reliability. The outsourced activities also cannot contribute to the focal firm's strategic capabilities anymore.

Furthermore, on-going outsourcing practices increase the necessity for interorganizational collaboration and improved contractual or relational governance mechanisms. Factors such as understanding the organization's goals and objectives, selecting the right sub-contractors or partners, properly structuring outsourcing contracts, openly communicate with outsourcing partners and the continuous management of outsourcing relationships are considered as critical for success in outsourcing.

British Airways and poor inter-firm relationships

When British Airways (BA) outsourced its catering service to an external service provider, a poor management of the inter-firm relationship resulted in an overall reduction of customer satisfaction. BA missed the opportunity to properly evaluate the importance of in-flight catering to their customers and communicate their desired requirements to the service provider. BA realised later that in-flight catering actually was a core competence and more important to the customers than initially anticipated. Poor outsourcing decisions such as this can be reduced through proper collaboration and integration mechanisms as outlined in the next section. See van Weele (2009) for further discussion on these outsourcing issues.

Exercise

Explain the trend toward an increase in outsourcing practices.

■ Collaboration leads to integration

As outlined earlier, proper supply chain integration and collaboration practices reduce the danger that the associated risks of outsourcing failures outweigh the benefits from outsourcing (i.e. cost savings and service improvement). Collaboration can be determined by its scope (i.e. the length and intensity of a contractual relationship) and its level of interaction (i.e. how many activities and service offerings are shared and consolidated) amongst partners. Two types of collaboration have emerged since the 1970s and have proved to be common practice amongst different organizations within and across often competing supply chains.

Horizontal collaboration takes place between firms that offer similar products or services, and refers to the sharing of customers, assets, capacities, or any other operation between competing firms, operating at the same stage in different supply chains. For example, two logistics service providers that operate in different industries share their capacities or assets and therefore achieve further economies of scale.

Vertical collaboration takes place between firms that offer different products or services and refers to the exchange of information between partners at different stages in the supply chain. For example, transferring ePoS data from retailer to upstream supplier as soon as they are available increases supply chain visibility and reduces inventory.

Both vertical and horizontal collaboration practices (as illustrated in Figure 11.4) aim to help firms within and across supply chains to achieve mutually beneficial objectives.

11

		Vertical collaboration				
Supplier	Supplier	Supplier	Supplier	Supplier	Supplier	
Producer	Producer	Producer	Producer	Producer	Producer	
Distributor	Distributor	Distributor	Distributor	Distributor	Distributor	
OEM	OEM	OEM	OEM	OEM	OEM	Horizontal collaboration
Wholesaler	Wholesaler	Wholesaler	Wholesaler	Wholesaler	Wholesaler	
Retailer	Retailer	Retailer	Retailer	Retailer	Retailer	
Customer	Customer	Customer	Customer	Customer	Customer	

Figure 11.4: Horizontal and vertical supply chain collaboration

Horizontal collaboration between multiple partners can occur at any stage in the supply chain, i.e. it is not only OEM firms that collaborate, but also distributors, wholesalers, retailers and any other type of organization. However, these collaboration practices are very static in their nature and they cannot easily be applied to large-scale supply and demand networks. The rapidly changing and dynamic business environment asks for more sophisticated and complementary efforts that support horizontal and vertical collaboration. Concepts such as CPFR, S&OP, VMI, (discussed previously) and others aim to overcome the risks and uncertainties that are associated with global sourcing practices.

How Nestlé and United Biscuits are working together to share resources

In 2009 the two competing major food manufacturers Nestlé and United Biscuits combined their deliveries and joint forces in logistics collaboration. After analysing and comparing their individual distribution and transportation network, they found that most of their deliveries take place in opposite directions. A horizontal collaboration approach enables them to synchronise their deliveries across each of their regional distribution centres so that any part load orders that either company receives can be combined into one truck load. Since the two companies are only competing on the shelves in the supermarket but not on the back of a truck, an 11 week test trial resulted in combining over 60 loads, and removing some 7,500 miles of duplicate truck journeys. This example of horizontal collaboration illustrates the potential benefits in terms of reducing costs and emissions, as well as increasing vehicle utilization and saving time.

It is, however, worth noting that collaboration between supply chain partners and amongst competitors raises certain conflicts regarding goal incongruences and the willingness to share financial and operational risks. The phenomenon of opportunism needs to be carefully addressed in any dyadic or triadic relationships. Further reading on how to mitigate opportunistic behaviour and how to reduce goal incongruences can be found in Christopher (2011).

Exercise

Identify and critically discuss an example of horizontal collaboration between competing firms in the FMCG sector.

■ Logistics service providers

As a result of continuous outsourcing practices, the development and emergence of logistics service providers (LSP) has received increasing attention amongst practitioners and scholars in the past two decades. Since the high watermark of outsourcing during the 1980s and 1990s, third-party logistics (3PL) services are deemed to be a separate industry that creates value for customers. The market for logistics services can be segmented into different services offered by LSPs, which have developed over time, and range from basic carrier activities to the integration of logistics systems and advanced service offerings.

☐ **Transportation carriers** represent the most basic and standardized category of logistics firms. These firms own physical assets, such as warehouses, handling equipment and vehicles. They concentrate on the supplying function of transporting raw materials, packaging or finished products. Typically, these carriers specialise on one particular transportation mode, such as road, rail, sea or air freight.

☐ **Freight forwarders** offer more coordinated services to the customers by consolidating and bundling transportation and warehousing operations. Their focus, however, is still the physical supply of combined warehousing and transportation services, including additional value adding services, such as planning and managing information flows.

☐ **Third party logistics (3PL) providers** offer more integrated logistics solutions in the form of a European or global distribution network, including end-to-end supply chain services. These services entail pickup and delivery of products at different stages in the supply chain. 3PL providers, however, do not own all of the physical assets and rely on the coordination of freight forwarders and transportation carriers. The core competence of 3PL providers is the coordination of logistics functions across the supply chain, resulting in more customized service offerings.

11

☐ **Fourth party logistics (4PL)** or so-called **lead logistics providers (LLP)** offer services that span beyond the conventional logistics functions of transporting and storing products. These provider firms concentrate on and specialise in supply chain wide integration, including all parties from the upstream supplier to the downstream end-consumer, without owning any physical assets or operations. 4PL services operate on a much more strategic level and strongly focus on information technology and supply chain alignment. The concept, however, offers rather abstract and transcendent characteristics and there is no universal definition of what a 4PL provider actually is.

Rusthon *et al.* (2010) provide further reading on supplier selection criteria and the particular benefits and risks of outsourcing logistics functions to LSP firms.

UPS Supply Chain Solutions

Recently, the global leader in the sporting goods industry, Adidas, hired UPS Supply Chain Solutions to help streamline and enhance its distribution operations. The challenge for the service provider UPS was to improve the supply chain performance of Adidas to accommodate rapid growth and efficiently meet the requirements of major retailers throughout North America. The solution was to consolidate the distribution system into a single, streamlined network, supported with automated inventory and order fulfilment systems that allow the company to rapidly scale its services and add enhancements to the supply chain as needed. The benefits of hiring and implementing such a logistics-led approach include increased order accuracy rates, boosted on-time delivery performance, enhanced visibility throughout the supply chain, improved customer satisfaction and added flexibility in operations. (*Source: http://www.ups-scs.com*)

Exercise

What are the different services offered by different types of service providers in terms of their degree of supply chain integration?

Managing the global supply chain

Recently, the business environment has become increasingly challenging due to emerging megatrends, such as the internationalization of procurement, production and sales, and increasing resource scarcity and energy costs, as well as the development of emerging and competitive markets. Today, such dynamic trends on a global scale challenge organizations and managers in maintaining customer satisfaction and defining an organization's supply chain competence. Based on the fact that these megatrends are difficult to forecast and adapt to, global sourcing and supply chain strategies receive increasing attention and deserve serious consideration.

■ Global sourcing as a business trend

Following the trends of globalization, organizations tend to focus on the efficient delivery of products and services around the world. Global sourcing describes the strategic sourcing practices that organizations include as part of their internationalization strategy. Examples of globally sourced products or services might be furniture from Scandinavia, call centre services in India, software and IT development from Eastern Europe, or manufacturing components from Asia. However, global sourcing is not necessarily related to the outsourcing of manufacturing to low-cost countries but can be extended and perceived as actively integrating and co-ordinating common items, materials, processes, technologies and suppliers across worldwide manufacturing and operating locations (Monczka, 2010). For example, Dell Computers sources hardware components, such as hard drives, memory sticks, screens, batteries and laptop cases from different countries around the world and assembles the final product in a central location. Most enterprises, especially in the high-tech or computer industry, (e.g. Apple and IBM) follow such practices.

The logic behind global sourcing, which is also referred to as offshore sourcing, is clear: companies seek to grow their business by extending their markets in the form of their suppliers and customers. At the same time, cost reductions are anticipated through the benefits of economies of scale in purchasing and production, and also the distinct positioning of manufacturing and assembly operations around the globe.

Global sourcing, however, also presents certain threats and challenges that need to be addressed by a local firm. First, global markets are not homogenous and show different requirements in terms of product variations and unique customer behaviour. Second, the complexity of logistics operations increases and the management of global supply chains results in higher transportation costs and longer lead times. There is also a danger that companies only seek short-term cost advantages within their production and purchasing functions through global sourcing. This danger must be addressed by considering all supply chain related costs that occur through longer supply lead times and is commonly referred to as the cost trade-off in global logistics (see Figure 11.5) (Christopher, 2011).

11

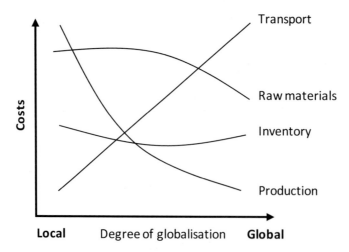

Figure 11.5: Cost trade-offs in global logistics. Adapted from Christopher (2011).

As global trends and the globalization of industrial activities emerge, the complexity of logistics operations increases and supply chain related practices find increasing attention amongst practitioners and scholars. Therefore, excelling in logistics management seems to be of critical importance as the key for maintaining a competitive position and profitability in any business context.

Exercise

Explain why certain operational costs increase whilst others decrease depending on the degree of globalization?

■ Coordinating global supply chains

As the trend toward outsourcing of non-core activities increases, so too does the need for global co-ordination. The demand for global supply chain control is, however, highly dependent on the organization's ability to find a balance and manage this trade-off between central control and local management of operations. Scholars and practitioners repeatedly refer to this phenomenon as *"think global, act local"*. Christopher (2011), amongst others, highlights the challenges that global organizations experience by trying to find the right balance, as is summarized in Table 11.2.

Extensive research has been conducted into the correct and most efficient sourcing and purchasing strategies and practices. Kraljic's (1983) purchasing model represents a comprehensive portfolio approach for purchasing and supply management. This well-known and widely accepted strategic purchasing framework follows the general idea of minimising supply risks and exploiting a focal firm's buying power. Further reading about the classification of a focal firm's product range within the Kraljic (1983) framework can be found in van Weele (2009).

Table 11.2: Challenges for global co-ordination and local management

Global co-ordination challenges	Local management challenges
Network structuring for production and transportation optimization	Human resource management and employee scheduling and planning
Developing and controlling information systems	Liaison with local sales and marketing management
Re-locating and positioning of storage facilities	Managing the local warehousing and distribution operations
Decisions about transport modes for international transportation	Gathering and synthesising local market requirements and intelligence
Sourcing decisions and supplier selection	Analysing customer profitability
Cost trade-offs and supply chain control	Customer service management

Source: Adapted from Christopher (2011).

Exercise

Describe the different methods of purchasing and the purchasing techniques managers should apply to products in each of the quadrants in Kraljic's framework.

Who to read?

On the subject of logistics and supply chain strategy, we recommend Martin Christopher; Martin has written several books and published papers on topics including supply chain agility, market responsive supply chains and supply chain risk and resilience.

We also recommend the works of Professor Hau Lee in the areas of global value chain innovations, supply chain management, global logistics, and environmental and social responsibility.

For a more in-depth understanding of global sourcing and purchasing we recommend Arjan Van Weele as a starting point.

11

Further reading and references

Barney, J. B. (1991). Firm resources and sustained competitive advantage, *Journal of Management*, **17**(1), 99-120.

Christopher, M. (2000) The agile supply chain: Competing in volatile markets, *Industrial Marketing Management*, **29**, 37-44.

Christopher, M. (2011). *Logistics and Supply Chain Management*, 4th ed., London: Pearson Education Limited.

Fisher, M.L. (1997) What is the right supply chain for your product?, *Harvard Business Review*, **75**(2), 105-117

Holcomb, T. R. and Hitt, M. A. (2007). Toward a model of strategic outsourcing, *Journal of Operations Management*, **25**(2), 464-481.

Kraljic, P. (1983). Purchasing must become supply management. *Harvard Business Review*, **61**(5), 109-117.

Monczka, R. M. (2010). *Purchasing and Supply Chain Management*, South-Western Cengage Learning.

Rushton, A., Croucher, P. and Baker, P. (2010). *The Handbook of Logistics and Distribution Management*, 4th ed., London: Kogan Page.

van Weele, A. J. (2009). *Purchasing and Supply Chain Management: Analysis, Strategy, Planning and Practice*, London: Cengage Learning.

Williamson, O. E. (1985). *The Economic Institutions of Capitalism: Firms, Markets, Relational Contracting*, New York, London: Free Press.

12 Corporate Social Responsibility and Corporate Governance

Julie McFarlane and Keith Gori

It is almost inconceivable that you have not used at least one of the following items today: a computer, a notebook, a tablet, a mobile phone, a video game console, a television or another electrical item. You probably did so without considering the social impact of the product upon people and natural resources, perhaps automatically, or possibly because you trust the manufacturers and retailers of these products to have made these considerations on your behalf. Unfortunately, in recent years, various incidents have brought their negative impacts to public attention, damaging trust in them and the companies that produce them. The trust placed in business organizations represents a form of social contract between businesses, customers and wider society. It is central to the successful functioning of business organizations. Several processes and measures are utilized by businesses to manage these relationships, and two of them – corporate governance and corporate social responsibility – are explored in this chapter.

Foundations of CSR and Corporate Governance

In 1824, John Cadbury, a young Quaker, opened a shop in Birmingham selling tea, coffee, and other goods. Cadbury believed that alcohol was the main cause of social degradation and that his products would serve as an alternative to its temptations. He also held the strong religious belief that all human beings should be treated equally, and was a major advocate of social reform. Following his lead, his two sons sought to improve working and social conditions for their employees and the community by providing good quality low-cost homes for their workers in the Bournville Village away from the squalor of city slums (Dellheim, 1987). They believed that if people could have their own, secure home a better quality of life could be created. Further, 'one-tenth' of the Bournville estate was to be used as open recreation space for residents to use and to promote exercise and healthy lifestyles. Cadbury have also been seen as instrumental in developing the Garden City Movement (see below) along with others such as Sir Ebenezer Howard, the father of modern town planning (Hall, 1998). Each advocated a need for decentralization and de-concentration in order to avoid the negative effects of urban life such as poverty, overcrowding, environmental decay and alienation (Chatterton, 2000).

Over the years, the Cadbury family legacy has remained apparent and subsequent generations have ensured that their workers' rights remain at the forefront of thought, from setting up pensions to founding colleges in the local community, and while the family have not owned the company since the 1960s they still maintain close ties with the local area. Here, then, we have a company that has shown how business can have a positive impact upon the community and society (Bryson and Lowe, 2002). During this period of development of better conditions for their workers, Cadbury continued to be a successful company, providing financial returns and growing their output to become a globally known brand (Rowlinson and Hassard, 1993).

Cadbury's confectionary rivals, Rowntree and Fry, were also central to efforts to highlight the plight of workers in Victorian Britain, with Seebohm Rowntree's reports in particular seen as providing significant impetus for the reforming activities of Liberal governments in this period.

Such was the business and social success of these companies in the period that Fitzgerald (2005, 2007) has argued that a corporate culture centred on both efficient production and management practices, and broad service to the community developed within the British confectionary industry. Though the modern terms for such practices were only introduced long after the Victorian period, we can see examples of both CSR and corporate governance in the case of Cadbury's, and other British confectioners.

Exercise

Think about the examples of the British confectionary companies discussed so far, what motivations might lie behind the actions of these organizations?

Businesses operate within, and are part of, wider communities and societies at a number of levels (local, national, global, etc.), and they therefore have a responsibility to act according to social expectations and norms, particularly since doing so will allow them to 'sustain, survive and grow' (Sethi, 2003, p.48). The ethical considerations which underpin much of contemporary corporate governance and CSR have roots in ancient philosophical debates, such as those surrounding Aristotle's integrated property rights in Ancient Greece (Hall, 1998) or the moral considerations relating to business and capitalism raised by Adam Smith in his seminal works the *Wealth of Nations*. Writing during the 18th Century Enlightenment in Britain, Smith grappled with the difficulty of transferring moral considerations into free market economic ideas (Bolton, Kim and O'Gorman, 2011). Ethics are concerned with the driving force of the moral agent (whether it is an individual or a firm) as opposed to the act itself or its outcome, and it is the role of the business as an active agent and the moral concerns surrounding its resulting impact that underpin academic debates surrounding CSR and corporate governance. Though both concepts have their roots in ethics and philosophy, it was only in the post-war period that they developed significantly into the position that they now occupy within modern business environments.

For a more detailed review of ethics and ethical theory, please see Jack, Glasgow, Farrington and O'Gorman's chapter on 'Business Ethics in a Global Context' (MacIntosh, and O'Gorman, 2015).

Outlining corporate governance

Corporate governance is essential to ensuring confidence in democratic market economies, and does so through strengthening the relationship between a company's management, its board, its shareholders and other stakeholders (OECD, 2004, p.12). In order for large corporations to ensure investment, they must display an ability to manage resources in such a way that a return on that investment can be considered likely. They also have to be self-regulated and able to clearly display this. This is not just a modern problem, but it is only in recent decades that the techniques through which it is addressed have been referred to as corporate governance (Tricker, 2000). In summary, corporate governance broadly refers to the manner through which companies are directed and controlled and, if handled appropriately, it should ensure that businesses operate successfully, legally and ethically, while remaining transparent and accountable to both internal and external stakeholders.

12

Example definition

Corporate governance is the system by which companies are directed and controlled. Boards of directors are responsible for the governance of their companies. The shareholders' role in governance is to appoint the directors and the auditors and to satisfy themselves that an appropriate governance structure is in place. The responsibilities of the board include setting the company's strategic aims, providing the leadership to put them into effect, supervising the management of the business and reporting to shareholders on their stewardship. The board's actions are subject to laws, regulations and the shareholders in general meeting.

Corporate governance as defined in *The Cadbury Report* (1992, paragraph 2.5).

Although corporate governance is a form of self-regulation, a number of governmental and non-governmental organizations at both national and trans-national levels have produced codes, frameworks and guidelines to assist companies with its implementation (for example, see HM Treasury, 2011; OECD, 2004). These codes often include common features, such as:

- ☐ **Leadership:** the board holds collective responsibility for the long-term success of the company with responsibilities clearly divided amongst its members. A chair of the board is responsible for its leadership but no one individual should have unfettered powers of decision.

- ☐ **Effectiveness and capability**: Corporate boards and committees should have appropriate skills and knowledge of the company to scrutinise the corporation's activities and should ensure these are refreshed appropriately. Board members should be appointed and re-elected through fair and rigorous selection procedures.

- ☐ **Accountability and transparency**: fair and balanced assessments of a company's prospects and progress should be produced and made available.

- ☐ **Relations with shareholders**: measures should be taken to ensure that there is an open dialogue between shareholders, boards and managers.

- ☐ **Sustainability**: businesses should be guided to create and allocate value fairly and sustainably to reinvestment and distribution to shareholders.

(Adapted from HM Treasury, 2011; OECD, 2004; please note that other codes may include different or additional principles).

Corporate governance is a concept which has to be reactive to public perceptions of corporate practice, and the effectiveness of codes such as the one outlined above often become the focus of fierce debate following high-profile corporate scandals which have apparently involved poor governance (Santomero, 2003). Corporate governance is therefore a concept that evolves over time and companies are required to constantly reassess and adjust it in order to ensure success and transparency.

What is CSR and why has it become so important?

CSR is a concept which, despite its significant presence, is extremely difficult to define in a simple way. It is a concept that is constantly reassessed by academics and it is used in a number of ways in the business world.

Example definition

Corporate social responsibility is essentially a voluntary commitment by companies to contribute to a better society and a cleaner environment. At a time when the European Union endeavours to identify its common values by adopting a Charter of Fundamental Rights, an increasing number of European companies recognise their social responsibility more and more clearly and consider it as part of their identity. This responsibility is expressed towards employees and more generally towards all the stakeholders affected by business, and in turn can influence its success.

CSR as defined by Commission of the European Communities (2001, p.4)

Carroll (1999) reviews the academic development of the concept in definitional terms, outlining that it has its roots in the social responsibility debates in relation to the role of business in the 1950s and 1960s. During this period the term covered notions of responsibility involving a wide range of issues including the welfare of employees, use of resources (natural and human), the impact of operations on local communities and environmental considerations. See Carroll (1999) for a more in-depth discussion of definitional debates surrounding CSR.

Much like corporate governance, CSR has attracted increased attention in recent decades, from academics and practitioners alike, and attempts to develop definitions, measures and frameworks have accordingly proliferated. Many national and trans-national organizations have addressed the concept and set out frameworks and standards (BIS, 2014; BITC, 2015; the Commission of the European Communities, 2001). Though numerous definitions of CSR have been proposed, a number of common themes have emerged including, most importantly, that it covers a wide range of broadly 'social' issues and considerations, and that it largely (if not entirely) refers to practices that are not addressed by legislation and state regulation but which are brought about voluntarily

12

by businesses (Carroll, 1999; Dahlsrud, 2008). A very broad definition of CSR would, then, highlight that it concerns the actions through which a business successfully carries out its core function in a manner that does not actively harm stakeholders, communities, environments and economies. In this sense Drucker's (2007) use of the Latin phrase *primum non nocere* (which means 'first, do no harm') to describe CSR is of value here.

Exercise

Thinking about the definitions of corporate governance and CSR discussed above try and think of firms that you believe to operate ethically. Justify your choices.

Models of corporate social responsibility

A number of scholars have attempted to conceptualise and create models depicting CSR and its elements. One of the most popular views is Carroll's (1979) dimensions of corporate social performance. This perspective claims that businesses tend to adopt four types of social responsibility: economic, legal, ethical, and philanthropic.

- ☐ The **economic** dimension of social responsibility refers to the requirement upon businesses to make a profit through the provision of goods and services that consumers seek in the marketplace. In this view, organizations will be profitable, maintain a competitive position, and a high level of operational efficiency.

- ☐ The **legal** dimension expects business organizations to conform to the government's laws and regulations of the places within which they operate.

- ☐ **Ethical** responsibilities refer to those responsibilities that are not societal norms, that are not imposed by law, and that involve adherence to the fundamental ethical principles of moral philosophy, such as justice and human rights.

- ☐ Finally, Carroll (1979) touches on the **philanthropic** dimension, referring to actions which are not expected but which involve going above and beyond the business organization and 'doing good' in a wider sense. This can include active participation in voluntary programs that promote human welfare or goodwill, from charities to the arts and education (Figure 12.1).

Dahlsrud (2008) identified in his research that numerous definitions of CSR have been proposed and suggested that this collection of definitions characterized CSR as being made up of five broad dimensions, as Figure 12.2, illustrates. These are: **environmental, social, economic, stakeholder and voluntariness**.

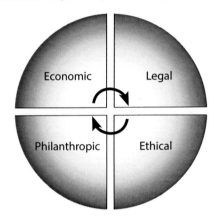

Figure 12.1: Carroll's Four Dimensions of CSR. Adapted from Carroll, A. (1979), A three dimensional conceptual model of corporate performance, *Academy of Management Review*, 4(4,) 497-505.

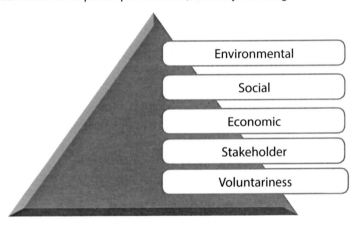

Figure 12.2: Dahlsrud's Five Dimensions of CSR. Adapted from Dahlsrud, A. (2008), How corporate social responsibility is defined: an analysis of 37 definitions. *Corporate Social Responsibility and Environmental*. Management, **15**(1), 1–13.

The **environmental** dimension is concerned with ensuring that business operations have environmental concerns at the forefront of all their operations. The development of industrial capitalism was transformed by the development of the coal-powered steam engine, invented by Scottish engineer James Watt in the late 18th Century. Since then, fossil fuels have been at the centre of the manufacturing and transportation which lies at the heart of a significant proportion of industrial and business development. The impact of the CO_2 emissions over this period on climate change has in recent decades become well-known

12

and businesses have come under increasing pressure to 'green' their operations. Against this backdrop of increasing environmental concern, CSR has therefore increasingly included environmental elements such as emissions reduction, and the sustainable use of land and sea resources.

☐ The **social** dimension is represented by the view that all business organizations must integrate both the social and the technical dimensions (socio-technical view) of their business operations. By integrating these social-technical concerns, business organizations can track and consider the full scope of their impact on the communities in which operations are based, and in doing so, contribute to a better society.

☐ The **economic** dimension in its narrowest sense is, of course, about making profits. For Carroll (1979), the economic dimension in his pyramid is about operating for profit, while for Dahlsrud (2008) this dimension contributes to how business organizations contribute to broader economic development in some way whilst ensuring that ability to generate profits is maintained in the organization.

☐ The **stakeholder** dimension is concerned with the relationships with those who have a vested interest in the business organization, including investors, shareholders, employees, suppliers, and partners. This is closely aligned with elements of corporate governance which are designed to ensure shareholders and investors receive transparent information and fair, socially just remuneration, and ensuring that stakeholders, such as suppliers and partners ensure best practice in regard to sustainability, treatment of employees and other responsible business considerations outlined in the chapter.

☐ The **voluntariness** dimension relates to actions which lie beyond the legal duties of the organization. As discussed above, this notion of voluntary actions which go above and beyond the legal and regulatory requirements imposed upon business organizations has been central to many accounts of CSR (Carroll, 1999).

Exercise

Thinking critically about the examples above, how would you assess the companies' claims to be acting in a corporate socially responsible manner?

Dimension	Examples
Environmental	Furniture and home-ware giant IKEA place a large emphasis on the measures taken in their production, supply chain and retail processes in order to reduce their environmental impact (see http://www.ikea.com/ms/en_GB/this-is-ikea/people-and-planet/index.html). Ice Cream producer Häagen-Dazs have initiated a campaign to increase awareness of the threat to the global population of honey bees, and donated profits to research aimed at addressing the problem (see http://www.haagendazs.us/Learn/HoneyBees/).
Social	Toms Shoes donate a pair of shoes to a child in need, for every pair of shoes they sell through their 'One for One' campaign. (http://www.toms.com/corporate-responsibility)
Economic	Nissan emphasise the economic contribution that their activities make as part of their CSR reporting. (http://www.nissan-global.com/EN/CSR/STRATEGY/ECONOMIC_CONTRIBUTION/)
Stakeholder	Coca-Cola have used a collective approach to water stewardship to engage some of their stakeholders in a programme to increase efficiency and sustainable use of a resource that is central to their product but also an indispensable human global resource (see http://www.coca-colacompany.com/sustainabilityreport/world/water-stewardship.html).
Voluntariness	The BMW group is notable for its commitment to transparency beyond that required by law and for going to extra lengths to protect internal whistle-blowers. As a result the group consistently scores highly in CSR assessments (see http://www.bmwgroup.com/com/en/responsibility/index.html and https://secure.ethicspoint.com/domain/media/en/gui/7825/index.html).

The business case for CSR

Having reviewed the areas that CSR is commonly thought to address, this section moves on to look at the gains it can provide for business. According to Zadek (2004), there has been a move away from a view of CSR as something organizations do just to mitigate risk, towards seeing it also as something they can use to create value for their business. This is not an entirely new idea; in an early attempt to conceptualise it, Davis (1960) noted that though incorporating social responsibilities within a business organization may come at a short-term financial cost, it would often produce long-term competitive and financial advantages. In this vein, CSR is seen as a corporate level strategic objective that focuses on how acting responsibly can add value to the business and the brand. For example, making the supply chain more efficient and therefore less damaging to the environment and less costly to the company, or CSR's role in retaining employees and building customer loyalty (Griseri and Seppala, 2010).

12

In addition, CSR has been analysed as a means through which businesses can respond to demands from stakeholders to avoid any ethical infractions. Some organizations use their ethical stance as a way to gain market position or even to gain competitive advantage over their rivals (for example the Body Shop's stance on animal testing has been seen as a key driver of their success). The argument that CSR is a way to maximise profits remains ongoing; though the business case for its incorporation into operations has become increasingly apparent. This is a controversial view, however, and there are those who argue that once CSR becomes engaged in activities more concerned with the interests of the company than of society, the activities cease to be CSR activities at all. Others believe that by doing so, firms have ignored the 'social' element of CSR in favour of functionalist, instrumentalist and business case rationales (Brammer, Jackson, and Matten, 2012). In summary, the business case for CSR incorporates a number of arguments:

☐ **Employee and customer satisfaction and loyalty**: Positive engagement in CSR can secure satisfaction in both customers and employees, with the first ensuring long-term income and the latter reducing staff turnover and the associated costs

☐ **Risk and reputation management**: This is linked with and contributes to a number of CSR and governance concerns, such as contributing to employee and customer retention, operational capacities and ensuring legal compliance. It also plays a central role in ensuring investors are attracted and retained.

☐ **Market position/competitiveness**: Investment in a variety of CSR engagements allows organizations to ensure they position themselves ahead of market competitors.

☐ **Operational efficiency**: In several areas (including employee retention and environmental savings, for example), CSR can contribute to increased operational efficiency in organizations.

Exercise

Thinking about what has been discussed in this chapter so far, can you name any companies you would now consider to be 'unethical'? Justify your suggestions.

■ Putting CSR into practice: larger vs smaller companies

CSR is not a universally accepted concept in business. While large business organizations tend to rely on high levels of standardization and formalization, smaller firms are more likely to follow an organic structure which rests on looser, more informal working relationships (Perez-Sanchez, Barton and Bower, 2003). Each tends to approach CSR differently (Williamson, Lynch-Wood and Ramsay, 2006). For example, while large organizations may make CSR an integral part of their business operations and adopt formal CSR strategies and policies, smaller businesses are often motivated by different factors (Vives, 2006) and often view CSR as an 'add on' activity (Schaper and Savery, 2004).

How CSR differs from MNCs to SMEs

For a large organization the implementation of CSR is part of a formal strategy. It is essential in the supply chain and its effective management. Multi-national corporations (MNCs) are also under pressure from shareholders and other interested parties to act in a responsible manner. For example, sports brand Nike has global reach and must ensure that its supply chain is not only efficient but also ethical. In addition, previous criticisms of unfair working conditions also means the brand is under constant pressure to improve its image. For smal to medium-sized enterprises (SMEs) this is not the case. They are less likely to formalise procedures and focus on environmental and social responsibility. They have looser controls and are less likely to document procedures and processes. While ethical behaviour may be part of the strategy and may be reflective of shareholder interests, the lack of resources means this proves difficult to implement. However, there are exceptions to this rule. In some cases, SMEs will go into partnership or supply to a larger organization with formal structures. In this case, the SME will have to standardise its approach to CSR in the supply chain in accordance with the MNC's code of conduct.

Research into CSR has mainly been focused at the large organizational level, where CSR is incorporated into the business from the top down; however, this is not the case for small businesses, which cannot simply be treated as little big businesses (Tilley, 2000). It has been successfully argued that the CSR dimensions applied to large organizations cannot be simply scaled down to fit smaller businesses (Jenkins, 2004; Tilley, 2000). The most telling difference is their size and structure. The owner-manager usually has a more prominent role in a small company, and in terms of the stakeholder dimension, the relationships of a large organization are complex and involve a large number of parties in a number of locations; thus, standardized practices need to be in place. For smaller businesses these relationships may be more informal, and characterized by personal engagement.

There is no 'one size fits all' approach to CSR and this is especially the case when it comes to smaller businesses (Thompson *et al.*, 1993). Castka, Balzarova and Bamber (2004) found that few small businesses have produced statements of their objectives or set out formal procedures for CSR. Elsewhere, Perrini (2006) has been argued that many small firms are in fact conducting CSR, but

12

may not realise that they are doing so, while Roche (2002) found CSR generally to be at an earlier stage of development for many smaller businesses than it is in large corporations.

Exercise

Take five minutes to think of ways in which CSR differs for larger corporations and smaller businesses, and note down the differences.

Corporate governance and CSR: A social contract between business and society?

During this chapter, we have identified that notions of responsible business are not new to academic or public debate. The terms used to conceptualise them and their definitions may have changed, however the foundations of CSR and corporate governance are firmly rooted in debates as old as the history of business (Bolton, Kim and O'Gorman, 2011). Corporate governance and CSR focus on the avoidance of exploitation of workers, communities or resources; transparent financial activities; and maintaining open relationships with stakeholders. When handled effectively, corporate governance and CSR are important activities that can foster a social contract between businesses and the people they serve, from customers to employees and shareholders. The link between the two concepts has been the subject of much academic attention (Aguilera *et al.*, 2006; Jamali *et al.*, 2008), with the nexus between the two a productive one: CSR decisions are heavily influenced by governance characteristics and, further, these decisions can bring significant additional performance value for organizations (Harjoto and Jo, 2011; Jo and Harjoto, 2011).

McWilliams and Siegel (2001) state that the actions of a business organization, regardless of its size, should go beyond the bare minimum required by law. The World Business Council for Sustainable Development (1999) have stipulated that all business should "behave ethically and contribute to economic development while improving the quality of life of the workforce and their families as well as of the local community and society at large." Thus, the recognition and embracing of corporate governance and CSR and their roles represent a commitment to best practice in business doing 'good' and acting with concern for the community (Kotler and Lee, 2005). Corporate governance and CSR are becoming more important because consumers, investors and other stakeholders are increasingly looking to do business with organizations of all shapes and sizes that provide more than just an excellent product or service or the likelihood of a good financial return. Business organizations need to be perceived as good corporate citizens by supporting good causes and ensuring that the environment they work within is protected while operating ethically and transparently. Some examples of companies that have made notable efforts in these areas, according to the Forbes 100 list online, are Microsoft, Google, Walt Disney, BMW and Apple.

Type of CSR engagement	Example organization/initiative
Social progress	Microsoft Youth Spark – providing access to education, employment and entrepreneurship opportunities to millions of American youngsters
Employee wellbeing	Google – noted for a strong emphasis on employee wellbeing and the working environment it provides
Environmental/sustainability	Walt Disney World (Epcot) – produces energy from waste products to reduce fossil fuel dependency
International development	BMW Group – investment in HIV/AIDS initiatives in South Africa

Exercise

Take 20 minutes to research some stories of both good CSR practice and bad. Outline what these businesses do and how these organizations have implemented CSR. Consider their motivations for engaging in these activities and their impact, both on the company and their wider social impacts.

Conclusion

This chapter has outlined the academic debate surrounding corporate governance and CSR, and the difficulty with which they have been defined and utilized in academic and practitioner circles. A discussion of how CSR has been modelled and conceptualized was used to outline the basic components that are often now associated with CSR and which are used to assess the CSR credentials of business organizations. Debates surrounding the business case for CSR, and the controversies this arouses have also been addressed to reflect the on-going debate within the literature across management disciplines. Corporate governance and CSR were then discussed together as forming part of the social contract that exists between business and society to create a sustainable, lasting relationship that serves the interests of both parties.

12

■ Who to read

Although this chapter provides a basic grounding in CSR and corporate governance, there is a range of contributions from the literature that offer greater insight. Carroll (1979, 1999, 2000a, 2000b) has published widely on the subject of business ethics and CSR on topics including its defining characteristics, its evolution, its conceptualization and implementation, and the value it creates for business organizations (Carroll and Shabana, 2010). Several excellent texts interrogating corporate governance in greater detail can be found, but in order to understand its relationship with CSR more fully, the work of Harjoto and Jo is of value (Harjoto and Jo, 2011; Jo and Harjoto, 2011).

■ References

Aguilera, R. V., Williams, C. A., Conley, J. M., & Rupp, D. E. (2006). Corporate governance and social responsibility: a comparative analysis of the UK and the US. *Corporate Governance: An International Review*, **14**(3), 147-158.

BIS (2014) *Corporate Responsibility: Good for Business & Society: government response to call for views in corporate responsibility*, Department for Business, Innovation & Skills.

BITC (2015) The Corporate Responsibility Index, Business in the Community, http://www.bitc.org.uk/services/benchmarking/cr-index, [last accessed 29/05/2015].

Bolton, S.C., Kim, R.C., & O'Gorman, K.D. (2011) Corporate social responsibility as a dynamic internal organizational process: A case study, *Journal of Business Ethics* **101**(1), 61-74

Brammer, S., Jackson, G., & Matten, D. (2012). Corporate social responsibility and institutional theory: New perspectives on private governance. *Socio-Economic Review*, **10**(1), 3-28

Bryson, JR. & Lowe, PA. (2002). Story-telling and history construction: rereading George Cadbury's Bournville Model Village, *Journal of Historical* Geography, **28**(1), 21-41.

Carroll, A. (1979), A three dimensional conceptual model of corporate performance, *Academy of Management Review*, **4**(4), 497-505.

Carroll, A. B. (1999) Corporate social responsibility: evolution of a definitional construct, *Business & Society*, **38**(3), 268-295.

Carroll, A. B. (2000a). A commentary and an overview of key questions on corporate social performance measurement. *Business & Society*, **39**(4), 466-478.

Carroll, A.B. (2000b). Ethical Challenges for Business in the New Millennium. *Business Ethics Quarterly*, **10**(1), 33-42

Carroll, A. B., & Shabana, K. M. (2010). The business case for corporate social responsibility: a review of concepts, research and practice. *International Journal of Management Reviews*, **12**(1), 85-105.

Catska, P., Balzarova, M., & Bamber, C. (2004). How can SMEs effectively implement the CSR Agenda? A UK case study perspective. *Corporate Social Responsibility and Environmental Management.* **11**(3), 140-149.

Chatterton, P., (2000). Will the real creative city please stand up? *City*, **4**(3), 390-397.

Commission of the European Communities (2001) *Promoting a European framework for Corporate Social Responsibility*, EU Commission Green Paper COM(2001) 366.

Dahlsrud, A. (2008), How corporate social responsibility is defined: an analysis of 37 definitions. *Corporate Social Responsibility and Environmental Management*, **15**(1), 1–13.

Davis, K. (1960). Can business afford to ignore social responsibilities? *California Management Review*, **2**(3), 497-505.

Dellheim, C. (1987). The creation of a company culture: Cadburys, 1861-1931. *The American Historical Review*, **92**(1), 13-44.

Drucker, P. F. (2007). *People and Performance: The Best of Peter Drucker on Management.* Boston, MA: Harvard Business School Press.

Fitzgerald, R. (2005). Products, firms and consumption: Cadbury and the development of marketing, 1900–1939. *Business History*, **47**(4), 511-531.

Fitzgerald, R. (2007). *Rowntree and the Marketing Revolution, 1862-1969*. Cambridge University Press.

Griseri, P., & Seppala, N. (2010). *Business Ethics and Corporate Social Responsibility.* Cengage Learning.

Hall, P. (1998). *Cities and Civilization: Culture, Innovation, and Urban Order*. London: Weidenfeld and Nicholson.

Harjoto, M. A., & Jo, H. (2011). Corporate governance and CSR nexus. *Journal of Business Ethics*, **100**(1), 45-67.

HM Treasury (2011), *Corporate governance in central government departments: Code of good practice 2011*, London: Cabinet Office.

Jamali, D., Safieddine, A.M., & Rabbath, M. (2008), Corporate governance and corporate social responsibility synergies and interrelationships. *Corporate Governance: An International Review* **16**(5), 443-459.

Jenkins, H. (2004). A critique of conventional CSR theory: An SME perspective. *Journal of General Management*, **29**, 37-57.

Jo, H., & Harjoto, M. A. (2011). Corporate governance and firm value: The impact of corporate social responsibility. *Journal of Business Ethics*, **103**(3), 351-383.

12

Kotler, P. & Lee, N. (2005) *Corporate Social Responsibility: Doing the Most Good for Your Company and Your Cause*. New Jersey: John Wiley and Sons, Inc.

MacIntosh, R., & O'Gorman, K. D. (2015) *Introducing Management in a Global Context.* (Global Management Series). Oxford: Goodfellow

McWilliams, A. & Siegel, D. (2001) Corporate social responsibility: a theory of the firm perspective. *Academy of Management Review*, **26**(1), 117-127

OECD (2004), *OECD Principles of Corporate Governance*, Paris: OECD.

Perez-Sanchez, D., Barton, J. R., & Bower, D. (2003). Implementing environmental management in SMEs. *Corporate Social Responsibility and Environmental Management*, **10**(2), 67-77.

Perrini, F. (2006). SMEs and CSR theory: Evidence and implications from an Italian perspective. *Journal of Business Ethics*, **67**(3), 305-316.

Roche, J. (2002). CSR and SMEs: chalk and cheese? *Ethical Corporation*, **9**(1), 18-19.

Rowlinson, M. & Hassard, J. (1993). The invention of corporate culture: A history of the histories of Cadbury. *Human Relations* **46**(3), 299-326.

Santomero, A.M. (2003) Corporate Governance and Responsibility, *Business Review*, Q2, 1-5.

Schaper, M. T., & Savery, L. K. (2004). Entrepreneurship and philanthropy: the case of small Australian firms. *Journal of Developmental Entrepreneurship*, **9**(3), 239-250.

Sethi, S.P. (2003) *Setting global standards: guidelines for creating codes of conduct in multinational corporations*, Wiley, Hoboken, New Jersey.

Thompson, J. K., Smith, H. L., & Hood, J. N. (1993). Charitable contributions by small businesses. *Journal of Small Business Management*, **31**(3), 35.

Tilley, F. (2000) Small firm environmental ethics: How deep do they go?. *Business Ethics: A European Review* **9**, 31-41

Tricker, B. (2000). Editorial: Corporate governance–the subject whose time has come. *Corporate Governance: An International Review*, **8**(4), 289-296.

Vives, A. (2006). Social and environmental responsibility in small and medium enterprises in Latin America. *Journal of Corporate Citizenship*, **2006**(21), 39-50.

Williamson, D., Lynch-Wood, G., & Ramsay, J. (2006). Drivers of environmental behaviour in manufacturing SMEs and the implications for CSR. *Journal of Business Ethics*, **67**(3), 317-330.

World Business Council for Sustainable Development (1999) *Corporate Social Responsibility: Meeting Changing Expectations*, Geneva: World Business Council for Sustainable Development.

Zadek, S. (2004) The path to corporate social responsibility, *Harvard Business Review*, **82** (12), 125-132

Index

absenteeism 138
ACAS *see* Advisory, Conciliation and
    Arbitration Service
advertising 108
Advisory, Conciliation and Arbitration
    Service 121, 126
analysis of data 91

barriers to entry 155–156
behavioural segmentation 99
bespoke services 102
Big data 83
Bill of Materials 175
Bournville Village 216
British Standard (BS) for quality 186
Business Model Canvas 15
business organization
    as a socio-system 10
    as a sociotechnical system 11
    as a techno-system 10
    as a transformative system 9
    internal environment 1–20
    types 2
    unincorporated or incorporated 41
    vision/mission 1–3
business process, defined 188
buying power 156–157

Cadbury 215–216
cellular layout 173
change management 123–124
    Kotter's 8-Step Process 123–124
channel length 111

channels to market 111
Christensen, Clayton
    disruptive and sustaining innovations 24
collaboration between firms 207–208
common law
    definition 60
    and employment rights 66–67
communication mix 108
companies 48–52
    legal person 53–54
    members and directors 48
    shares 51
Companies House. 41
competitive advantage, and supply chain
    197
competitive rivalry 153–154
consumer value, elements 15
continuous improvement 185–186
contract law, definition 60
contract of employment 62
contract of service 62
corporate culture 9–14
corporate governance 215–230, 217–218
    definition 218
corporate social responsibility 215–230
    and business size 224–225
    business case 223–224
    definition 219
    dimensions 220–222
    models 220–222
cost leadership 162
creative destruction 22

creativity 21–40
  and innovations 23
  defined 21–23
CSR *see* corporate social responsibility
data analysis 91–92
de Bono, Edward 22
decoupling point 199
delict, definition 60
demographic segmentation 99
Disability Discrimination Act 1995 128
dismissal, unfair 69–72
distribution 110

effectuation 34–35, 35
EFQM (European Foundation for Quality
    Management) model 177
Electronic Data Interchange (EDI) 204
employees and workers, distinction 63
employment
  implied duties 67
  tests of 64–65
Employment Appeals Tribunal 61
employment contract 62, 120
  common law rights 66–67
employment law 59–76
  history 59–60
  institutions 60–62
employment legislation 127–128
employment rights
  employees and workers 63
Employment Rights Act 1996 60
employment tribunals 61
  and unfair dismissal 70–71
entrepreneur
  definitions 29
  motivations 28
  role identities 31–32
entrepreneurial opportunities 27
  and serendipity 28
entrepreneurial process 33–34
entrepreneurship
  economic theories 30
  theories and concepts 31–35
Equality Act 2010 128

Equal Pay Act 1970 127
ethics and business 217
ethnography 88
exchange, nature of 97

factory layout 171
Feldman, on creativity 22
Five Forces model 151–160
  criticisms 160–161
flexible working 136
flow line layout 172
flow of work 188
focus groups 87
forecasting techniques 203
four Ps 98
fraudulent trading 54
freight forwarders 209

Gartner, William B. on entrepreneurship
    31
gender 135–150
geographic segmentation 99
global sourcing 211
global supply chains 210–212

health and safety 129
Health and Safety at Work Act 1974 129
health of employees 139
human resource management (HRM)
    117–134
  administrative objectives 124
  change-management objectives 123–124
  external influences 126
  health and safety 129
  pay/reward 125
  performance objectives 121–122
  role 118
  staffing objectives 119–120
human resources (HR) 117–134

incorporated businesses 41
industrial revolution 170
industrial sectors 5

innovative organizations 26
innovation 21–40
  and creative problem solving 26–27
inputs and outputs 9–11
insolvency 54
inventory management 183

job evaluations 125
job-sharing 136
Just in Time (JIT) manufacturing 175

Kotter's 8-Step Process 123–124

laws on companies and partnerships 42
layout planning 171
leading and lagging indicators 191
lead logistics providers 210
lead-time gap 200–201
legal person 44, 53–54
  attributes 52
  problems and solutions 54–56
legal structures for enterprises 41–58
liability and business structure 41
lifecycle of products 181
lifestyle segmentation 99
Likert scales 84
limited companies 49
limited liability 41
limited liability partnership 46
Limited Partnerships Act 1907 46
logistics 195–214
  definition 197
logistics management 111
logistics service providers (LSP) 209–210

manager, roles 12–13
managerial processes 189
manufacturing, relationship between
    volume and variety 182
marketer 97
marketing 95–116
  definition 95, 96
  positioning 102
  targeting 100–102

marketing budget 112
marketing mix 98, 103–109
marketing plan 112
market(ing) research 77–94
  defined 78
market segmentation 5–7, 98–99
mass marketing 101
Materials Requirements Planning 175
Mintzberg, Henry on chief executives 13

names for products/brands 104
niche marketing 101

observation research 87
omnibus surveys 81
operational processes 189
operations management 169–194
  balancing supply and demand 183
  delivering products/services 180–182
  evolution 179
  key concepts 169–179
opportunity
  discovery and exploitation 27–28
  entrepreneurial 27
Optimized Production Technology 175
organizations, innovative 26
outsourcing
  and logistics 205–208
  benefits and risks 205–206

partnership 43–48
  fiduciary duties 45
  liability for debts 44
Partnership Act 1890 43
pay 125–126
performance management 121–122
performance measure 190
place 110–112
Porter, Michael
  Five Forces 151–160
  generic strategies 161–164
  'stuck in the middle' organizations 164
  value chain model 16
positioning in market 102–103

postponement in supply chain 200–201
price 105–107
pricing 106
  differential 106
  dynamic 107
private companies 50
process layout 172
process management 187–190
products 103–105
  differentiation 163
  functional versus innovative 198
  lifecycle 105
  name 104
  types 104
product development process 190
production line concept 170
production line layout 172
production lines 171–173
productivity 171
product lifecycle 181
promotion 107–110
  tools 108
promotional goals 107
public companies 51
public limited company (PLC) 51

quality assurance 174
quality control 174
quality management 185–186
questionnaire design 85
questionnaires 84–85

Race Relations Act 1976 127
recruitment 119
redundancy 72–74
  eligibility 73
  payments 74
research 77–94
  brief 81
  design 79–80
  ethics 92
  ethnography 88
  focus groups 87
  interviews 86

is it necessary? 78
  methods 81–82
  observation 87
  primary 83
  qualitative and quantitative 83
  questionnaires 84–85
  reporting 92
  sampling 89–90
  secondary 82
retirement 126

sampling techniques 89–90
Sarasvathy, process model 34–35
Schumpeter, Joseph
  creative destruction 22
  definition of an entrepreneur 29
  five types of innovation 25
segmentation of markets 98–99
  criteria 100
  variables 6–7
semantic differential scales 84
Sex Discrimination Act 1975 127
Single Minute Exchange of Die 176
Smith, Adam 217
social contract 226–227
socio-system theory 10–12
sociotechnical theory 11–12
sole trader 42
Stewart, Rosemary on managers 12–13
strategic decision-making levels 4
strategy 3–7
  corporate, business, functional 3–7
substitutes 158–159
supplier power 157–158
supply chain
  collaboration 207–208
  decoupling point 199
  global 210–212
  integration 207–208
  market-responsive 198–200
  planning 202–205
supply chain management 184–185,
    195–214
  definition 196

supply networks 196
support processes 189

targeting markets 100–101
Theory of Constraints (ToC) 175
third party logistics (3PL) providers 209
threat of entry 155–156
Total Preventative Maintenance 175
Total Quality Management 177
Toyota Production System 170
transportation carriers 209

unfair dismissal 69–72
unincorporated businesses 41
unlimited companies 49
unlimited liability 41

value, types of 96
value added work 171

value chain model 16
value creation 7–8
value proposition 15–18
VAT threshold 43
veil-piercing 55
Vendor Management Inventory 204

waste management in production 176
women in labour market 136
work-life balance 135–150
    and gender 144–146
work-life balance practices 136–138
    barriers 141–142
    benefits 138–140
    case study 143
    costs 142
    women and care responsibilities 144
work measurement 171